DEUTERO-ISAIAH

DEUTERO-ISAIAH

A THEOLOGICAL COMMENTARY ON ISAIAH 40–55

GEORGE A. F. KNIGHT

ABINGDON PRESS · NEW YORK · NASHVILLE

DEUTERO-ISAIAH

Library of Congress Catalog Card Number: 65-20363

SET UP, PRINTED, AND BOUND BY THE PARTHENON PRESS, AT NASHVILLE, TENNESSEE, UNITED STATES OF AMERICA

FOR THOSE STUDENTS
AT McCORMICK THEOLOGICAL SEMINARY
who have stimulated me as much as I hopefully have stimulated them when we explored together the riches contained in Deutero-Isaiah

CONTENTS

ABBREVIATIONS

DI	Deutero- or Second Isaiah, or Isaiah 40–55
DSI	Dead Sea Scrolls Isaiah, technically known as IQIsa
KJV	King James Version of the Bible
LXX	Septuagint (the Greek Version of the Old Testament)
RSV	Revised Standard Version of the Bible
ANET	Ancient Near Eastern Texts Relating to the Old Testament, ed. by J. B. Pritchard (2nd ed.; Princeton: Princeton University Press, 1955)

INTRODUCTION

No section of the Old Testament has attracted more attention than has Isa. 40–55. The literature on it is more extensive than any one man could hope to read and digest in a decade. Yet Deutero-Isaiah will continue to attract exegetes so long as men study the Bible, for these sixteen chapters are as decisive and significant for an understanding of the Christian faith as are the sixteen chapters of Paul's Epistle to the Romans. Yet far less *theological* interest has been paid to Deutero-Isaiah than to the Epistle to the Romans.

The reason for this is that few scholars have cared to venture beyond the critical issues which lie behind these chapters; nor have they ventured to expound them as part of the biblical revelation as a whole. An inhibiting factor has been the difficulty of agreeing upon the true provenance of the book. Apart from oddities of position like that of Torrey, followed by Elmslie, Simon, and others, the majority of scholars agree that these chapters come from the period at the end of the Babylonian exile. There are those even today, however, who cling to the view that chs. 40–55 were written by Isaiah of Jerusalem.

Without attempting to answer this traditional but uncritical view of the provenance of Isa. 40–55, I would take my stand with the present generation of biblical theologians who, from a study of the Old Testament itself, believe that to interpret it we must take seriously the historical events in the midst of which its prophets and writers lived and spoke. We might ask ourselves what Jeremiah and Habakkuk would have given to have possessed these sixteen chapters, for these two prophets would surely have found in them the answers to their torturing problems. Their task was to interpret the mind of God as the might of Babylon closed in upon little Judah a century after Isaiah's death. If he had been able to read Isa. 40–55, the tortured cry of "Why?" would hardly have been wrung from Habakkuk's heart (1:3) as he witnessed the destruction and violence of his time. Nor would Jeremiah have complained as he did (12:1) at the prosperity of the wicked if he had known DI's answer. But then, these chapters were not in existence in their day.

Again, we can see that God, in his wisdom, continued to raise up an interpreter-prophet to expound his actions at each of the great crises in Israel's story—at the Exodus, at the loss of the ark to the Philistines, at the creation of the monarchy, at the crisis connected with Baal worship, at the fall of the Northern Kingdom, at the fall of the Southern Kingdom, during the exile itself in Babylon, and so on. It would surely be strange then if God had omitted to raise up a prophet at the vitally significant moment of the return from Exile, since this marks the climax of Israel's historical experience. Moreover, each one of the Old Testament prophets spoke out of the midst of a situation existentially, as we would say today, or as participants who were wholly involved, bodily, mentally, and spiritually, in the crisis in question. The prophets took no balcony view of events, but belonged with their brethren down in the arena, where the heat of the battle was most intense. There they were able to feel the response of their own people to their words, as they all faced the particular situation together. In fact, the prophets needed just such a living contact with the minds of their fellows if their own minds were to work fruitfully upon the events which they knew God meant them to interpret. Such an experience and understanding of sixth-century events were denied to Isaiah of Jerusalem if he was merely peering from the eighth century into the future with a spiritual telescope. The prophets were no diviners or prognosticators of the future. Our prophet in fact heartily denounced those Babylonian prophets who professed thus to peek into the future. Even though they knew God only in terms of the gods, by prognosticating exactly what God was going to do the Babylonian seers were not allowing room for God to "repent," or "change his plan," and shower blessings on his rebellious world. So DI took them to task for not being able to interpret contemporary events, much less future events. Perhaps the day may come when we shall learn that the author of these chapters also happened to be called Isaiah. The name occurs commonly in the OT, even as John, James, and Jesus do in NT times (cf. I Chr. 25:3, 15; Ezra 8:7; Neh. 11:7).

In the Hellenistic period, after about 300 B.C., when the material that comprises our OT was being edited and recorded in the form of "books," certain standard-size scrolls seem to have been available. On one of those scrolls Matthew, Luke, and John are each written, as well as the Minor Prophets, or the Book of the Twelve. Now, if we omit the historical section of Isaiah, that is chs. 36–39 (an insertion from II Kings), then the remainder of the sixty-six chapters would fit approximately on two such standard scrolls. It is quite feasible that if, owing to their common name, these two scrolls were later associated, a heading bearing the name Isaiah might have been dropped from before what is now ch. 40. But there is a much more cogent reason for the two "Isaiahs" to be later transcribed onto one large scroll. We receive the impression that DI has steeped himself in the works of his illustrious predecessor. Isaiah had proclaimed certain things about the *ʿetsah,* or plan, of God that was yet to be worked out in Israel's life and experience. DI now proceeds to show how that *ʿetsah* was taking form and reality in his own day and generation and even declares that it will continue to work in Israel's life in a unique and extraordinary manner in days to follow.

Ever since the days of Hermann Gunkel at the beginning of this century, many scholars became so concerned to place the separate paragraphs of our chapters in their various *Gattungen,* or types, that they lost all sense of the unity of the book as a whole. It is of course instructive to see how DI's work can be classified within the various categories that are to be found either within Israelite literature, or else in Ugaritic or Babylonian. But DI was first of all a theological giant. He conceived his work in terms of a literary and theological whole. He was in fact a theologian worthy to be set alongside of that yet more famous name of Paul, who wrote his most noted work, his Epistle to the Romans, in sixteen chapters too. The *Gattungen* that we can isolate today in DI's work are not therefore separate essays on his part. Rather DI used a number of ancient forms of artistic writing for the sake of variety, but he has threaded these units together to form one closely knit argument and developing thesis.

We cannot neglect the work of those scholars who have succeeded in effectively isolating the various forms in which a prophetic oracle could be couched in the days of Israel's prophets. Yet DI was the greatest mind of all the prophets of the OT. In contrast with him we can observe how some of the prophets, even as they made use of a particular *Gattung,* could become prisoners within the form that they were using. But DI seems to have been big enough to dissociate the various *Gattungen* available to him from their normally accepted *Sitz im Leben;* he has cleansed them of their usual associations and then, within the bounds of his own freely conceived pericopes, let them serve as media for the development of his sustained thesis.

DI is obviously well versed in the literature of his people; yet his references to past events presuppose that his readers know to what he is alluding. "Readers" is used deliberately, for DI's work is a written unity. It does not appear to have been spoken piecemeal in short, memorable, prophetic utterances, as most of the prophecies of Isaiah of Jerusalem were. As we read DI's work with attention to detail, we become aware of the brilliant manner in which his argument advances from point to point. Ch. 40, DI's first, is written like the headlines of a newspaper; in it the great themes of his message are splashed across the page. Thereafter, DI brilliantly lets drop hint after hint, in the shape of linking passages or individual words or phrases. By means of these he reminds us that he has not forgotten these central issues, but will develop them later in detail. The whole book thus gives the impression of being carefully produced in the study; and even though sections of it may have been tried out on local audiences, its final form is that of one sustained and unified thesis.

Ever since Bernhard Duhm in 1875 isolated the so-called "Servant Songs," a disproportionate amount of interest has been paid those chapters, to the detriment of the book as a whole. The reader will notice that herein the "scissors-and-paste" method adopted by many commentators is not employed. The so-called "Servant" passages (42:1-4; 49:1-6; 50:4-9; 52:13–53:12) are to be understood best when we read them in the setting in which DI actually placed them, for they each in turn advance the total argument just where they stand. Therefore the "Servant Poems" as such are not discussed. The whole sixteen chapters together in fact are a poem about God's relationship to his "Servant" Israel, in whom he has determined to glorify himself.

This is a theological and exegetical commentary. To say that it is theological, however, does not exclude the necessity for its being critical first. But since this commentary is meant to be of practical use to the nonspecialist within the Christian Church, there is no need to fill its pages with discussions of questions that are ably dealt with elsewhere in the many existing "introductions" to Deutero-Isaiah. This is not meant to be an introduction. For example, an introductory critical commentary that informs us that the Hebrew word *shalom,* "peace" (45:7; 48:22; etc.), has its roots in the worship of a Canaanite god of that name is not helping the reader to get past the prolegomena to biblical study. Important, nay essential as those may be, sufficient of that study is being made elsewhere. Here we spend no time asking where the land of the Sinim is to be located geographically (49:12), or in discussing the New Year festival held in Babylon in DI's day. Such questions ought to be faced in a critical commentary, and these exist in sufficient number. Here we take for granted the results of the work of the critical scholar. Our task is to apply the knowledge he has given us to the problem of what DI is actually seeking to say, and to the elucidation of a text which is the unique revelation of God to man.

Although this is a theological commentary, it also seeks to be exegetical. Let us see what the use of this word implies. The word "exegesis" means "leading out." The exegete has the duty of setting forth to the best of his ability and in modern terms what he believes the author was saying to his contemporaries. There is an aspect of neofundamentalism abroad which claims that a Jew, a Protestant, and a Roman Catholic ought all to be able to reach the same exegesis of a given book or text, provided they approach it with complete objectivity. We can dispute the validity of such a point of view. The Bible is not in the same category as, for example, either the sectarian documents of Qumran or *The Republic* of Plato. In a study of these scrolls Jew, Catholic, and Protestant do in fact work in complete harmony and are able to face together the problems of interpretation with great objectivity. This is because these scrolls are not source books of the faith of any one of us.

The text of DI, on the other hand, is part of Holy Scripture. As such it is the book both of the synagogue and of the Church. Therefore Jew and Christian alike come to its study already conditioned by the book itself. That is to say, both of them can be comparatively objective about the prolegomena to the study of the book, but scarcely are able to be so in the case of its interpretation. Interesting evidence of this fact is offered when we read the semiofficial interpretation of Isaiah made in the early Christian centuries in the Aramaic Targum of the synagogue. Some of its peculiarities will be noted later.

Then again, the chapters we assign to Deutero-Isaiah do not contain static statements about God. DI is not a collection of doctrines which could mean the same in the twentieth century as they must have meant in 540 B.C. In fact, it is the very vitality of the book that prevents the Jew and the Christian from reaching an identical exegesis of it.

The text of the Old Testament is the vehicle of a two-way traffic between God and man. It informs us, in the first place, about the thoughts of its writers on the ways of God with Israel. These thoughts can be relatively objectively studied; and the scholar, with evidence of much self-satisfaction, is able to set forth in scientific form the growing understanding of God that is apparent as the story of Israel proceeds. But, secondly, the text of the Old Testament is the vehicle of the Word of God to Israel. Moreover, that Word is heard not just through the intellectual grasp of God's thoughts which the prophets were able to make, but rather in and through the misunderstanding, the folly, the resistance, the unbelief, and even the apostasy of that Israel whom the prophets represent.

The reader of DI's pages today is a member himself of this Israel of God, this backsliding, apostate people. The degree to which he hears the Word of God addressed to Israel through these pages therefore is bound up with his degree of awareness of his own apostasy, and with his acceptance of that forgiving and renewing love of God that the pages of DI reveal.

The great commentators of last century, Duhm, Marti, Nowack, and the others, pursued a line of study which is as essential today as it was then. The establishment of the text so as to discover exactly what the writer is saying is the first project any commentator must essay. But the majority of scholars of a former day applied their criticism only within the context of the first of the two ways of traffic mentioned above. They held the view that the text of DI is telling us something about the religion of Israel that is important for us to know. Their view is valid, for the text of the Old Testament does give this information. What they did not realize, however, is that the text of the Old Testatment has more to tell us than that. For example, no commentator on one of the Gospels who approaches its text with the presuppositions of a Christian would be content to limit his exposition of the text to interpret the religion of Jesus. This is because the commentator believes that the Gospels are the Word of God, and that they reveal the incarnate Word as the subject and not merely as the object of faith. In the same way, then, there is such a two-way traffic over the Old Testament text, for the OT is the Word of God as truly as the Gospels.

On the other hand, the interpreter must rigorously free himself from any tendency to allow dogma to dictate the exegesis. To a degree that the linguistic and literary critic can ignore, objectivity for the theological commentator means allowing the Word of God, as it meets him from the pages of the text, to judge him—with his theological position and confessional standpoint, even his sociological setting—instead of his judging the text of the biblical book in question and reading into it his own human limitations.

Therefore the text of Isa. 40–55 offers an encounter not just with the faith of a man whom we name by the initials DI, but also with the Word of the living God. We meet this Word in the pages of his chapters as it begins to become flesh in an historical situation that we can pinpoint and quite accurately describe. Acceptance of such a view obviates the danger of seeking for Christian dogmas within the text, or of trying to interpret what DI has to say in a christological manner. The interpreter who attempts the latter can only bring himself under censure for offering his readers an eisegesis rather than an exegesis of the text. For it is Israel that we read of in DI's text, and not the person of Christ.

DI's great contribution to our biblical faith is his insistence that the living Word of the living God began to be united—though still in a proleptic sense—with the very flesh of God's son Israel at that specific period in which DI himself was participating. Through the Word which he was then uttering on God's behalf, this fantastic union would become event. In other words, DI believed that this Israel which was even then the subject of the Word would finally, by God's grace and for the sake of God's ultimate purpose for the world, become the Word itself.

The line between exegesis and homiletics can be only thinly drawn. Exegesis will be set forth in such a manner in this commentary that it will speak for itself homiletically, although on occasions there are a few tentative hints along homiletical lines. For exegesis and exposition, while remaining two separate disciplines, are necessarily mutually interdependent.

A final note on the structure and procedure of this commentary would be in order. The reader of the above discussion will realize that an exegete has already made an exegesis of a passage in his own mind before he finds words in English to translate the original language. The principles behind my translation of the biblical passages and the form that the commentary has taken therefore are these:

1. The language used in the translation already goes part of the way toward the interpretation that follows. Every time a Hebrew word occurs, therefore, it is not necessarily rendered by an identical term in English. The words *mishpaṭ* and *ts*ᵉ*dhaqah*, for example, each mean several things in English; thus the word chosen for their rendering will depend primarily upon the context in which they occur.

2. Unlike the majority of commentators, I have kept as closely as possible to the received Hebrew text; that is to say, I take a conservative view of the Masoretic text. There are places where scholars have made countless suggested emendations; the majority of these are now superfluous. This is not because of a superstitious reverence for the work of the Masoretes. Rather it is because once one assumes that the sixteen chapters of DI form an entity, then many of the scholars' suggested emendations are no longer necessary. What had appeared to be good and even essential changes in the text when the line belonged within the context of one isolated pericope are no longer required. On the other hand, we must pay good heed to the witness of the Versions. On occasions they appear to have preserved a better text than that which the Masoretes have left us. Yet the authors of the versions were not averse at times to altering the meaning of the original text. They might have done so not just deliberately, as is the case quite frequently in the Targum, but also quite unwittingly. Like all of us they were necessarily prisoners of the zeitgeist in which they were living and drawing their breath. Accordingly, we are bound to scrutinize their offerings just as critically as we are able.

3. While the lines of the original verse of DI are retained in this translation, no attempt is made to produce corresponding verse in English. The correct meaning of the original wording is surely more important than mere elegance of English style.

4. For the convenience of the reader, the sixteen chapters of DI's work retain the numbering that they have received in the English versions; but for ease of handling, these chapters are now divided into small "sense sections" of necessarily unequal length. The reason for this is to enable the succeeding words of the commentary to follow as closely as possible upon the translation of the passage they discuss. The reader will understand that these sense sections will probably but not necessarily correspond with such divisions of the text in *Gattungen* that other interpreters may have already made. For what is obviously one pericope may be too long to be handled with ease as one sense unit.

5. Square brackets [ ] are employed when it is necessary to add words that do not occur in the original. Their use may result in paraphrase. Rounded brackets ( ) enclose words necessary to complete the sense.

6. References to other works can become a hindrance rather than an aid to the reading of a commentary. So these have been reduced to a minimum.

7. All Hebrew students are aware that what we call the "modal" forms of the verb in a modern language cannot be represented in Hebrew, viz., words like would, could, should, etc. Therefore my choice of such auxiliary forms rests upon a subjective decision. Each verb was scrutinized in the light not just of the pericope in which it occurs but of the total message of the book. Also, the tenses of the verb in Hebrew are still not fully understood. My choice of tense in English therefore does not necessarily agree with the choice of the English versions (cf. 42:1).

8. The word *ki,* when it introduces a statement, has been traditionally translated "for," e.g., "For his mercy endureth forever" (Ps. 136 *passim*). But frequently this particle represents an unspoken oath or other emphatic verb of asseveration. As such it has been rendered in the translation by "realize that" (cf. 55:8 *ff.*), or "it is true that" (cf. 49:19), or even just "indeed" inserted in the sequence of the sentence. This usage is discussed by Köhler in "Deuterojesaja stilkritisch untersucht." [1]

9. Stress is placed upon the vitality of Hebrew nouns and verbs. It can be a mistake, of course, to interpret a word by what it may have meant in its root usages centuries before, or even as we think we understand it from cognate languages. But there is another aspect of the content of Semitic words to which reference is seldom made. The Westerner who reads the classical Arabic poets for the first time is surprised at a particular form of the Semitic poetic genius displayed there. This cannot be shown in English translation. An Arab poet could employ a word, written as it was without vowels, which could be construed to mean two, three, or even four different things at once. Each of these meanings had then to make sense by itself. The homonym is a feature of the Semitic languages, whereas it is a rare phenomenon in English.

It could be only a genius and a master of his own tongue who could contrive to employ triple and even quadruple homonyms successfully. DI was just such a poetic genius, for his carefully executed verse bears the marks of this style of writing that was common later amongst the Arabs. It has long been recognized that the prophets enjoyed creating puns. But DI went further than that in his artistry. He packed some of his words with more than merely two meanings. Thus he produced a highly condensed form of writing that cannot always be translated verbatim, but which has to be interpreted and explained in detail.

[1] (*Beiheft zur* ZAW, 1923), pp. 63-64.

10. The number at the left side of the page in the exegetical section of the commentary corresponds to the number of the verse in the translation made above it.

11. This commentary may give the impression of being repetitive; a discussion of the significance of words and ideas may occur more than once. But this is to help the reader who scans only a section of the book for his immediate use.

12. To facilitate a group of DI's theses, I have sought to summarize his argument in a closing chapter.

Isa. 40–55 is a document of fundamental importance. The roots of most of Christian theology are to be found in it. Therefore its study is both essential and very rewarding.

CHAPTER 40

1 **"Comfort my people, comfort them," says your God.**
2 **"Speak to Jerusalem's heart, and call to her**
That her forced labor is ended, that the punishment
due her for her iniquity has been accepted;
That she has received from Yahweh's hand double in
payment for all her sins."

1.

It is often said that the main factor in revelation in the OT is the action of God within the life of Israel. This is true only to a point, however. For accompanying the action must go the Word. In fact the Word is noticeably conjoined with the action at each of the great moments in Israel's story. This is because a prophet is normally found at each moment, interpreting the action that he is witnessing. Moreover, the prophet in question is more than a mere mouthpiece; he is the channel through which the Word reaches into history; and without his faith and obedience, we cannot see how God would have acted in any of the historical situations recorded in the OT.

DI is here the channel for the inbreaking of a new divine Word into Israel's consciousness. This particular Word, which comes down like the rain from heaven (cf. 55:10), results in that historical incident in which the Israelite exiles are set free from servitude in Babylon by King Cyrus and are permitted to return home to Jerusalem, there to rebuild their ancient city and to reconstitute their ancestral worship.

The Word is the ground and basis of all life. So at least believed the author of Gen. 1:3—"And God said," he declared. Sharing in such a heritage, DI now conceives of this reality pictorially. Thus he interposes angelic personalities between the Word of God and the word of the prophet. It is as if the whole universe is filled with God's Word. Here at vs. 1 the air seems filled with living creatures. As the servants of the Word, these exist to execute God's will and purpose both in heaven and on earth. In DI's thought, we should notice, there is no line between heaven and earth.

God speaks first, as he gives his commands to these angelic agencies. The Word mediated through angelic lips is heard on earth as a message of comfort and joy. Elsewhere it resounds on earth as the words "Do not be afraid." So the Word came to Hagar (Gen. 21:17), to Elisha's servant (II Kings 6:16), to the shepherds at Bethlehem (Luke 2:10), to the sorrowing women at the open grave (Mark 16:6). When the veil grows thin between this area of God's world that we inhabit and that which we cannot see, then the sound which meets our poor human ears is the Word, "Do not be afraid."

In line with this general biblical revelation, we hear the twice repeated command to *comfort*. The word does not mean to comfort or console another in his trouble; it means to comfort him out of his trouble into joy, obviously, that joy in which God himself continually dwells. The angelic forces (the verb is plural) are here to bring joy to God's own special people. The latter have, of course, been such ever since God chose them in the days of Moses. All the peoples of the earth belong to God; all men are his creatures. Yet Israel is God's "peculiar treasure above all people" (Exod. 19:5). They are in fact *my people*. The word used here, *'am*, is that normally used for the people of Israel alone. Obviously they are no longer "Not-my people" of Hos. 1:9, or even just "this people" of Isa. 6:9. So what we hear is the word of grace revealing constant concern that Israel should be aware of the significance of the covenant relationship by which Yahweh has bound her to himself. Though the destruction of Jerusalem, the scattering of *my people*, and the harsh subjection of the nation to the rule of the Babylonians had seemed like a breaking of the covenant which God had made of old, yet our author now declares that behind and through and within that overwhelming tragedy God is still present as Israel's God, and the basis of God's purpose for the whole universe is still his Word of comfort and of joy.

2.

DI is fully aware of the teaching of the great prophets who preceded him. We shall note his dependence upon them and agreement with their words as we proceed. Hosea for one, closely followed by Jeremiah, has already used the astounding metaphor of marriage to set forth the distinctive relationship between Israel and her God. The language here follows upon the acceptance of such a figure. *Speak to Jerusalem's heart* is a phrase belonging within this sphere of thought. It occurs eight times in the OT, and of these, five refer to the wooing of a lover (cf. Hos. 2:15-20; Jer. 2:2). The figure of God's husbandly love is later developed in detail in Isa. 54:1-8. It is also taken over in the NT to describe the relationship between Christ and the people of God as, for example, in II Cor. 11:2; Rev. 19:7; 21:2-9. This means that the special relationship that obtains between Christ and his Church in the NT is recognized to be in continuity with that between God and Israel in the OT.

At this point, however, it is not God himself but the angelic agencies who are to convey the words of husbandly devotion. The angels are to *call to her*. God is evidently convinced that Israel is capable of making a response, hopefully one of joy and obedience; for it is God who has completed the act necessary for her redemption and not she herself.

The word for *forced labor* has special meaning for those who have known an era of slave labor camps and depressed exiles cut off from all that they hold dear. It is basically the word for army or military service, and is to be found in the divine name "Lord of hosts." DI's use of the word is thus in itself part of the Good News. For the dispirited Israelites would naturally remember how the word belonged in this title of their God. He was truly their *Lord,* and as such was in full command of his hosts. On the other hand, occurrences of the word such as Job 7:1 bring out the meaning that we have here. In the Job passage it means "daily laborer," one who is virtually doing forced labor. The idea of forced labor, however, does not compel us to believe that in Babylonia the Hebrews were as cruelly and oppressively treated as they had been in Egypt before the Exodus (cf. Exod. 1:11-14). The Greek translation, *tapeinosis,* in fact emphasizes rather the sense of moral degradation and mental humiliation which the exiles had perforce experienced. In his famous letter to the exiles Jeremiah presupposed that his readers could live and were living normal lives though in a strange and alien land (29:1 *ff.*). The LXX's choice of term may however have been deliberate, for it occurs elsewhere in parallel with *douleia,* which means both forced labor and military service at the same time.

Yet the word has still another overtone. The conscript soldier in Israel performed a religious duty when on service. His obedience when under arms could be likened to the service enjoined upon the fully grown male Israelite when he took his turn at the sanctuary (cf. Num. 4:3). Putting these ideas together, we might say that the forced labor that Israel had been doing for the last fifty years in a land of alien gods was in reality a service she had to render to God. Now, however, the angelic message sounded, Israel's long term of military conscription was *ended*. This last word is an instance of the perfect tense of the verb used to declare a future action, in that God has declared it will happen. DI is only copying his predecessor, Isaiah of Jerusalem, when he uses such language. For example, Isaiah could declare with total assurance about the future, "Unto us a child has been born" (9:6).

Punishment due her for her iniquity represents one word in Hebrew. It is an interesting fact that many nouns and verbs in that language appear to be pregnant with a double meaning, or potent to the point of expressing more than one idea. So DI with one word can imply that sin indubitably brings its own reward. This, he believed, is because iniquity cannot pass unnoticed in God's ordered world. DI would have agreed with our modern proverb: "Be sure your sin will find you out." By this language, DI is opening a window into the wonderful nature of Israel's God. His next word, *accepted*, means something like "satisfaction" or "expiation has been made"; and of course it can be God alone who can accept Israel's sin in any sense; Israel cannot make satisfaction for her iniquity herself. It is true that she had suffered *double*, twice over, for all her sins, so that in fact she had made double payment for her past disloyalty. But even if she were to suffer ten times as much as she had done, she could never pay them up in any sense at all.

In the OT sin is not fundamentally a thing, an object, that can be dealt with objectively. Sin as a thing in itself cannot be atoned for. In the last resort there is even no such thing as sin—there are only sinners. This is because sin is primarily a breaking off of personal relations. Sin is rebellion; it is pride; it is the belief by man that he knows better than God (cf. Gen. 3:3). Therefore God alone is in the position to deal effectively with it. DI would know of the statement by God to this effect as it is now incorporated in Lev. 26:41, 43. On such a basis, therefore, he could see how God could accept the forced service of the exile as if it were divine service which God had asked Israel to perform in payment for her apostasy. On Israel's part, the basis of her sin lay in her breaking off relations with her divine Husband, the figure DI uses in later chapters. Those relations only God himself could now restore, even though Israel had now completed her service to that end. *Double* therefore does not imply that Israel had now expiated her own sins plus those of the gentiles among whom she had been dwelling. Rather the word is a strong Hebrew expression for something like "she has suffered terribly," as indeed was true. Again, the word "cup" is probably understood after *she has received*—a double cup, a twice-filled cup. We find the idiom at 51:22, but also at Jer. 25:15 and at Lam. 4:21-22, and it forms the background to similar NT usages at Matt. 20:22; 26:39; I Cor. 11:25. The translation *in payment for* is obtained by taking literally what the grammarians call the *beth pretii* that lies before the word for *all*. Here are three perfect tenses in succession, each of them revealing a completed action, completed by God and not by an Israel that sought to work out a satisfaction for *her sins*.

We have before us, then, three thrilling statements, all of them proclaimed so matter-of-factly: (1) Israel's forced labor is ended; (2) Israel's punishment has been accepted; (3) Israel has now received from *Yahweh's* hand the payment which he has exacted. Only later, at 47:6, does our writer identify this hand of Yahweh with the instrument that he uses, viz., Babylon. If Israel had indeed deserved to be doubly punished, then in forgiving her in this total manner God must have been pouring upon her a double portion of grace. Two centuries before, Amos had declared that since Israel had received more light than her neighbors, in that God had given her special revelation in the Torah, then Israel was doubly responsible when she rebelled against that light (Amos 2:4, 6; 3:1-2). But this was all now a thing of the past, declared DI; Israel's punishment God himself has now *accepted*. How he has done so is not yet shown. DI, however, has much to say about this tremendous reality in later chapters.

Israel is here addressed as *Jerusalem*. The city of course symbolizes the people, even though the latter are presently some seven hundred miles from home, and the walls of the city are lying in ruins. But this figurative use of the word Jerusalem is important in the context of DI's exposition. Like all cities, or ships in modern English, Jerusalem was regarded as a feminine entity, and so was known as "she." The feminine singular can be shown in the Hebrew verb, though it is not possible to do this in English. DI employs this figure consistently when he has in mind to speak of the people of God as Yahweh's bride.

3 [A voice crying:]
"In the wilderness prepare the way for Yahweh;
In the desert straighten out a highway for our God!
4 Let every valley be filled in, and every mountain and
hill be leveled down;
Let steep areas be evened up, and mountain chains
become a plain;
5 For the glory of Yahweh is to be revealed; and all
flesh will see it together.
Verily Yahweh's mouth has spoken it."

3.

Obedience belongs at the heart of worship. This reality must be applicable to the whole of God's universe and not only to man. An angelic voice promptly passes on the divine command that has resounded in the heavens. It is as if the host, *tsabha,* above was with military precision obeying the Lord of hosts, just as Israel was meant to do below when she was called to bear obediently the forced labor, *tsabha,* which God had laid upon her.

Now the whole heavens are ringing with shouts and commands as God's generals prepare the way for the King of kings, and DI's language soars as he speaks of the majesty and dominion of God. What follows is of course poetry, and no poet expects his words to be taken literally. What the poetry expresses, however, is no less than this: when God completes the rescue of his bride from her exile in Babylon, his action will have cosmic significance. His method in rescuing her DI discusses only later. But once she is released, God will walk beside his people as they face the vexations and pains of life, and will lead them back home to Judah, even as a shepherd leads his sheep home to the fold. For of course Yahweh is no mere local deity; he is the King of all gods and kings.

4.

When in DI's day an Eastern monarch traveled through his dominions in his slow and simply constructed chariot, sappers were accustomed to go ahead virtually in order to build the road that the king had to travel. Later Persian monarchs ordered the construction of a fine network of royal roads that led to the far ends of their kingdom. But Babylonia did not possess such roads in 540 B.C. So DI knew how these sappers in a primitive sort of way had to level the hillocks and build up the ditches and fill in the holes so that the royal chariot might make some kind of speed. With this picture in mind, DI then invites us to imagine what is involved in the astonishing idea that the living God will march beside his people across the deserts and hills that lie between Babylon and home.

The command *prepare* means to push obstacles out of the way. However, the words *in the wilderness* come first in the command. This is to remind his hearers that God has already come through the wilderness of Sinai along with his people in the days of Moses (Ps. 68:7). Israel ought then to be confident that nothing now can stop him this time. Yet the Hebrews used the word *wilderness* in a metaphorical sense as well as a literal. The wilderness represented for their thinkers and prophets the concept of chaos and disorder; it figured for them that area of life where God's ordered world was set at nought; thus it could even be a state of soul as well as a geographical area. The fact therefore that the angelic host was ordered to prepare a way through chaos is significant for a theological understanding of this important chapter.[1] DI later returns to this issue. All four of the Gospel writers, on the other hand, regarded this passage in the theological light suggested above (Matt. 3:3; Mark 1:3; Luke 3:4; John 1:23). Evidently they recognized that, poetry though it was, this voice speaking five hundred years before their day was heralding both a factual and an eschatological situation at the same time. This reference to the Exodus again shows that not just here but throughout his whole work DI is concerned with the Mosaic tradition. Yet nowhere does he make any direct quotation from the Pentateuch. He seems to take for granted that his hearers know the traditions as well as he does. He handles the traditions in freedom and seems to be unhampered by any preconceived dogmatic interpretations. On the other hand, this is where he lays the emphasis: He argues, since God has acted before and has already used Moses to interpret and declare the meaning of his actions to Israel, God can therefore be trusted to act again in the days to come in similar ways. Thus these coming actions must not be regarded merely as local events or as ends in themselves; rather they are actions which will affect in their outcome the whole of God's creation.

5.

Next follows an even more astonishing declaration: *The glory of Yahweh is to be revealed*. *Glory* is the word that earlier writers had used to describe

[1] The Qumran sectaries later understood this "way of the Lord" as "the study of the Torah by which God gave command through Moses for acting according to everything that is revealed from time to time, and according to what the prophets revealed by His holy spirit." See Matthew Black, *The Scrolls and Christian Origins* (New York: Charles Scribner's Sons, 1961), p. 120.

the visible manifestation of God, who is yet essentially invisible and incomprehensible. No man can see God and live, DI's predecessors had declared. But later OT writers postulated a concept which they called "glory" and regarded it as the visible medium through which God's presence reveals itself to man.

Glory was therefore frequently visually conceived in terms either of light or of fire, as at the Mount of Revelation in Moses' day (Exod. 19). Ps. 97 for example interprets the visible nature of glory in this very manner. This kind of interpretation, however, is not a new thing in human thought, for such a psalm is closely related in genre to the psalms used by the Canaanites in their cult in earlier centuries. There too light and fire are figures for the radiating power of the being of the deity. Such figures were easy to conceive, since fire obviously radiates the heat which issues from its heart. When Israel took over the concept from the Canaanites, however, she employed it in a new and paradoxical manner. The paradox lay in her view that glory was actually revelation of the invisible heart of God. In Israel's early days it had been easy to confuse the concept of glory, envisaged as it was under the form of fire, with various meteorological phenomena such as lightning or volcanic eruptions. But as time went by, Israel's prophets had purified and moralized the content of glory. It remained now for DI to establish the ultimate meaning the word would ever offer. Later in his work he maintains that the glory of God is to be understood in terms of redemptive, recreative, and suffering love.

God's glory *is to be revealed,* declares DI. By the word "revealed" he employs a pun. The verb means "to be uncovered." But to go into exile was also described as being uncovered, because one went naked and exposed. Perhaps DI is here hinting that there is a connection between the two meanings of the word.[2] In fact the connection later on is one of his central themes. *All flesh* means all mankind. *Together* is one of DI's favorite words. Sometimes he appears to employ it just to fill up a line of verse and make it scan. On the other hand there may be substance in the LXX's rendering of the word, as here, by "the salvation of God"; for those words must mean "God's saving action." Later we shall see that DI uses the Hebrew term *tsedheq* to mean this very thing.

The angelic voice now concludes his command by giving the sanction for the orders he has passed on. His sanction is: "God has spoken." Amos

[2] See p. 17.

the prophet had declared, "The Lord God has spoken, who can but prophesy?" (3:8 RSV.) But a sinful man may resist the will of God and refuse to pass on the Word. The angelic voice, on the other hand, is not a sinful personality. In DI's day the angels were regarded as the will of God in action so to speak—God's will merely made visible to the eye of the human mind, either in the form of flames of fire or else in human form. In themselves, however, the angels of the OT were nothing. They were just the voice through which the divine Word came to man. Thus the whole emphasis here is upon the Word and not at all upon the bearers of the Word. Yet the Word of God is to be identified with the will of God that has now been uttered, and which is therefore now moving along its creative path. The Hebrew language has only one word for our two, "word" and "thing." In translating the OT, sometimes one English word must be used in preference to the other; only the context can decide. But ideally the two meanings for the Hebrew thinker cannot be separated, just as in the OT world of thought no separation can be made between matter and spirit. The essence of man's sinfulness follows from his rebellion against God's will for him. Thus it reveals itself in his selfish unwillingness to make God's Word become flesh. On the other hand, this separation between word and thing cannot be maintained of God. When God utters his Word, then the thing becomes: "God *said:* 'Let there be light' and light became." The Word of God cannot return unto God void, but must accomplish that which he utters as his will. DI has more to say of this at 55:8-11. Meantime his wholehearted conviction is that the eschatological redemption announced by the Voice is bound to become event, and when it does, that event will take place in history. Yahweh's mouth has spoken it.

6 A voice saying: "Call!" "What am I to call?" I replied.
All flesh is grass, and lasts no longer than the
wild flowers.
7 Grass dries up, flowers wither, when Yahweh's breath just
blows upon them. [Surely the people is grass.]
8 Grass dries up, flowers wither—but the Word of our
God remains forever.

6.

DI now hears another angelic voice telling him to cry aloud his message in his turn. But he still has to learn what that message is to be. In fact man can never conceive the right message in his own heart and mind.

The religions of the world each imagine that they know the answer to this problem. The word "religion" does not exist in the OT, however. There alone we meet with a people that believes it has received revelation not religion. So here is the message, in vss. 6-8. It comes as a word both of revelation and comfort at the same time to discomfited Israel in exile in Babylon. In doing so it enters into the realm of history, thing, or flesh. In vs. 5 *all flesh* meant "all mankind" (cf. Gen. 6:3; John 17:2; Rom. 3:20).

The date is now somewhere between 545 and 540 B.C. About forty-five years before this time the end had come upon Jerusalem. In those days, before there was medical care and social security as we know it, human life was nasty, brutish, and short. Thus it is likely that very few of DI's present hearers would even remember the events of 587 B.C. when Jerusalem was destroyed. Most of those who had gone into exile in that year would now be dead. Those who were still alive must have had little hope of finding any meaning in their remaining unhappy years. When the brevity of the human span is seen in its stark reality against the vanity of human existence, then the meaninglessness of human life becomes even more apparent. Some of us have known the experience of going back on a second occasion a few weeks later to view a beautiful hillside that had been covered with spring flowers, only to discover that not one of those flowers has survived.

The word rendered by the phrase *lasts no longer,* in connection with the wild flowers, is a noun in the original Hebrew. Its use here has troubled translators all down the centuries. It is the noun *ḥesedh,* a word which the KJV translates in many ways, such as "mercy," "lovingkindness," "goodness," or even "piety." The translators of the RSV sought to render it consistently by "steadfast love." But none of these translations will suit here with reference to the short-lived nature of grass. Normally the word is used to describe the content of the covenant relationship that obtains between God and Israel. Thus its many-sidedness reflects the continuing and undeviating nature of the loyalty and devotion that is the mark of those who have covenanted together. But the continuing loyalty of grass to its true nature and purpose is a chimera, for grass is too short-lived to remain what it was created to be. This is a frequent theme in the OT (cf. Isa. 37:27; Job 8:12; 14:2; Ps. 90:5-6). This noun cannot be translated by such words as "beauty" (RSV) or "goodliness" (KJV) or "glory" (LXX). The *ḥesedh* of nature is to die. So is that of human empires; so too is that of all dictatorships. When those who live under a dictatorship remind themselves of this, the cry becomes a word of comfort instead of a cry of despair.

7, 8.

The words "surely the people is grass" (KJV) read like a gloss that has been written onto the margin of the text. As they stand, they spoil both the rhythm and the balance of the line. The contents of vs. 6 are sufficient to remind us that it is the deliberate providence of God that human life is short. It is God's breath that creates man (Gen. 2:7); so too it is God's breath that withers man, just as the hot wind from the desert—"breath" and "wind" are identical in Hebrew—withers the sparse grass of the dry Babylonian sand dunes. How odd to make part of the Good News the devastating fact that man is as short-lived as grass. But the angelic message of DI does not end with this sad but obvious fact. The simple truth is, that in contrast to all that has been said, the Word of God is ever constant, reliable, and steadfast, and is alive forevermore. It is alive and endures on the ground that it is the Word of the living and enduring God. In fact, the Word is God because it has issued from the heart of God, which is the center of his being. It has now become his will made known in creative activity. As such it is the Word uttered, and consequently now become objectively independent of the God who uttered it.

The doctrine of the Word had been developing steadily within Israel before the Exile had even begun. We see it hinted at in the case of Samuel (I Sam. 3:19), and by Hosea (6:5); Isaiah (11:4) furthermore uses the concept in connection with his messianic Figure; some of the psalms moreover personalize the Word almost to the degree that the psalms of Solomon understand it after the completion of the OT writings (cf. Pss. 107:20; 147:15). There the Word continues to perform a saving, healing action, just as it does here in vs. 8; this is because the God who speaks the Word is himself the Savior and healer of men (Isa. 43:11; Exod. 15:26; Ps. 103:3; Jer. 17:14).

Herein lies the only ultimate hope that man can ever entertain. Of and by himself man is nothing. On the other hand he is created from the breath of the ever-living and enduring God. Man thus lives by the Word that cannot return unto God void. The *hesedh* of nature is that it should die; but the *hesedh* of God is such that he must necessarily remain. Accordingly man too will remain. The ultimate eschatological outcome of this statement of DI is of course to be found in John 1:1. There we have the statement that the Word actually becomes man. Yet this ultimate vindication of the angel's Good News would not have appeared as a strange thing to a man like Jeremiah (see 17:5), or to the writer of Ps. 8:4-5 when he asks, "What is man?" for his answer is, "Thou hast made him a little lower than divinity," or to the writers of Pss. 102:26-28; 103:15-17. Yet DI will later draw the contrast between God and man more strangely still. For at the point where his argument reaches its climax he declares that the Word becomes not just man, it becomes suffering man. Yet DI must establish many links in the chain of his argument before he can raise that unexpected issue.

9 Get up, Zion, on a high mountain, and tell forth the
good news;
Raise thy voice aloud, Jerusalem, and tell forth the
good news;
Say to the towns of Judah: "Behold your God!"
10 Behold, Lord Yahweh is coming with power, and his arm will rule
for him.
Behold, he has his wages with him, and his payment by him.
11 Like a shepherd he will feed his flock, gathering up
the lambs in his arms, carrying (them) in his bosom, and
gently leading the pregnant ewes.

9.

That then is the good news. Consequently Jerusalem dare not keep it to herself. At the moment of speaking *Zion*—God's people—is dwelling on the flat Mesopotamian plain. But Jerusalem, the ancient capital city of the exiles, straddles a ridge that seen from the west seems to be along the skyline above. Of nearby hills, only the Mount of Olives is higher than Zion. So the people of God is to get back somehow to Zion and climb onto the top of its high hill, so that when she proclaims the good news her voice will carry further. She is not to be afraid about her task; she is to shout her message at the top of her voice—as surely she ought. While grammatically it is possible to translate this as "O herald of good tidings to Jerusalem," such a rendering would leave the problem that the herald as well as Zion is spoken of in the feminine. That understanding of the words is obviously out of the question. While DI the prophet is certainly the mouthpiece of the angelic message to Israel, yet it is Israel herself, under the feminine figure of either Zion or Jerusalem, who is to be the missionary instrument to all the world. Moreover, a city set on a hill itself signifies mission. We shall see, as his sermon develops, that Israel's missionary task is one of DI's major themes.

Included in Zion's constituency are naturally the small towns and villages *of Judah.* Not all the people of Judah had been removed to Babylon by Nebuchadrezzar in 587. Many peasants had been left to continue their simple and brutish life in the hill country of the little area known as Judah, then part of a province of the Babylonian Empire. However, as recent archaeological evidence shows, the country districts of Judah were at that time terribly decimated and impoverished. Yet these poor folk were God's people and so were still one with the exiles to whom the angelic message, first of comfort, secondly of challenge, was now being addressed. The people of Judah, then, were to be the first to hear the good news. The remnant, now in Babylon, was to shout it to them the moment they succeeded in getting home to Judah. Little did the remnant realize, however, that they were actually God's *ecclesiola in ecclesia* within Israel as a whole, that they were that element within Israel which had been specially fitted for their missionary task just because they had suffered doubly, as the towns of Judah had not. This too is another of DI's important themes, merely hinted at as it is in this first chapter of his thesis. Here at the beginning of his book, he makes a number of unexplained statements of this nature. It is as if he were the editor of a newspaper whose task it is to provide the headlines to the subject matter. In the small type below, the topics splashed across the page are then dealt with in detail.

The verb to *tell forth the good news* means in origin to "smooth," and then to "smooth out the wrinkles" on a human face. The remnant itself in Babylon has now been given the comfort of God, and it has now heard that *the Word of our God remains for ever* (vs. 8). The natural sequence is that she in her turn should pass the good news on to her poverty stricken brethren back home. What she is to say is: *Behold your God!* When she does so, then those careworn and impoverished villagers will know a joy such as they have not known for a generation; they will learn that, despite all appearances to the contrary, their covenant God is still alive, and that he cares for them still as the Father of his people (cf. Exod. 4:22).

10.

The above message is no mere philosophical idea. DI is concerned not with ideas but with historical facts. The word "God" which he has used before he now defines by the name Yahweh, i.e., by the name of the covenant God who had already revealed himself to Moses within history

(Exod. 6:1-8). The transcendent God, he now declares, is about to stoop to enter history once again with *power*. Here we have an instance of the *beth essentiae* of the grammarians. DI means that God is coming in the shape of, *qua*, power. This power he portrays by the anthropomorphic picture of God's arm ruling for him. This symbolic sense of arm occurs only in Isa. 40–66. An arm is for stretching out, it is for action, it is for doing the task determined upon by the whole man.

Yet it is not enough for Israel to know that God is all-powerful. Israel wants to know if the all-powerful is also essentially good. The answer comes in the next cry: *Behold, he has his wages with him*. Lord Yahweh is a God of justice, whose power will never be used arbitrarily but always for defined ends of love and justice that conform to his absolute will. The double name, Lord Yahweh, had been a favorite of Amos' two hundred years before. He too had delighted to stress the justice of Israel's God. Ezekiel immediately before DI's day had used this double title also.

11.

The connection between the words *power* and *wages* is now explained in an astonishing metaphor. The argument runs like this: (1) The strength of Almighty God is the strength of the gentle giant. It is the strength of tenderness and love and care. This is good news indeed. (2) God's *wages* and *payment* are his own abiding presence with the poor exiled Israelites, his covenant people of old. This second theme DI will also develop greatly as his message unfolds. Meanwhile we see how God's action in picking up the lambs in his arms is actually an act of salvation (cf. 59:16; John 10:28). DI is not the first to make this plain. Israel had long since learned to picture strength and gentleness as necessarily conjoined in the Good Shepherd who was their God (cf. II Sam. 5:2). Yet the picture unfolds from a situation that appears to the human eye as what we would call a complete loss. Israel's God had been finally defeated, it seemed, when Nebuchadrezzar's god had strengthened him to destroy Yahweh's temple and people, and had brought about the negation of the promise made to Israel's father Abraham. This was the promise that through his descendants the whole world would be blessed (Gen. 12:1-3; 17:6; 18:8), and the covenant which God was making with Abraham to that end would stand forever (Gen. 17:7).

Now, declares our prophet, despite all appearances: (1) The Word of God does in fact still stand (vs. 8). (2) God himself is still "thy shield and thy exceeding great reward" that he had promised to be to Abraham

(Gen. 15:1) and in consequence to all Abraham's descendants. (3) Therefore, as a result of God's intimate fellowship with Israel through the reality of the covenant, God himself, *qua* Israel's *wages*, has so identified himself with her in her tribulation that the pain and suffering which Israel has been going through, and which Israel has been suffering to her cost, has now become God's costly redemptive experience. For he is carrying Israel *in his bosom,* and so he is meeting the buffetings of fate in her place. The words *his payment by him* (vs. 10) mean that God himself has paid the wages, has paid the price that Israel should have paid, but obviously could not do.

DI must have had access in exile to manuscripts from the hand of Jeremiah and of the other prophets of the preexilic period. Jeremiah (31:15-17) had spoken of the pain and sorrow let loose when the northern tribes were torn away from their home—"Rachel . . . weeping for her children, and refusing to be comforted." Yet Jeremiah had declared that, despite all appearances, their exile contained meaning and purpose, for they all still belonged within the plan of God. "Stop weeping," Jeremiah had told his contemporaries, "for there are wages for thy work." Even the experience of suffering punishment for one's sins was thus evidently a "work" of God. However, DI now declares, the moment of comfort has arrived, because God has now used the Exile with all its sorrows and trials to reveal his own nature as that of saving love. Such therefore is his exceeding great reward.[3]

The picture here of the Good Shepherd embodies the reversal for Israel of all the horrors of the past—of the siege and destruction of Jerusalem, of the bitterness of separation from dear ones, of the agony and thirst of the desert march, of the sense of hopelessness they had known, and of the purposelessness of their life in exile. The word for lamb can also be used for a little child; in fact its feminine form in Aramaic was used by Jesus when he raised up Jairus' daughter. DI here makes the striking point that it will be no effort for God to lift his *lambs in his arms,* for he can raise up—the verbs are identical—and fill in valleys with equal ease. It is a continuing question whether DI was personally acquainted with Ezekiel in exile. Certainly Ezekiel delights to use the same picture as DI does, of God as the Good Shepherd of his people (Ezek. 34). On the other hand, not until his last chapter does DI make the suggestion which Ezekiel de-

[3] See also Trito-Isaiah on this theme at 62:11.

velops, that God will use a descendant of David as the agent of his shepherding care (Isa. 55).

12 Who ever measured the waters in the hollow of his hand?
Or marked off the heavens with a span?
Or enclosed [the dust of] the earth in a measure,
weighed the mountains on scales, or the hills on balances?
13 Who could ever ascertain Yahweh's mind? As for a man—
Would he ever let a man know his plan?
14 Whom did he consult so as to give him understanding?
Whom did he teach the way of judgment?
[Whom did he teach knowledge], and to whom did he reveal
the way of understanding?

12.

Many commentators have worked upon the assumption that DI is a collection of independent oracles which have been rather oddly strung together to form the sequence we now possess. Scholars have therefore classified the types of oracles under various heads, and have compared and contrasted those types with their fellows elsewhere in the OT as well as with those found in extrabiblical literature. But the work of DI is to be understood quite differently from the prophetic material left us by the preexilic prophets, including even Isaiah of Jerusalem, whose name has been set above the whole sixty-six chapters of the book of Isaiah. DI undoubtedly made use of the various types or *Gattungen* of prophetic utterance which were his literary heritage as a Hebrew. But unlike the great prophets before him, whose material has come down to us in short and pithy utterances consisting sometimes of only a few lines at a time, DI has penned a sustained theological treatise in verse. In doing so, he has brilliantly rung the changes of style possible in his day by weaving into his narrative several of the various *Gattungen* that the earlier prophets had employed. But the important point to note is that there is a logical sequence of thought throughout his whole sixteen chapters, and that each of the pictures he paints, independent of the whole as it may appear to be at first glance, is necessary for the continued advancement of his argument just at that point where he has placed it. It would be nonsense to declare for example that Rom. 9–11, being a separate *Gattung* from chs. 1–8, was therefore an inset in the Epistle to the Romans made by a later scribe. In the same way the verses that now follow should not be regarded as a brilliant but irrelevant picture portrait of the majesty of God. They follow naturally after vs. 11. For at vs. 12, DI sets out to teach what the power and the arm of the Lord that he has mentioned really mean. And his reason for doing so is to assure Israel that the loving purpose of God Almighty is such that he can permit himself to stoop to carry his lambs without losing his right to be known as the Creator of all.

Who then is the Good Shepherd to whom DI has referred above? It is he who has *measured the waters in the hollow of his hand. Waters, mayim,* is a deliberate choice of a word instead of "seas," for it sounds in assonance with the word *shamayim,* heavens. Yet DI may also have intended, by avoiding the word for seas, to suggest that even the waters above and below the firmament lie secure in the hollow of God's hand (see Exod. 20:4). For of course DI lived in that three-decker universe which the whole ancient world accepted as a scientific description of the cosmos it knew. The ancient Hebrews feared the sea and seldom ventured on it. But they dreaded still more the waters of chaos under the earth, and saw them as the symbol of all that was evil and inchoate. It is doubtful whether DI possessed our first chapter of Genesis. But he refers frequently to the same description of the creation of the world that that chapter so magnificently portrays. If, on the other hand, Jeremiah had known Gen. 1, as we might imagine he did from Jer. 27:5 and 31:35-37, then of course DI too would know it half a century later. Whatever the truth of the matter may be, it is interesting that nearly all the features of Creation which DI describes in these chapters are to be found in Gen. 1–3. Vss. 12-14 have formed the basis of Paul's citation at both Rom. 11:34 and I Cor. 2:16.

13.

The word translated by *mind* is really the word for "wind" and consequently also for "spirit." It is rendered this way, however, on the ground that Paul, in the above two quotations, translates it by the Greek word *nous.* The theologian Bultmann offers a further interpretation of the word when he expounds this verse with the words: "Who has recognized God's wonderful plan of salvation?" Bultmann probably does this on the ground that DI raises this issue in later chapters, where he reads this meaning into the word *ruaḥ.* God's *plan,* his *'etsah,* is that which Isaiah of Jerusalem had spoken of long before, when he declared that God's messianic Figure would utter the very *'etsah* of God (Isa. 9:5-6; 11:2). But in all DI's long and intricate argument he assumes that it is Israel herself who is to become God's messianic agent and incorporate within her own unique relationship to God the plans and purposes of God for the redemption of the world. This, of course, is a highly important theological assumption, and one that must be kept in the forefront in any Christological discussion.

As in Job 38, a poem similar to this one, the mind of God is indeed unfathomable to man. Who could have suggested that the Creator of all would think it part of his plan to pick up lambs in his bosom? What DI offers here is certainly not a man's findings who has searched for God. Rather what he gives us is revelation, the revelation to man of God's mind and purpose for him. Therein lies the essential difference between the biblical faith as here expressed and the many human philosophies of all the ages of man.

The word *ascertain is* identical with the word rendered *marked off* in vs. 12. Thus does DI with both wit and sarcasm force his readers to take seriously the blasphemy of man. Man in DI's day was just as apt to imagine, as any astronautical scientist today is tempted to do, that humanity may one day measure the mind of God.

14.

It is ludicrous to suppose, he declares, that any human mind could ever fully understand either the mysteries of this mysterious universe, or the depths and fullness of God's total revealed way of life for men. This word *mishpaṭ* here obviously means more than just the way of judgment, or even the right way to live, as we shall see later.

15 Behold, the nations are like a drop [spilling] from a bucket, or they are regarded [by him] as specks of dust on the scales.
Behold, he handles islands as if they were fine powder.
16 Lebanon does not offer sufficient firewood,
Nor enough wild animals for a burnt offering.

15.

Language nowhere offers more striking pictures than do these lines of the greatness and power of God. And even though we today live in a vastly more expansive universe than DI could ever have imagined, his similes resound as validly now as ever.

The first picture is of a *bucket* being drawn up from a well; the drop or two that spill back into the well are not worth catching in comparison with the water in the bucket. In the second picture the significance of the word *dust* is even enhanced for us by the passage of time; for we today are very conscious of living in a world that is an agglomeration of infinitely tiny atoms.

16.

Lebanon was the mountainous area to the north of Palestine on whose slopes grew coniferous forests. These forests included the famous cedars, which Solomon had used for the interior decoration of the Jerusalem temple (I Kings 5:8-10). Neither Lebanon's mighty forests nor its many and various wild animals could ever be sufficient for a human act of worship of such a mighty God. Man from the beginning has instinctively offered sacrifice to the divine. But this greatest of mountaintops known to the Hebrews was not sufficient as an altar for the God who was now revealing himself to Israel in all the glory of his majesty.

17 All the nations are as nothing before him;
They are regarded by him as less than nothing,
or even as negation.

17.

Yet God does not so much reveal himself as hide himself in nature. For before its intricacies and wonders man's mind is both numbed and awed. Man realizes even while he muses, that since he can never know God, he will never come to know what degree of sacrifice he therefore ought to offer God. For is any sacrifice of any significance at all, if the human race which seeks to offer it is itself *as nothing before him?* The significance of the word that follows in the poetic parallel, the one translated most unpoetically by the word *negation,* is important. DI is once again using the language of Gen. 1. At Gen. 1:2 we read: "And the earth was without form, and void," i.e., *tohu wa-bhohu. Wa* means "and"; *bhohu* is merely a poetic doubling of the word *tohu,* used for emphasis and effect. Our author, DI, employs this word *tohu,* without the unnecessary doubling, on seven occasions in his sixteen chapters. What he is obviously concerned to do by this frequent use of the word is to declare the great reality, viz., that it is God who is all in all, and that all else must therefore be less than nothing. As the Genesis picture puts it, in the beginning God created order out of chaos. DI has much to say later on this concept of God's order. Here his emphasis is upon the fact that man and man's human forms of government and ordered life are actually so far from being in conformity with

God's order that they belong rather to the realm of antiorder, to what tends toward disintegration rather than to integration, to destruction rather than to construction, to the concept of negation or darkness rather than light and positive value. No more need be said at present of this idea, for DI returns to it with force in later lines.

18 With whom then would you compare the Divine Being?
Or what would you liken him to?
19 An idol? A workman pours it, then a goldsmith stamps gold leaf all over it; then he welds silver chains to it.
20 But the man who has been reduced to poverty must just select a piece of mulberry wood that will not rot;
He seeks out for himself an ingenious craftsman, and has him set up an image that will not fall over.

18.

In order to assure the exiles of what he has now said, that God is quite capable of accepting their suffering as an adequate punishment, of putting an end to their *forced labor* (vs. 2), and of leading them home as a shepherd leads his sheep, DI has first shown his hearers how their covenant God Yahweh is mighty beyond all human thought (vss. 12-15). This led to the view that man cannot respond in any adequate sense to God's demands (vs. 16); that in fact the human order is wholly different from God's order and purpose (vs. 17). Now DI shows how puerile are the efforts of men—and he obviously exemplifies the Babylonians among whom the exiles were perforce living—to conceive of divinity in any adequate manner.

19.

Man has first to make his gods, or create his concepts, before he can bow down to them and worship them. DI reminds his readers, however, of the truth that we find expressed in the second commandment. So wholly other is Israel's God, so positive when man's thoughts and life are merely negative, that if man essays to conceive of God in any form at all, his thoughts must necessarily eventuate as blasphemy. The negative cannot possibly conceive the positive. Thus when man does try to create a likeness of the divine, all that he can produce is the fatuous gold-lacquered image which the Babylonians imagined to be a god, and yet which they had to chain to a wall to keep upright.

20.

With biting sarcasm DI suggests that if a man is too poor to rise to a gold-plated image, then he can be happy making do with a piece of wood, provided only that it does not *fall over* (see also 44:12 *ff.*; Jer. 10:3-4).

21 Do you not realize? Do you not understand? Has it not
been told you from the beginning?
Have you not understood since the foundation of the world?
22 It is he who sits upon the vault over the earth.
Its inhabitants are like locusts.
It is he who spreads out the sky like gauze,
and stretches it like a dwelling tent.
23 It is he who brings dictators to nought,
and makes earthly rulers like negation.
24 No sooner are they planted; no sooner are they sown;
No sooner has their stem taken root in the ground,
Than he has breathed upon them, and they shrivel up,
or the desert wind carries them off like stubble.

21.

Sweeping all this Babylonian nonsense aside, DI returns to ask questions in the Socratic manner, such as every living soul must seek to answer if he is to remain a sane and purposeful creature. He implies first that the greatness of God is self-evident, and would agree that "the heavens declare the glory of God, and the firmament showeth his handiwork" (Ps. 19:1). Yet natural revelation is never stressed in the OT. Sometimes it even seems to be denied (cf. 45:15). DI is well aware that the Babylonians gazed at the same sky his own fathers had seen over Jerusalem. Yet the Babylonians had developed no conception of an incomparable, wholly other God as the author and sustainer of their lives. That is why DI later refers to what ultimately speaking is God's chosen method of revelation to man, the special relationship into which he had entered with Israel at the time of the historical event of the Exodus and at the giving of the Law at Mount Sinai. DI himself of course belonged to this people whom God had chosen in this way. That means he is here speaking out of a situation of grace, out of the experience of redemption which Israel had already known in the days of Moses. Only later did she philosophize upon what God had done for her at that time.

The word *the beginning* (*ro'sh*) is a technical term in DI's vocabulary which he employs to describe the beginning of revelation and this first act of redemption in the days of Moses. It could read "for a long time back," but does not seem to mean this anywhere else in DI's writings. Should this be its meaning, then DI understood God's control of the universe in the light of the exodus from Egypt. Yet DI seems to go further back than the days of Moses. For God's promise to Abraham had preceded his redemptive act in Moses' day. Ever *since the foundation of the world,* when God put man in control of this mysterious universe under himself, God had been revealing himself to Adam's sons—as indeed Noah knew, and as Abraham, Isaac, Jacob, and Joseph had also certainly known. But since the word *foundation* may refer to the occupation of Canaan, for *ha-'arets* can mean the land (of Canaan) as well as the whole earth, it is quite possible that DI was punning. Thereby he implied that God's gift of land to Israel, theologically speaking, was one with his creation of the world. The world began when God's plan began to unfold in and through his people Israel.

22.

This plan had to do not with *locusts* but with people, the people of Yahweh. For what is the life of a locust? It is a life of destruction and the production of chaos (*tohu*); it is a life of rending and devouring. Unredeemed man has torn at the roots of the earth by felling trees en masse and so producing floods, by introducing rabbits where once was a balance of nature and so producing droughts, by obliterating not merely the moa and the dodo but also the primitive races of man in every continent of the world. And now once again man is setting at liberty forces he does not understand, so that he watches in fear and horror as a mushrooming cloud ascends above his head, and he is left with a waste of atomic detritus from which he does not know where to hide. Yet even *the sky,* to which man's mushroom ascends, God could effortlessly reduce to its original atoms when he no longer needs it for his plan, even as a man pulls down a *tent* which he has used as a temporary home.

23.

Man too is part of this universe that exists only because God wills that it should stay in being. *Dictators* therefore rule only by God's abundant sufferance. In themselves such men are vanity—nay, they are even *negation.*

24.

And so comes the logical question from contemplating the above: Why then should the exiles stand in awe of the silly power of Babylon? It might look as if the royal line of Babylon were well rooted in the soil of Mesopotamia, because for almost a century now the dynasty of Nebuchadrezzar had been ruling throughout the Near East, an area which included Israel's beloved Judah and the ruins of their ancient city of Jerusalem. But what is a human *root* when it has dug down merely into—negation? God has only to breathe on the dictator of Babylon and he will *shrivel up,* even as goes the *stubble* that is swirled into oblivion by the storm *wind* out of the *desert.*

25 **With whom would you compare me then? Whom am I like?**
asks the Holy One.
26 **Lift up your eyes on high and see—who created these?**
It is he who brings their host out by number;
each of them he calls by name,
By the greatness of (his) vigor and mighty strength:
none is ever missing.

25.

Is it not rather ridiculous to liken anything at all to the God who is absolute ruler of earth and sky? asks the Holy One. Here our poet borrows one of the favorite names of Isaiah of Jerusalem for God. DI uses it when he seeks to express the majesty and wonder of the Creator over against the sinfulness and pettiness of the creature. By its use, however, DI does not show that he believes in creation, far less that he believes in man. Unlike many present day philosophers he believes only in the Creator of the creation, and in the Creator of man.

26.

When the sun sets in the evening, out comes the *host* of the stars. It is as if God were the commanding officer of a vast army in the heavens. When he visits his units on parade and numbers them off, he finds that not one star *is ever missing* or out of its appointed place. In fact, fantastically numerous as they are, God knows them all—and not just by number but *by name.*

The word for *host* here, *tsabha,* is the word of vs. 2. It occurs also in the plural in the divine name "Lord of hosts." Those hosts were, as we see, the multitude of the stars. But often these were personalized in OT thought, as if each star were an angel acting as God's instrument on high. And so the word *host* also signified the heavenly host of angels and angelic powers that performed the will of God in a living manner, on the ground that they themselves were but emissaries of the living God (cf. Ps. 104:4). DI, by the way, knows of no disobedient stars, as do Isa. 24:21, which comes at least a century later, and Ps. 58:1, where the stars are "mighty lords" or even "gods." Enoch 18:15, from within the intertestamental period, runs: "And the stars which roll over the fire are they which have transgressed the commandment of the Lord in the beginning of their rising, because they did not come forth at their appointed times." [4]

But this is a sacramental universe, a fact which the Hebrews knew well. By that modern word we describe their belief that the universe is one entity and not two; that is to say, they believed we are not to speak of heaven plus earth, for there is but one unified cosmos. So it is natural that God's hosts should serve him throughout it all. That is why this word *tsabha* can be used both of the angels and of Israel. For Israel is God's host, that host which under Joshua fought its way into the Promised Land at the founding of "*the* land" (vs. 21). Yet the warrior God Yahweh is always at war against evil everywhere, and so he uses his hosts to this end both on earth below and in heaven above (cf. Exod. 12:41; Num. 10:14; and cf. Eph. 1:21; Col. 1:16; I Pet. 3:22). If God so cares for the host, *tsabha,* of stars on high that he knows each of their personalities as a distinct entity and can identify each by its own individual name (cf. Ps. 147:4), then how much more must he have counted the hairs on your heads, O you trembling *host, tsabha,* of Israel? It is true that you have had to undergo, in the providence of God, the *forced labor, tsabha* (vs. 2), of an army that needs disciplining. Otherwise it would be of little use to him who has chosen it out of all the nations of the earth. But since God is in control of the hosts of the sky, obviously he is also in control of your life in exile. By means of this word play on the noun *tsabha,* DI once more brilliantly drives home his point about the majesty of God's purpose. It is such that neither the sin of his rebellious host Israel nor the shouting of Babylon's dictator king could even

[4] *The Apocrypha and Pseudepigrapha of the Old Testament,* ed. R. H. Charles (London: Oxford University Press, 1913), II, 200.

faintly disturb. *Grass dries up, flowers wither—but the Word of our God remains forever.* (Vs. 8.)

27 Why sayest thou, Jacob, and declarest, Israel:
"My way is hidden from Yahweh, and my judgment is disregarded by my God"?
28 Hast thou not known? or hast thou not heard?
It is Yahweh who is everlasting God, who is the creator of the ends of the earth!
He never wearies, nor is he ever exhausted;
There is no way of investigating his knowledge.
29 It is he who gives strength to the weary; who offers bounding vitality to those with no strength.
30 Young men may indeed grow weary and be exhausted; and warriors can actually fall.
31 But those who eagerly look for Yahweh shall gain newness of strength; they shall put forth new pinions like eagles;
They shall run and never be weary; they shall march on and never be exhausted again.

27.

Naturally Israel has not yet known that God is like this. She has not yet heard the Word of God uttered through the mouth of his prophet, nor seen it take shape in a historical situation. Only then can the comfort announced in vs. 1 become meaningful to her. Israel in exile had supposed that Yahweh had forgotten her. The temple was lying in ruins, and the temple was that spot alone where God and man could meet in sacramental worship. Jerusalem was now destroyed, and Jerusalem alone was God's chosen city, and as such was as much the medium of unfolding revelation as had been the line of David. The Holy Land, which God had given his people forever (Gen. 17:8; 28:13) was now overrun by hordes of heedless pagans. Much that DI has to say later is virtually a wrestling with the significance of these very problems. He is triumphantly able to show how Israel could lose her temple, her city, her land, even her very raison d'être, and yet discover that God could be wholly faithful to the promises he had made.

DI begins this section of his argument by addressing the despondent nation first as *Jacob* and then as *Israel.* By reminding them of their eponymous ancestor in this way, DI is alluding to the promise that God had made to Jacob. That promise was that Jacob's seed would be as numerous as the dust of the earth (Gen. 28:14). A few lines back DI had been declaring the insignificance of the nations of the earth in God's sight, and saying that they were like mere *specks of dust on the scales* (vs. 15). But now Yahweh, through DI, assures his people that though they share the common human lot and as such are also dust, they are precious in his sight. Their continued existence as a people even in far-off exile ought to show them that God has not repudiated his promise to Jacob. God is such that he cannot go back on his promise, for *the Word of our God remains forever* (vs. 8). This linking of vs. 27 with vs. 15 is not a piece of ingenious exegesis, even though in vs. 15 DI uses for *dust* a noun different from that employed in the tradition about Jacob in Gen. 28:14. The whole of DI's work is in reality a closely knit argument. His method is to make constant reference backward and forward as he proceeds, and bit by bit he binds his book together in one sustained and developing argument.

Then again, in the words of the divine promise, Israel's numbers are to be likened not only to the dust of the earth but also to the stars of the sky (Gen. 15:5). DI's teaching now becomes very clear. If God has indeed full control over the stars of heaven (vs. 26), he argues, then he is also in control of the seed of Abraham, Isaac, and Jacob.

Making use of a poetic parallelism, DI now addresses his people by the other name that Jacob had won for himself, once he had wrestled with God and had prevailed, viz., *Israel* (Gen. 32:24-32). Before Jacob had undergone his distinctive spiritual experience which earned him this new name, though chosen by God he had been a mean, selfish, and despicable man. His nature had in fact been *tohu*, negation, destructively false. But now, by God's grace and through the faith God had awakened in him in the encounter, he had become a new man altogether. He was thus worthy of a new name to describe the new man he had become. So there at Peniel God had blessed him. That blessing was the utterance with power and purpose of the Word of God which remains forever. The people who now bore Jacob's name had necessarily become the blessed people Israel, "strong with God." Why then should Israel, strong with God, so runs DI's argument, imagine that because of fleeting circumstances, her way *is hidden* from her God? Even in Babylon Yahweh was surely still her God, and Israel was still "my people" (vs. 1).

28.

The truth of this amazing good news DI drives home in a final magnificent word picture. Even as Israel cast her eyes upon all the ridiculous gods of Mesopotamia she should be reassured that her own national, covenant God was no other than the Creator of all things. *Everlasting, ʿolam,* is a word that is not primarily connected with life beyond the grave. It comes from the root meaning "hidden." And so it speaks of the mists of the past, hidden from the thought of man, and it looks toward the mists of the future, into which man's mind cannot even begin to pry. And so it speaks of the God who is Lord even of the hidden realities that human beings can envisage only in terms of infinite time. Moreover the word *creator* is that which occurs at Gen. 1:1. There we see no philosophical speculation about the origin of the earth such as we make today. We moderns speculate about how the universe came into being, and whether God produced it *ex nihilo* or in some other way. The significance and emphasis of the word before us is rather upon the continual creative activity of God—the word is an active participle—who never ceases to do what no man and no heavenly power can do. God has given man the power to refashion stuff that is already there; but man cannot *bara'*; only God can create. In fact this verb is reserved by both Genesis and DI for the action of the Almighty alone.

29, 30, 31.

DI thus draws attention to the effortless ease God displays as he continually creates a universe that no man can fathom. God is wholly other even than the strongest of his human creatures, whether they be lusty young athletes or highly trained *warriors.*

Now note DI's deliberate choice of words once again. The phrases *grow* or *be weary* and *be exhausted* occur twice. On the first occasion they refer to God—in the negative—in the second to man, when they are shown to be a significant reality in his life. The contrast is clearly made. DI has just established the absolute otherness of God from man. Now he proceeds to depict the grace of God leaping over the chasm that he has made between himself and man. In vs. 26 God has been revealed as *strength* itself. Now DI tells us that God gives this very *strength* of his—the words are identical—and his *bounding vitality* to those who are most in need of it, the *weary* and the *exhausted* among Israel. Yet once again God requires the cooperation of human faith, just as in the case of Jacob, before his gift of *vitality* can be appropriated by the weary exiles. It is *those who eagerly look for Yahweh* who find a miracle taking place in their experience. If God, says DI, was able to create in the beginning and can keep on creating this vast and complex universe, then he can as easily create a new thing in the life of those who passionately seek him. He can make pinions grow where there were none before.

The Targum translates: "They will lift up pinions as eagles." But the LXX best guides us to what may have been the original meaning of the Hebrew if not the original text; for it reads, "They will put forth new pinions." This means that new feathers sprout as the old ones crumple and die. *Lift up your eyes on high and see,* DI had said at vs. 26. Raise your sights. Believe that God is alive and can give you his own vitality too; for if you do make this act of faith, you will find that you do in fact possess the *strength* of God himself, for it is his will that you should have it. Faith means possessing not the mere physical energy of youth, but utter assurance that God is strong with the strength of the Good Shepherd. Anyone then, be he young or old, once he possesses the *pinions* of *eagles,* may find that he need no longer trudge along the road of life, for he will now be swept into a run by the pinions of faith (cf. Ps. 84:5-7). And in the long and wearisome march to the Promised Land that the *tsabha,* the army, of the living God must make, no soldier in that army need ever feel exhausted again. For he may be sustained by the vitality of God himself and by the promises of the enduring Word. Even the humdrum experience of daily living, with God now becomes by faith an eschatological exercise. And it is Israel's special joy to know that the meaning of the latter will be made clear at the end.[5]

[5] Throughout the later biblical period and into the Christian centuries the eagle was used as a symbol of new life. The eagle can soar till it is lost to sight. Like the phoenix it was also a symbol of release from bondage and of resurrection to newness of life. See George Ferguson, *Signs and Symbols in Christian Art* (New York: Oxford University Press, 1954), pp. 13-14, 23-24.

CHAPTER 41

1 **Turn and listen to me in silence, you coastlands;**
Let the nations gain new strength;
Let them come near; only then let them speak—
So let us enter into judicial proceedings together.
2 **Who is it who stirred up from the east the man whom victory meets at every step?**
Nations he lays low before him, kings he subdues beneath him;
His sword makes them like dust, and his bow like driven stubble.
3 **He pursues them and passes on intact, his feet (scarcely) touch the road.**
4 **Who has done this and acted thus? He who has been summoning the generations ever since the beginning—**
It is I, Yahweh, who am the first; and I am He who will be at the last.
5 **The coastlands have already seen and been afraid, the ends of the earth have panicked.**
6 **Each man now helps his neighbor and says to his brother, "Cheer up."**
7 **Craftsmen are now urging on goldsmiths, and those who smooth the gilt on with a hammer encourage those who do fine work with awls.**
One man says about the soldering, "That's fine." Then they set it up firmly with nails so that it will not fall over.

1.

Our chapter divisions are, of course, quite artificial. While DI used strophes that may be classified by us today under the titles of the various

Gattungen that we have invented, yet his whole epic poem is clearly a unity. It does not even use stanzas or cantos as do Milton's *Paradise Lost* and Dante's *Divine Comedy*. Vs. 1 follows directly from what precedes.

Here is the Lord of history speaking. He who stoops to give *newness of strength* (40:31) to the weary can obviously just as easily command the nations to obey him and so to gain *new strength*—the choice of language is the same in both cases. The strong of this world gain strength from God alone just as much as do the weak though they may not know it. It is as if God were calling the nations to a court of justice to hear him pass judgment, something which is his right to do. "Forget your wars for a moment, and be serious, and try to learn what is the meaning and purpose of life. I can destroy in a moment the best laid schemes of mice and men, and of generals and princes, and turn the end of a Maginot Line with ease. So don't speak your mind till first you turn and look at me and see what is my power and plan." The LXX translates the word for *the nations* by "rulers." This leads us to suppose that the LXX has the other meaning of *le'ummim* in mind, viz., a cognate word of the Akkadian *limmu,* which can be used of a ruler. The Targum of Genesis and the LXX of Isaiah also seem to know this meaning of *le'ummim*.

2.

What is this plan of God then? Again DI hints at it, without naming the person of Cyrus, king of Persia, who even as he was speaking was carrying forward a triumphant campaign of conquest in Asia Minor. But DI insists that Cyrus' advance was primarily God's doing and only secondarily the action of a man. He comes both *from the east* and from the north (41:25). That is actually the route that Cyrus took. The translation of the next few verses as it is here is only one of several possibilities, as the reader can see by referring to other commentaries and the various versions. DI's Hebrew is so condensed and poetically expressed that no one should lay claim to making a definitive translation. But the picture of Cyrus' steady advance causing all powers to collapse before him is historically accurate if we place DI in the second half of the 540's B.C. *Victory* is of course an equivocal translation. The word means "righteousness" or "justice" in other contexts, but it also has the pregnant sense of rightness taking effect by the power of God; so it comes to mean at times deliverance, victory, prosperity, as these represent the justification for or outcome of clashing with one's foes. Or again, in the sphere of morals, the word may be used as a virtual synonym for salvation, since salvation is deliverance from evil.

3.

Once again more than one translation is possible; yet the purport of them all is the significance of Cyrus' victorious advance: (1) "By a route which they are not aware of," i.e., Cyrus' intelligence corps finds ways by which his army circumvents the enemy. (2) "By a route which he does not enter with his feet." This might mean, as in the case of (1), that Cyrus avoids the beaten tracks. DSI seems to favor this interpretation. (3) "A path with his feet he does not tread," or in modern words, *his feet (scarcely) touch the road*. So fast does he advance that he goes like the wind. In other words, Cyrus is a kind of miracle man who never tires—for the reason that Israel's God is with him.

4.

Israel's God who has been doing all this—we have two perfect tenses of two similar verbs in succession, of which the first may mean to initiate an action, the second to realize and carry it out—is no parvenu among the gods. It is he who has been active since the beginning, because he is the beginning, *the first*, himself; consequently he *will be at the last*. But DI does not conceive of Yahweh as static being. He is the active, purposeful, creative God. For *I am He* is the emphatic assertion of Yahweh's personality. As we proceed it will be noted that DI makes use of innumerable active participles in relation to Yahweh to describe his vitality. An active participle is part of a verb, which in turn is the action element in human speech. Yahweh then has been active ever since *the first*. This is probably DI's technical term for the Exodus period when God chose Israel as his son (Exod. 4:22 and Hos. 11:1). Since then God had been calling generation after generation of Israelites to hear and obey his voice.

Our author has Yahweh make this great declaration about himself in the light of what the Israelites were probably learning at that time about the religion of Cyrus the Persian, the man on whom DI was calling his people to pin their hopes. It is a matter of controversy whether Cyrus was a Zoroastrian by religion or not. This is because we are not yet certain when Zoroaster lived. But when formulating his faith, he adapted into his system the very exalted religious beliefs of the early Persians which were similar to his own. This matter will be discussed further at 45:7. The Gatha 31:8, a paragraph from Persian literature quite as old as Cyrus, runs: "I recognized, O Mazda, that thou art the first and the last." But here, however, Yahweh is not called the last himself. He is to be at or with the *last,* curiously enough a plural word. The term seems to signify the "outcome" of particular historical events in space and time. Its use links the world of word and thing that has been mentioned at 40:5 and requires their unity. To use present-day theological jargon, this word "outcome" might be translated by the phrase "eschatological significance."

All the prophets of the OT were convinced that this life is meaningful. To this end they emphasized the word "now" in every human relationship with which they dealt. Not only did people matter to God, they believed, so also did things. This world, they were sure, was not but an empty dream, nor was it a mere passageway to the real world still to come. Since God's universe is one, on the ground that God himself is one, then the life we live now in the flesh is but one side of the coin which represents the whole of reality. The other side we have not yet seen. But the coin that has the two sides is still the one coin, so that what happens to the one face of the coin affects the coin as a whole. Since this life here and now is important and significant, on the ground that God is speaking and uttering his Word within it, then what man does with his time and his things here and now must have an outcome in the world beyond. In our Lord's parable of the last judgment (Matt. 25:31-46), his whole emphasis is upon the outcome of ordinary human actions performed here and now. Feeding the hungry in this world he regards as an eschatological act. This verse then presents an awesome statement; it is that God will be there at the end, or at the outcome of all our everyday actions. Behind this solid world of things is not an it, but an "I." This "I" has already revealed himself as such to Moses (Exod. 3:6; 6:2). This *I, Yahweh,* must therefore necessarily continue to be identical with the "I" by which men know him now, and by which he has revealed himself in his relationship to Israel (cf. Ps. 102:27; Jer. 5:12).

There are some modern scholars whose linguistic competence in the sphere of pre-Israelite origins is undoubted who get caught themselves in the toils of the radical fallacy. For example, some scholars suggest that the name Yahweh means in Israel's historical period what it meant when it was first uttered by the human voice. Not so DI. By the year 550 B.C. the ancient name of Israel's God, Yahweh, had become linked with the conception of his vital, purposeful activity in and through the unique covenant relationship he had formed with this one people of his choice. That is why

DI can affirm that the whole relationship of God with Israel in terms of "now" must carry within it eschatological significance, since God himself will be there at the end. But having been there also at the beginning, he thus encloses all history in a ring. The rise of Cyrus was now the great historical event of the day. One could see that the whole balance of power in the known world was about to alter. Yet these catastrophic events were tightly enclosed within the divine plan, and were therefore under the control of the living God.

5, 6.

By 546 B.C. Cyrus had fought his way victoriously to the west coast of Anatolia, before which lay the islands of the Aegean, the Dodecanese, with Cyprus, Crete, and the Peloponnesus not far away. So there arises a natural human reaction to this common enemy. Old quarrels are forgotten, and men encourage and help each other to resist the conqueror. These lines offer us a cameo, showing how men will whistle in the dark to keep their courage up.

7.

Cyrus' most powerful opponent in Anatolia was King Croesus of Lydia, known till today for his fabulous wealth. Croesus' workmen had executed his orders well. This was to outdo all other kings in the production of golden gods such as the world had never seen before. Like a drowning man, Croesus was clutching at straws—in the shape of lucky amulets or silly, gold-lacquered charms—but even these fabulous gods were helpless before the advance of Cyrus, whom the God of Israel was using as the instrument of his plan. It may be that the three oracles preserved in Isa. 21:1-10, 11-12, 13-17 were all uttered by other prophetic voices about this time. Their authors belonged to the poverty stricken inhabitants of Palestine, and were not speaking from the milieu of Babylon, where DI was living. Yet together they witness to the widespread fear that Cyrus' victorious advance was creating.

At vs. 7 DI makes a pun upon the word rendered in vs. 6 by *cheer up*. This translation can give it only by the words *urging on;* by this means our author makes his message more telling and expressive. Yet English cannot reproduce the vitality of DI's language. His whole picture is a comment on what he has already said at 40:19-20 about the futility and stupidity of making one's own gods. This is a subject to which he returns in extenso at 44:9 *ff*. There are editors of DI who suggest that vs. 7 has slipped in by mistake from 40:19-20. But once we see the continuity of argument which DI so brilliantly employs, we recognize his genius in returning to the theme he has already raised. For whenever he can work it in, he uses it as a foil to his descriptions of Israel's God. He is aware that human nature is naturally superstitious. He would agree that the Lydians and Babylonians of all ages are eager to turn to such stupidities as yoga, astrology, and lucky charms, even when their rational minds inform them that belief in such things is futile. For just like the gods spoken of here, all such props to the human spirit, in the final analysis, *fall over*.

8 But thou Israel, art my Servant, thou Jacob, art he
whom I have chosen, the seed of my friend Abraham.
9 Whom I took firm hold of (and brought) from the ends
of the earth, and whom I called from its farthest
bounds;
To whom I said: "Thou art my Servant: I have chosen
thee, and so cannot have rejected thee."
10 Do not be afraid, for I am with thee; do not gape in
astonishment, that it is I who am thy God.
I have been holding thee firmly, and helping thee too;
I have actually been supporting thee with my
saving right hand.

8.

Suddenly DI's message changes. He has been describing above how Cyrus the Persian monarch is the instrument of God's plan; the nature of that plan, however, he has not as yet revealed. What he has to say now is even more surprising than what he has already reported, yet it too must be part of the Good News. His message is that the poor, stricken, downtrodden, exiled people of Israel is no less than, first, *my Servant;* secondly, God's *chosen* one. Yet DI has God address Israel here as Jacob. He evidently must remind his people that they are the true son of their father Jacob the unlikable, as we read of him in Genesis. DI's declaration can be paraphrased at this point with words from the NT: "You have not chosen me, but I have chosen you," adding, "but I chose you, because Jacob is the grandson of Abraham my friend" (cf. Gen. 15:18; II Chr. 20:7; Jas. 2:23). DI employs the word *seed* as a collective singular. He makes God address all Israel as one single, collective entity.

9.

Though not mentioned at this point, it is now obvious that the city of Jerusalem is in DI's mind; for it is from above it that God sends forth his voice. Jerusalem, as Ezekiel had believed, was the navel of the earth. Thus from the point of view of Jerusalem, both Egypt and Mesopotamia lay at *the ends of the earth*. DI is saying that God has already been faithful to Abraham's descendants when he called them out of Egypt in days of old. He is therefore to be trusted to look after the contemporary generation that is now in Babylon. Thus the significant statement about God's election of Israel is affirmed twice.

The term "servant of the king" is a Near Eastern technical term for a royal official. Many a jar and seal revealed by excavation have these very words stamped on them. Israel therefore knew what she was meant to be when God the king called her to be his Servant. She was called, in short, to serve unquestioningly and eagerly, and to be ever ready to execute the will of her royal master.

Israel, however, is here called to be God's Servant in a unique capacity. So DI raises the issue of the mystery of the divine election. Why is it that God has *chosen* Israel and *so cannot have rejected* her? Why not any other nation on the face of the earth? DI does not need to discuss the mystery, since Deut. 7, which has already dealt with it, was written well before the Exile. In light of such a discussion, therefore, DI cannot imply that a nation such as Babylon was outside of God's purpose and care. The Babylonians were just as much in the grasp of God as was Israel, yet only on the level at which they could be grasped, i.e., at the level of the experience of the divine to which they had reached. Their religion was a distorted religion, but it was not irreligion. This fact prevented the election of Israel from being made wholly in isolation; and it enabled the chosen people to make contact with their pagan neighbors. But it equated the religion of Babylon, which here has a small degree of positive value, with the negation that is the opposite of God's purpose of love. We shall see later (at 47:10) how DI deals with this interesting contradiction.

DI therefore lays full emphasis not on Israel herself as the elect, but on election as the action of God alone: *whom I have chosen, . . . whom I took firm hold of*. The phrase *took firm hold of* is another of our author's highly pregnant phrases. It focuses our eye upon, first, the action of gripping the hand, and, second, the action of leading by the hand that is now held tight. Then the words *whom I called from* (the earth's) *farthest bounds* remind Israel that God had led them before now from faraway Egypt into the Promised Land. God had thus called Israel from service to Pharaoh to enter into free, responsible service to himself (cf. Exod. 3:12). This service was the service of one whom God now called a *friend* (vs. 8); and as Deut. 4:37 had explicitly stated, this meant that God in his turn loved this people whom he had chosen. That of course was an extraordinary notion for anyone in the ancient world to entertain. Imagine any one of Babylon's gilt-plastered gods loving individual poor peasants huddled in their sordid mud huts on the banks of the Euphrates.

10.

But Israel's God includes in his Word of love the call that echoes through the pages of both the Old and New Testaments: *Do not be afraid* (cf. 41:13-14; 43:1, 5; 44:2, 8; 54:4; also 51:7, 12). This is surely good news to those (1) who are in the depths of despair and in fear of what man can do to them, and (2) who have become aware that they are standing on holy ground, because they are now in the presence of the all-holy and ever-living God. *For I am with thee*. No wonder, therefore, that DI's next words are, *Do not gape in astonishment*. For here we are presented with an amazing exegesis of election. Election, DI infers, means to be bound up *with* the God of heaven and earth. DI may be making explicit reference to God's words at Exod. 3:12, when he said to Moses, "Certainly I will be *with* thee." And God's declaration "I will be" is to be linked in turn with the words of divine self-revelation two verses later at Exod. 3:14. The words "I will be" are identical in Hebrew with the name "I am" of vs. 14, though rendered differently in English, and the concept of being is normally expressed in Hebrew by the use of the noun *yesh*. Martin Noth declares, "It is in any case important to note that the verb *hyh* does not express pure 'being,' pure 'existing,' but an 'active being' which does not take place just anywhere, but makes its appearance in the world of men and primarily in the history of Israel."[1] It bears the sense of becoming rather than of being. When this verb is used of God, it exhibits the purposeful, creative essence of his Being. Unite this concept with the preposition "with," and the words "I shall become with you" then appear as the essence of the divine plan that is to unfold within God's covenant relationship with Israel. Not only so, but since God has laid hold on Israel,

[1] *Exodus: A Commentary*, Noth, ed. (Philadelphia: Westminster Press, 1962), p. 45. Cf. also my *Christian Theology of the Old Testament* (rev. ed.; London: SCM Press, 1964), ch. 3.

something must have happened not only to Israel but also to God. The mutual relationship within the covenant must necessarily affect both parties to it. The last words of the line—*I have actually been supporting thee with my saving right hand*—define in what direction God's dynamic action is moving. God's essence is to save, i.e., to bring about a state of rightness, normalcy, justness. All of these words seek to represent the norm that Israel's relationship to God ought to demonstrate.

Now, the words "I shall become with you" have already been used by more than one of the prophets to exemplify the content of the covenant. So DI is merely bringing into play a conception which his informed hearers have already realized is basic to the election doctrine known to their fathers. Hosea (1:9) had employed it in both its positive and its negative aspects to further his interpretation of Israel's duty within the covenant relationship; and Jeremiah (30:11) had handled the same words and ideas.

Then another point to note about Israel's election is that though it is God who has chosen Israel *first,* his choice does not preclude the necessity of Israel's choosing him in return, in joyous response to his act (cf. Josh. 24:22). It is just this factor of Israel's responsive choice of Yahweh which prevents the biblical doctrine of election from postulating any view of divine predestination such as would overrule the human will. Jeremiah (1:5) could believe that God had elected him while he was still in his mother's womb, and DI can believe that Israel is called to be God's servant before she could know what her task and calling are to be. But in choosing to call the elect people first Jacob and then second Israel, DI reveals how OT thinkers such as he are able to hold this balance between predestination and free will. God had indeed called Jacob before he was born; for Jacob was the grandson of the Abraham to whom God had given his promise. Yet just like the infant child of Christian parents who has been presented for baptism, Jacob later could and did object to his calling and could and did rebel against the gracious purpose of his God for him. Even while he remained in a state of rebellion, he continued to be the called of God. Then came that night when he wrestled with the angelic manifestation of God's presence "with" him, and in full freedom of will had "power with God and prevailed" (Gen. 32:28). It was only then that Jacob gained the new named of Israel. In those days the name, ideally at least, was meant to be a description of its owner. That is why Jacob now received a new name, for he had become a new man.

It is not important to discover the real etymological origin of this word "Israel." Our concern is to know how the later OT writers used it and what *they* imagined its meaning to be. Now Gen. 32:28 takes it to mean "he who strives with God." Yet we are to note that Jacob—and therefore all Israel, the people of God in Jacob—is found striving with God in freedom of will only within the context of the relationship which God has already imposed upon him. Thus we may say that Almighty God can and does weave into his great plan every action of sinful Israel, even when, in complete freedom and in a spirit of rebellion, she continues to obstruct and to fight against the evolution of his loving purpose. God does not therefore rule Israel so much as overrule her. And finally God reaches his goal *despite* Israel, and in face of, and even by means of, her continuing enmity to and apostasy from him and his love. So in calling her freely to give up all fear and to trust his *saving right hand,* God exhibits toward Israel his sovereign grace. DI wants it known that God has already called Israel to serve him; so it is that call, and nothing that pertains to Israel herself, which is the ground of her being. That is why God must continue to forgive Israel for her continued state of rebellion against her calling. God in his grace will continue to weave into his overall purpose the outcome of the sins which his elect people continually commit.

11 Behold, all who are incensed against thee shall be
ashamed and humiliated,
Those who took thee to court shall become as nothing,
and shall perish.
12 Thou shalt look for them, but never find them—those
who have been struggling with thee;
Those who have been warring against thee shall become
as nothing at all.
13 For I, Yahweh, thy God, am gripping thee by thy right hand.
It is I who say to thee: "Don't be afraid; it is I who have
been helping thee."

11.

Behold, says God again; look and realize how all those who are fighting against Israel are fighting against the gracious purpose of God *in* Israel. This must be so, since God is "with" her, in the unique sense noted above. The prophets had long since claimed that God can be only either with or against his people. There is no third way he can act (cf. Hos. 1:9, 10;

Amos 3:1; Isa. 7:14; 8:8, 10). To be *incensed* is to grow hot and burn, or as we might say in today's jargon, "all who get het up against you." Since the verb can carry this meaning, some would vowel it so as to read "those who snort with indignation at thee." Thereupon, *those who took thee to court* before the world assize which DI has already described (41:1) will hang their heads with shame, and be accounted with those who are pure negation.

12.

For if they are not with God, then they can only be against him, and consequently they will disappear. But in grand contrast to this negative eventuality, the positive revelation of God in his loving, purposive relation to Israel DI now repeats to make it doubly clear. Yet he warns us that Israel will gain the joy that God is offering her only after constant *struggling*. Even though she has been redeemed, Israel is still to know wars and rumors of wars, for the life of the covenant people, as God's Servant, is destined to be one of toil and contradiction.

13.

But fundamentally she need never be afraid. Her God is the living God; and it is the living God who is even now holding her by her right hand; and so the faithfulness, or reliability, or rock-like quality of God is thus conveyed to Israel whom God holds; and this becomes in turn the basis of her whole life and historical existence, no matter what contradictions she may have to face in days to come.

> Let me no more my comfort draw
> From my frail hold of thee:
> In this alone rejoice with awe—
> Thy mighty grasp of me.

The above is said by DI not once as here, but again and again. This call not to be afraid is one of the basic elements in OT revelation.

14 Do not be afraid, thou worm Jacob, thou louse Israel;
I have been helping thee, is Yahweh's utterance;
it is the Holy One of Israel who is thy redeemer.
15 Behold, I have made thee into a sharp threshing sledge,
new, mounted with teeth.
Thou art to thresh mountains and beat them small,
thou art to make hills like chaff;

16 Thou art to winnow them, so that the wind will carry them away, and the sirocco will scatter them.
Then shalt thou exult in Yahweh, and glory in the Holy One of Israel.

14.

Here we return to the feminine form of "thou," for the reason that the word for *worm* is feminine. DI now gives us an astonishing line. He has been emphasizing the wonder of God's grace for a sinful people descended from the sinner Jacob. But now he makes God say: *Thou worm Jacob, thou louse Israel.* Those who oppose God's plan are negative, in that they are against God. On the other hand, Israel has no cause for boasting, merely because she knows herself to be the chosen people. Yet what a couple of words for God to use! *Thou louse Israel* is a much stronger expression than our modern "You lousy Israelites," for the emphasis is upon Israel's smallness, unimportance, and bestiality. The word *m*ᵉ*thē* in the Hebrew text has long been a puzzle. It may mean just "men of," but if so, it is a very weak parallel to *worm*. Some expositors therefore have suggested it means "little group of men." Three important ancient versions translate it by a form of the word for "dead." This translation should not be dismissed out of hand, as most interpreters do. If it is valid, then in the light of the discussion later at 42:23 and 43:28 we might say here "you dead Israelites." Others have invented a parallel to the word *worm* and understand the word for "grub." Their intention may be correct, it seems, for it is only in this generation that an Akkadian word has become known to us—and it was the language of Israel's Babylonian masters—a word built from the same consonants as the Hebrew word for "men of." It is this word meaning *louse*. Perhaps then DI is merely quoting the term that the Babylonians used when they referred to conquered and depressed Israel. Yet the phrase may be an instance of DI's fondness for the double entendre. By it he could be suggesting that Israel in exile has become a corpse, as Ezekiel had already done (37:11-13), so that as a corpse Israel is also to be pictured in terms of worms and grubs. However that may be, it is the name that God himself gives to Israel. The word *worm,* however, occurs also in Ps. 22:6, where we have, "I am a worm and not a man." If it is the case that our Lord repeated this whole psalm on the cross and not just the first line, "My God, my God, why hast thou forsaken me," a sentence which is only the key to the whole, then we are presented with a challenging problem in our

Christology. For in both Ps. 22 and at Isa. 41:14 it is undoubtedly *Israel* that is the worm. Our Lord seems to have recognized that this psalm spoke of himself. An aspect of his self-emptying was his identifying himself with all Israel and her calling. But now we see he identified himself not just with Israel the "son" (Exod. 4:22), but actually with Israel the *worm.*

In light of the above, the gracious words that follow have all the deeper intent: *I have been helping thee, is Yahweh's utterance; it is the Holy One of Israel who is thy redeemer*—the redeemer of a louse.

These words contain an ultimate insight. They contain the truth that between God and man there is a great gulf fixed. Men say that man is after all really quite good, morally speaking, that he is able in his own strength to build an equitable society, that he is essentially capable of rising to meet God and lift himself by his own bootstraps. In the light of DI's words we see how such beliefs are nothing short of blasphemy. Worms cannot behave except as worms; they cannot raise themselves from crawling on the ground. On the other hand, if by God's grace man can become aware that he is a worm, then God can begin to do something with him. In various places in the OT, the human experience of the worship of God is patterned upon this and similar passages, for example, upon the call of Isaiah in Isa. 6. First, as in Isaiah's experience, there comes adoration of the living God. But immediately thereafter follows confession. For even as he sings the praises of God, elect man becomes aware that he is unclean and "undone" (Isa. 6:5), that is to say, taken to pieces or reduced to his constituent atoms in the presence of the all-holy God. Only thereafter do we see how God offers Isaiah his costly, burning forgiveness and commissions him for his service.

DI now uses three designations for God. (1) He is *Yahweh,* the covenant God, who has promised to be faithful to his chosen instrument, even if that people should be, in reality, as DI says, a worm or a louse. (2) He is Israel's *redeemer.* This is a word with a long association for Israel in the ordinary affairs of life under the Law of Moses. First, it could mean avenger of blood (Num. 35:12; etc.). But, secondly, the word was used for the male next-of-kin of a widow whose husband had newly died. A single woman could scarcely have maintained herself in ancient Hebrew society. She had necessarily to belong to a family group. So this *go'el* invited the widow into his home. Although the book of Ruth was written long after DI was dead, it deals with ancient practices; and in it we see Boaz, as was the custom in the days of the Judges, graciously receiving the widowed

Ruth into his home when the rightful next-of-kin was unwilling to do so. Thirdly, the word is used in Lev. 25:48-49 of redeeming slaves and in Lev. 25:25-26 of redeeming even property as well as persons. It is understandable therefore why the verb *ga'al* is a favorite word with DI, and why he uses it to describe the consistently loving and gracious activity of God. Later DI gives this ancient term a new theological content. (3) God is *the Holy One of Israel.* This is a title of God first used by Isaiah of Jerusalem. Our DI gratefully seizes upon it as a strikingly paradoxical name for God. Isaiah it was who had taken the ancient word "holy" and given it a new moral content. The word is as old as the Hebrew language, and was applied originally to cultic objects that were ceremonially set apart from profane usage. So it came to emphasize the great otherness of God from mortal man. But Isaiah gave this otherness a content that it had never possessed before. For Israel could easily have conceived of the divine otherness in terms of mere negative difference from man. But Isaiah had declared: "God who is holy shall show himself holy in the form of righteousness." (5:16.) In other words Isaiah made the great declaration that God's holiness is in reality his goodness, or better still, his saving purpose for man.

But DI transcends the thought of his master Isaiah. His word "holy" stands here in the construct state. That means it is construed as virtually one word with the noun it governs. Thus "Holy [the word 'One' is not in the Hebrew] of Israel" is one concept. And the word Israel has been newly defined in terms of worm and louse. By means of the accident of this composite form of speech, DI daringly offers a paradox such as no human mind could have invented, viz., that the utterly other and good God is the God-of-the-louse-Israel.

15, 16.

Still another paradox follows. It is hard to imagine a louse or a worm acting as *a sharp threshing sledge.* The latter was a flat piece of wood studded on the underside with *teeth,* that is to say, with an array of sharp stones or nails. Domestic animals dragged this implement over the wheat piled on the ground of the farmyard. But Israel is here called to be just such an implement herself to *thresh mountains* and *hills;* evidently she is called upon to grind these to *chaff* or dust; and this chaff Israel will not even need to sweep away, for the wind—God's wind—will do it for her.

What does this curious metaphor imply? First, the mountains and hills seem to be the difficulties lying in the way of God's purpose that has to come to fruition in Israel. Probably the phrase is the base of the similar NT phrase which speaks of a faith that can remove mountains. On the other hand, it is sin that is always declared to be the real obstacle to God's advance, not just mere difficulties and vexations. So again we have the kind of metaphor which the NT employs when it declares that "the gates of hell shall not prevail against it" (the Church; Matt. 16:18). In that passage the Church is shown to be synonymous with the people of God. Here in DI's writings, it is Israel that is the people of God. Then secondly, if a louse is to have all this strength, it is obvious that such strength cannot be her own but must be God's. If Israel can then actually exert *God's* strength through her *own* arms, then the next promise does not sound strange or unreal: *Then thou shalt exult in Yahweh, and glory in the Holy One of Israel.* Thus the joy of God, as he works out his plan of salvation through Israel, becomes communicated to Israel herself. The verb *exult, gil,* DI uses to represent not an ordinary but an eschatological joy. This is evident when we recognize that he uses the verb in a figure that parallels the last-judgment motif, when there comes the separation of the wheat from the chaff. The latter figure is used elsewhere too in both Testaments (cf. Isa. 65:17-19; 66:10; Joel 2:23; Mal. 4:1; Matt. 3:12; 13:30; etc.). Apart from the motif of judgment, however, the theme of rejoicing in Yahweh is one that is fundamental to the OT. We find it echoed for example in many of the canonical psalms.

There is an important issue to note here, one that is also of significance for our christological thinking. It is that Israel is to be the instrument of God's judgment upon the nations and upon the forces of evil in the world. DI has nothing at all to say about any messianic figure such as we read of in the works of Isaiah of Jerusalem. We wonder whether DI knew the words of our Ps. 80, for that psalm was composed either during the Babylonian exile or, with Weiser, earlier. For in Ps. 80:17 (RSV) the writer identifies "the son of man whom thou hast made strong for thyself" with the people of God whom God long before had brought up from Egypt and planted in the Promised Land (vss. 4, 8, etc.). Here then the Son of man is the corporate people of Israel. But now DI adds that it is this corporate Son of man who is to be the instrument of judgment upon the nations. Ought not we today to read the words of Matt. 25:31 *ff*. in the light of this verse before us?

17 Should the poor and needy seek water where there is none,
and their tongue goes dry with thirst,
Then I, Yahweh, shall answer them; I, the God
of Israel, will not forsake them.
18 I shall cause rivers to run down bare hillsides,
and springs in the midst of valleys.
I shall turn the wilderness into pools of water,
and parched land into springs of water.
19 I shall make cedars grow in the wilderness, acacias,
myrtles, and olive trees,
I shall set cypresses in the desert, along with both elms
and pines.
20 So that men may see and be aware, and take it to heart
and understand as well,
That it is the hand of Yahweh that has done this, and
that it is the Holy One of Israel who has created it.

17, 18.

We are not told who the poor and needy are. Certainly they comprise crestfallen Israel in exile in the first place. But they also comprise the destitute cities of Judah, whose people had survived in poverty since the fall of the state in 587 B.C. (cf. Jer. 12:7-13; 14:2-9; Lam. 5:4-5). Yet the picture here must also describe all of the wretched sons of men everywhere and at all times. So there follows another eschatological picture. It is similar to many in the OT such as those at Isa. 35; Ezek. 47; and herein at 43:18-21; 48:21; 49:9-11; 55:13. In accordance with his genius, DI has already hinted that he will develop this metaphor later (see 40:10-11). Note three points once again in connection with the wilderness theme. First, it spoke to the Israelites of spiritual stagnation, of an inner state of need for God. Thus the call to slake one's thirst in God was naturally understood in a spiritual sense (cf. 55:1; John 4:14; 7:37-38). Secondly, however, the theme was no airy sentimental concept. It rested upon the factual memory of how Yahweh had already given his people water in the wilderness journey under Moses. Its sweetness was peculiarly welcome in contrast to the waters of Egypt, which God had adulterated because of Pharaoh's unbelief. Thirdly, the two concepts had already been combined by DI's predecessors among the prophets, whose works DI would know. They had declared that if Israel were disobedient, and refused God's spiritual sustenance, then Israel's goodly land itself would become a desert (Hos. 2:12; Isa. 5:1-7; 7:23-25;

Jer. 12:7-13; Ezek. 6:14; 12:20; 33:29—all may be subsumed under one *Gattung*, which possibly is based on the words to be found in I Kings 8:35). This is due to the fact that the concept of desert or wilderness could represent in Israel's thinking the chaos that was there in the beginning (Gen. 1:2), and which God continues to employ as his instrument of judgment and mercy. But now, as DI announces, Israel's God will enter into dialogue (*answer*) once again with his people, for their good and not for evil; for out of their present evil situation he will actually produce good, just as water can bring life to a parched desert.

19.

So God is now about to surpass even the gracious acts he performed in the days of Moses, and once again the inconceivable God will reveal himself by coming to the aid of those of his humbly dependent children who declare their need of him.

The list of trees DI gives may not be accurately translated, for we do not know to which species some of them belong. *Myrtles,* if correct, were not found in Palestine, yet they were typical of Babylonia. This tree is named only in writings subsequent to the Exile (see Neh. 8:15; Zech. 1:8, 10-11; it is found as a proper name at Esth. 2:7). The Babylonian provenance of DI's words may be still further underlined if *bare hillsides* means sand dunes, as some suppose, rather than the rocky hill country of Palestine. But certainly the trees listed are all valuable and useful to man over against the harmful and useless thorns that characterize wilderness vegetation.

Could we therefore make the inference from DI's declaration that he believed God was going to make even chaos praise him? Yet DI probably does not infer as much here. We should not press the picture to reveal more than it is—a poetic representation of God's creative purpose, as the latter increases and grows even as the power of his Word takes effect. Yet the chaotic hearts of men are included in the wilderness theme. DI draws no line between God's actions in creation and his actions in redemption; for in DI's view, to speak of redemption is virtually another way of referring to re-creation. God's first creation DI knew was good. He would agree with the annalist in Genesis who pictured the newly created world as paradise. That is why, once the judgment spoken of at vs. 15 has fallen, DI presents us with a vision of God's purpose at its completion as paradise regained. The useful trees mentioned will then replace the thorns and thistles characteristic of the wilderness, and which are typical of "Paradise Lost" (cf. Gen. 3:18). This theme too DI has developed from the works of his predecessors (cf. Isa. 2:1-5; 11:1-9; Hos. 2:16-19). His successors learned it from him in their turn (cf. Isa. 65:17; 66:22; 25:6).

20.

Only God, he declares, can do all this—only Israel's God. And he will do it in order that the whole world of men *may see* and *take it to heart*. And that poor, dispirited worm Israel is to be the instrument whereby this transformation of the universe is to take place. So it must necessarily be Yahweh who will be the author of this great redemption. He will do it by stooping to make use of that peculiar chosen people, whom he has just addressed as worm and louse.

21 Set forth your case, says Yahweh; bring your grounds
of proof to light, says the King of Jacob.
22 Let them come forward, and tell us what has been
happening.
Tell us what the first things were, that we may
understand their significance;
Or let us hear about what is going to happen that we
may know their outcome.
23 Tell us about future events too, that have not yet happened,
So that we may know you really are gods!
[Please] do [something], either good or evil, that we may
gape in astonishment and be afraid at the same time.
24 Behold, you are made of nothing, and your actions are
therefore negation!
He who chooses you is repugnant.

21.

The priests and prophets of the gods of the nations, and any other mouthpieces that they can produce, are now called upon to defend their gods in court against Yahweh. Yet DI's tenses infer that Yahweh never ceases to present such a summons to the nations of men. *Grounds of proof* really means entrenchments or bulwarks on which one relies.

22.

The truth, God now declares, can easily be reached since it can be tested by facts. But of course neither idols nor those whose philosophy is idolatrous possess any clue to an exposition of the meaning of history. Yet

Yahweh humbly invites mankind to set forth their philosophical notions, and leaves man free to do so. Listening to Babylon's man-made theories, however, Israel is to learn with DI's help that the Babylonian religion is in the last resort merely a form of star-gazing, and star-gazing is a futile activity. Israel's God, *the King of Jacob,* on the other hand, has a plan working out through history which will find its ultimate *outcome* or fruition in God's good time. It becomes obvious, as the court proceeds, that this plan of God has had a beginning—what DI calls his *first things* —at that point in Israel's history when God raised up Moses to be his prophet. Israel's history, since it has had a purposeful beginning, is thus meaningful history. It is what we today call *Heilsgeschichte*. The Babylonian nation had no beginning in this sense, and therefore its continued story cannot be regarded as *Heilsgeschichte* as can Israel's. The nations are consequently summoned to apply their intelligence to this fact, and to think through its significance for the world.

23.

The Hebrews looked forward into the past. This is because they, like us, could see what had already happened like a road winding into the distance in front of them. What has not yet happened, therefore, lies behind one's back. *Have not yet happened* translates this word "back." On the other hand, Babylon's gods stare dumbly back at their worshipers when they ask them what the future holds. Therefore they are morally impotent. "[*Please*] *do* [*something*]—anything at all, just to show you are alive; better do *evil* than do nothing at all" (see also Zeph. 1:12; Jer. 10:5). "Behave as divine beings should. If you do, we'll gladly worship you, even in awe and terror. Only, act! But you can't, for you don't even exist in the first place."

24.

Thus the man who consciously chooses an idol as his god in face of that elementary fact must be *repugnant* to both God and Israel. It is in this sense that Babylon has chosen her gods. DI is saying that they did not choose Babylon; it was Babylon who chose them. Yet Yahweh undoubtedly chose Israel. Thus Yahweh rightly has power over Israel, yet, contrariwise, Babylon assumes that she has power over her gods. The Canaanites we know believed this kind of thing about their gods, for they sought to manipulate them by means of sympathetic magic. The Babylonians evidently sought to do the same.

This ancient view of what a people's relationship to its god should be is as alive today as ever it was in DI's time. For whenever a people deifies the state to which it belongs and vows loyalty to it beyond loyalty to God who created the state in the first place, then the same evil that DI saw before him in his day is reenacted in modern guise. This is true even of those who sing with Blake:

Till we have built Jerusalem
In England's green and pleasant land.

For any theory of the state that takes for granted that man can produce his own utopia, if only he applies his mind to it, is in line with the kind of thinking that DI condemns with the word *repugnant*. Even while DI impressed upon his Israelite hearers the centrality of this concept, many of them must have been tempted to believe that by the very nature of things DI was wrong; for it was as obvious as anything this world could show that, with the destruction of the state of Judah forty long, silent years before, the death of Yahweh himself had been announced. On the contrary, Babylon's man-made gods and philosophies were just as obviously alive as Yahweh was dead, for did not Babylon control the whole fertile crescent? Those who are hungry to know the truth of this mysterious universe, many Israelites declared, ought therefore to devote themselves to study the philosophies of a nation which was so obviously in the right.

25 I roused (him) up from the north, and he is coming,
from the rising of the sun I have been calling
him by name.
He has been trampling upon prefects of provinces like
mortar, as a potter tramples on clay.

25.

How different Israel's God is from any god that a man can manipulate; not only is he the living God—and thus not mere static Being—he is also the active, purposeful, creative One, who is constantly revealing himself in some form of saving activity. The evidence of this at the moment is the victorious advance of Cyrus. Cyrus *is coming. . . . He has been trampling* down all opposition in the creative way that the potter tramples the clay. How much more, DI means us to realize, must Cyrus' Maker be both the living and the creative God. *Roused up* is a strong term, for it throws responsibility for all Cyrus' actions upon Yahweh. In fact, if God has been *calling him by name* as DI says, then he is no less than Yahweh's child, and Yahweh is responsible for him. On the other hand, the Hebrew text has "he will call upon my name." If this reading is correct, what it says is to be regarded as the exaggeration of enthusiasm, for Cyrus never did acknowledge Yahweh to be *the* God, so far as we know. Yet DI is here looking to the outcome of Yahweh's coming action rather than to the state of Cyrus' mind either then or later. For DI's hope is that all men will know the Lord once the coming events have reached their victorious conclusion. The LXX also gives us an overenthusiastic translation, for it asserts that the inhabitants of the North and East are also to be called by God's name.

The phrase *prefects of provinces* represents the Babylonian term *sagan.* DI adopts this word and uses it for the local rulers of Anatolia whom Cyrus has overrun. It is characteristic of an exiled group in a foreign land to adopt the technical terms of the people around them and to employ them even when speaking their native tongue.

26 Now, who was it foretold this from the beginning, that
we should realize it? and from former times, so
that we might say: "That is true"?
Actually not one [of you] has been foretelling it,
actually none has been announcing it, in fact
no one could hear your words.
27 It was I who first told it to Zion; it was I who gave
Jerusalem a herald of good news.
28 I looked, and there was no one else, and of these [gods]
not one had a plan,
When I asked them to give me an answer.
29 Behold, they are all nothing, their deeds are emptiness;
their molten images are wind and negation.

26.

The Babylonian priests had given no sure oracle about the coming of Cyrus. On the other hand, ever since the days of Moses—*from the beginning*—Yahweh had planned the advance of this Persian conqueror. This word *ro'sh* is probably a technical term for the first actions of God in Israel's *Heilsgeschichte.* DI means that when God first chose Israel under

Moses, he had already foreseen what he would have to do centuries later; for Israel would later need to be disciplined by exile and then renewed through the instrumentality of a particular human agent whom God would rouse up at the right moment.

27.

That moment, says DI, has now come. God had announced it in advance. DI must mean that God's Word, addressed to the contemporary moment in Babylon, was implicit in the original Exodus events of centuries before. The first redemption—from the power of Pharaoh—was in his eyes a guarantee of that which was to come, in fact, that which was actually coming now through the instrumentality of Cyrus. Be that as it may, this interpretation of contemporary events DI believed to be the first element in God's *good news* (cf. 40:9). He returns to this theme at 52:7. Let us note, however, that the words *that is true* are only a tentative translation of the Hebrew word *tsaddiq*. The latter can mean several things in English, e.g., "he (it) is right"; "he (it) is victorious."

28.

Now God draws attention to the fact that none of the Babylonian gods has come alive or spoken at the court to which they had been summoned, so that there is no one else besides himself to produce *a plan*. The word *plan* Isaiah of Jerusalem had already used in his day, and now DI delights to employ it in his turn.

29.

The last line of DI's effective strophe comes to a striking conclusion by the repetition of the now obvious fact (cf. vs. 24) that the gods of the nations are as fatuous as are their priests. Yet the end of those gods is not to take place at once. The mills of God grind slowly. But DI's revelation of the inanity of the gods certainly spelled the beginning of the end of idolatry.

It is interesting that these verses are in the style of a Babylonian letter written from a superior to an inferior. DI must therefore have been sufficiently well educated, first, to read the Babylonian language and, secondly, to appreciate what he was reading. In him we have indeed Israel's Milton or Dante, for he is fully capable of writing in verse a complete theological treatise. Yet DI surpasses both those masters of the art, because his treatise is an existential and not just an academic work. Unlike the other two poets, DI did not know the end of the story which he was interpreting from the beginning. The end, about which he now begins to speak, through the power of the Spirit unfolds its meaning for him only as Cyrus advances toward the gates of Babylon, and only as he becomes aware in his heart, even before the great moment of release arrives, that God is even then using the sufferings of Israel for his plan.

CHAPTER 42

1 Behold my Servant! I am holding him firmly. He is my
chosen one, in whom my whole being takes pleasure.
I have put my Spirit on him; he is to offer the true
way of life to the heathen nations.
2 He is not to cry out nor raise (his voice); he is not
to shout at the street corner.
3 A broken bulrush he is not to break, nor is he to blow
out a smoldering wick.
But he is to offer faithfully the true way of life.
4 Yet he himself will neither smolder nor be crushed,
until he has established the true way of life on earth—
For the whole world is longing for his revelation.

1.

Israel's calling to be Yahweh's Servant DI has mentioned before (41:8-9). Now he develops his theme. Jeremiah and Ezekiel had both already described Israel by this title (Jer. 30:10; 46:27-28; Ezek. 28:25; 37:25). DI puts it at the center of his argument (cf. 43:10; 44:1-2; 45:4; 49:3-7). The title was that held by a royal plenipotentiary among Israel's neighbors, and so was a title of honor. It implied executive power in the king's name and by his authority, but it also implied total and absolute obedience on the Servant's part. "The root *ʿ-b-d* always contains two elements; action and obedience," says Lindhagen. In fact, "Servant of Yahweh," as Cheyne says, seems about equivalent to "Son of Yahweh" as it applies to the king in Ps. 2:7. Yahweh used many servants: The stars were his servants, for they were his "host," like the soldiers of a general (40:26; 45:12). Cyrus the king was his servant (44:28; 45:1), *whom victory meets at every step* (41:2). Isaiah had called himself God's servant (20:3). But the Servant

Israel is delineated here in total contrast to all other servants of God. The word *behold,* as a demonstrative interjection, marks the transition to a new subject and fixes our attention on the significance of the word *Servant* as it occurs here.

Israel is presently a pariah, sweating in a slave-labor camp and therefore totally unlike a royal vizier. And yet, DI wants us to see, Israel *is* a royal vizier. This is not because Israel has any value per se, but wholly because God holds *him firmly,* now that he has selected him from all other possible servants to execute his will. To that end, moreover, he has put his *Spirit on him* (cf. 11:2). Thus it is clear that Israel is no longer not-my-people but is truly "*my people*" (40:1), as DI said at the beginning. Other nations were accustomed to the idea of upholding their gods. Here is something new for Israel to understand, for this verb "to hold on to," with God the Good Shepherd as the subject, takes on the overtone almost of cuddling in the arms. There are two contrasting yet perfectly alignable concepts:

1. God's *whole being*—his *nephesh—takes pleasure* in Israel (cf. Mark 1:11; Matt. 17:5). In other words Israel is the elect, the chosen one, for the simple reason that God has fallen in love with Israel, it might be said. The mystery of election is well figured by such a phrase. To the eyes of an onlooker it appears to be a complete mystery why a young man should fall in love with one particular girl when she had several equally attractive sisters. DI would know the Deuteronomic discussion of this mystery (Deut. 4:36-37; 7:6-8). Part of the mystery is that the word "chosen" implies a prior test on the part of the chooser. Moses for example is spoken of in this way (Ps. 106:23). DI applies it now to Israel with reference, inter alia, to the call of Abraham, whom God did indeed test (Isa. 41:8; 44:1-2; 45:4). The word Servant is used elsewhere for individuals both within and without Israel, for such as Moses, the prophets (Amos 3:7), Nebuchadrezzar (Jer. 27:6), David the beloved king (cf. II Sam. 3:18) and so for the messianic David who is still to come (Hag. 2:23; Ezek. 34:23 *ff.*). In conformity with this last view of the word Servant, the Jewish Targum that arose in the early Christian centuries interpreted the word as it occurs here by saying he was *meshiḥi* meaning "my anointed" or "my Messiah." That is to say, as head of Israel, David bears the messianic function attached to Israel as a whole people. It is Israel as a whole, the chosen people as a whole, which DI regards as the Servant of God.

2. The second concept is this. Israel is chosen not merely for her own good but in order to do what a servant is meant to do, viz., *serve.* Israel's

service is to bring *the true way of life* to the rest of the world. *Mishpaṭ* represents the conception of a rule or law for life. So it points to the idea that God has revealed the right way for men to live together as brethren in peace and concord. Its root meaning has to do with the idea of judging, so the noun that we have here signifies the entirety of judgments that God has already delivered (cf. 51:4; Jer. 5:4-5). *Mishpaṭ* certainly does not mean "religion" in the modern sense of the word, for nowadays the word religion describes only one area or department of human life, its spiritual element, as modern man supposes, over against the everyday material affairs that occupy his attention. The Servant is to be the channel whereby God's revelation of his loving purpose for all men can reach them. To sum up—in himself the Servant Israel counts for nothing; yet Israel's God, acting in conformity with his saving purpose, has chosen this pariah and is actually now holding him up; it is God therefore who has empowered him to be what he is called to be, for by himself he is quite unable to fulfill his calling.

Since, however, this wholesome way of life is not to be mediated in a vacuum, Israel herself is called to be more than the mere mouthpiece of God. Two points arise here showing what she is meant to be. In the first place Israel is an empirical people, a people that lives within history. She is therefore condemned to face the vexations and tribulations that all men must face who live in a fallen world. Secondly, Israel is shown to be nothing in her own right, for she does not exist apart from her function, from her reason for existing. Apart from that she would be what the gods are—mere negation. Thus the Israel idea is to be equated with the idea of mission as such (cf. Jer. 15:19), a mission, however, that is motivated by the Spirit and which takes form within a given area of space and time. The awful judgment lying upon Israel therefore is that, should she reject her calling, she will revert to sheer negation.

2, 3.

What then is Israel's function? Curiously enough, it too is negation. It may be that the positive functions of God's other servant, the mighty Cyrus, are sketched as they are in 41:25, in order to offer a foil to the function that God has decreed for Israel. Three negatives in succession emphasize that Israel's wisdom, Israel's native strength, Israel's self-acquired knowledge, all of which are aspects of the threshing-sledge powers of the domineering human ego, are of no value to God at all (41:15).

4.

So now we are given the first indication of the important theme that DI will later unfold, that the way the Spirit chooses to operate is the way of self-emptying not of self-assertion, and that it is by that means and not another that the Servant will bring to the *whole world* the *revelation* for which it *is longing*. The word *torah, revelation,* here is not of course to be equated with the later meaning of the word when it is fully identified with the Pentateuch or the law of Moses.

On the other hand, since the revelation spoken of here is revelation of the eternal God, then Torah too must be eternal. The pictorial language of the rabbis, who in later centuries could speak of God studying the Torah each day in heaven, is thus not far removed from DI's world of thought. Such a midrash is designed to protect the OT vision of God from misrepresentation. For God is not lawless power. He is capable of doing only what he wills to do—and that will of his is made known to man through the revelation of his loving, saving purpose.

The above is not the accepted interpretation of the well-known words from the KJV, "A bruised reed shall he not break." The familiar English translation suggests that the Servant will not quench whatever good he finds in heathen hearts, but will gently fan it into flames. That meaning of vss. 3-4 may be obtained from the Hebrew, provided that the strophe at 42:1-4 is regarded as a separate utterance of the prophet unconnected with its context. But if we recognize that DI is offering us a sustained argument in this developing theological treatise, then we must interpret each section of his poem in the light of his whole argument as it reaches us in all his sixteen chapters. For this reason the Hebrew word that occurs in vs. 3, *l*e*'emeth,* has been translated by *faithfully*. This faithful way is evidently the way of renunciation. Thus, instead of choosing to fan the feeble flames, the Servant is meant to sit down alongside the brokenhearted just where they are to be found, viz., in the mire of this human life of ours; and in this way, by his very presence with them, he will become the instrument by which a strength and hope that is not their own will be transferred to them. He is to do this thing, moreover, just because God himself does it (40:29; 57:15; 66:2), and the Servant cannot be above his Master. Moreover, God's *Spirit upon him* will be the guarantee that this way will be effective. Vs. 4 deliberately and for effect applies to the Servant the verbs that are used in vs. 3 of the world as it lies in need. This means that the crushing which the Servant is to experience will not, nay cannot, go too far, for God's Spirit is resting upon him, and God is always in control. This, then, is what mission means.

5 Thus says Yahweh, the Divine Being, who creates
the heavens and enlarges them,
Who makes the earth evolve, and what grows out of it,
Who puts breath in the people upon it, and life in
those who walk thereon,
6 It is I, Yahweh, who called thee in (my) saving purpose.
I gripped thee by thy hand,
And I have kept thee, and made thee into a covenant for mankind,
into a light for the nations;
7 To open blind eyes, to bring prisoners out of prison,
and those living in darkness out of the dungeon.

5.

Yahweh is the God who speaks, and in speaking he continually *creates*—this is an active participle. That is to say, he creates by uttering his Word. We know more today about an expanding universe than DI could ever have guessed. He can only speak of God beating out the earth in the way that a silversmith makes a lump of silver expand until it is large enough to bend and so to *evolve* into the shape of a bowl.

6.

But God is also personal. He is *I, Yahweh*. That is one possible way of translating the divine name as it occurs here. Moreover, he feels concern for all his creatures. He puts Spirit in all mankind. *Breath* and *life* are here used as synonymous terms, and are placed in poetic parallel, but basically the word *life* means "spirit." This verse safeguards the doctrine of election, which DI introduced at 42:1-2 above, from leading to the conception of favoritism.

God has chosen and called Israel, he says, for a purpose; she is to be the agent of his plan of love, *b*ᵉ*-tsedheq*. This same word occurs at 45:13 where it applies to the call of Cyrus. The root of this word *tsedheq* comprehends two notions. The first is that of being normal, although it is doubtful whether DI knew that the word he was handling had this basic meaning, for in his day that sense applied only to such things as weights and measures. The transitive form of the verb from this root could then be understood to mean "to render normal." This is the verb which the KJV frequently renders as "justify." The state of sin is abnormal, however.

For the norm is what man knew and experienced before he fell into sin in the Garden of Eden. Thus "to render normal" must also mean "to make righteous," and that is why eventually, and with the NT, it can mean "to justify."

Tsedheq then includes within it the concept of rightness. But God's rightness or righteousness, like his holy love, necessarily involves his righteous dealing with sin and evil. That is why both of God's chosen instruments, both Cyrus and Israel, both state and Church, we could say, are used by God to establish his rule of saving love. Here, the soteriological emphasis is central to DI's argument.

> In a Unitarian conception of God, where there is no subject-object relation within the Godhead, the idea of creation inevitably comes to mean that the world is the necessary object of the divine activity, . . . and God is subjected to external necessity. If however there are hypostatic distractions within the Godhead, we can find in God the possibility of creative action without introducing such necessity.[1]

God does not require the nature he has created for his own fulfillment or perfection. While the universe without him is mere negation, yet he without his universe is still God. On the other hand, his being-as-God is revealed to man, as DI saw, not in terms of natural theology but in terms of saving love. Such alone is the ground of Israel's election. Thus we are led to recognize that, in a sense beyond the logic of our thought, the chosen people of Israel, *qua* God's mission through the Spirit to the world, is the necessary vehicle of his Word. For that Word was then in the process of becoming flesh, and such a vehicle was necessary to God for the fulfillment of his own perfect purpose.

A covenant for mankind may be translated in more than one way: (1) "I have made thee into the people of the [new] covenant," such as Jeremiah has already spoken of (cf. 31:31). (2) "I have made thee to become the means of my making covenant with [all] mankind." The word *'am*, people, is anarthrous. When it carries the article it is usually restricted to mean "*the* people of Israel." But here it is obviously used in parallel with the plural word *goyim, nations,* despite the Codex Sinaiticus which has had before it *'ammi*, my people. Thus people must here mean all *mankind*, and the construct relationship of *covenant* and people must lie

[1] L. S. Thornton in *Essays Catholic and Critical*, ed. E. G. Selwyn (London: S.P.C.K., 1926), pp. 145-46.

in parallel with that of *light* and *nations*. We ought therefore to accept interpretation (2) as the correct one, especially since DI has already raised the issue in this form at 41:8-10 and will do so again in 49:5. We find this form of language also in such a phrase as "wondrous counselor" in Isa. 9:6; and DI is indebted to the style of his great predecessor.

Israel has been chosen, then, not with the object of being saved, nor merely to be the covenant people as an end in themselves, but in covenant relationship with God, to be the channel whereby the world may be saved (cf. Luke 2:31-32). Humanity in God's eyes is one, even though as one ancient writer was aware, it shows a fissiparous tendency (cf. Gen. 11:9). As such it is the single object of God's concern. DI's language at vss. 5-6 is strongly reminiscent of the creation narratives of both P and J in Genesis. After creating the world, according to Gen. 2:7, God breathed the breath of life into man (cf. 42:5). But like his predecessor Ezekiel, DI understands the function of the breath of God or the Spirit of God soteriologically rather than ontologically, on the ground that, as in Ezek. 37, the Spirit of God has primarily a re-creative function.[2]

7.

This re-creative, or saving purpose, is actually meant to become flesh in and through Israel's obedience in mission. The illustrations used are typical of the whole biblical revelation, in that the poor and the depressed classes among men are to be the special object of God's continuing concern. So the poverty stricken exiles must have felt comforted indeed to discover that in their *dungeon* and in their *prison* God was concerned for them still. King Jehoiachin had spent many years in prison (II Kings 25:27-30). DI's audience would all know this fact. And they would remember that in the thirty-seventh year of the Exile, King Evil-merodach had finally brought Jehoiachin out and restored him to favor (Jer. 52:31-34). The exiles would thus realize DI's right to build a metaphor from an historical situation.

Finally, another word from Gen. 1:3, viz. *light*. Light is the opposite of chaos or negation (cf. 41:29). Thus out of darkness Isaiah (9:1-2) had expected that light would shine as it had done in the beginning. Through the hands and mouths of the chosen Servant people, light is to shine once again, re-creatively, into the dark places of a stricken world. It is interest-

[2] *A light for the nations* may have been added here retrospectively from 49:6 It is not found in some Greek manuscripts.

ing to note that this language would not come as too great a surprise to the educated among the exiles in Babylon. This is because vss. 6-7 echo a frequently repeated concept that occurs in what even in DI's day were then ancient Akkadian hymns with a royal messianic ideology.

8 I am Yahweh, that is my name; my glory I shall never
give to any other, nor the praise due me to graven images.
9 As for the first things, behold, they are passed;
It is new things I am now about to proclaim.
Before they spring forth, I am letting you hear of them.

8.

God's saving purpose is now identified with the *name* that describes his essence. For the theologians who have given us the book of Exodus, the name "Yahweh" had meant "he who becomes," because this name is evidently the third-person form of the word of self-revelation, "I am" (Exod. 3:14), or better "I become," for there is no verb "to be" in Hebrew (see discussion at 41:10). In Exod. 3:12 that name is expressed also as "I shall become with thee," viz. with Moses, but through Moses with all Israel of whom Moses was but the representative. "I shall become with thee," says God even in exile.

The word glory in its developed, theological usage at the time of DI was used to signify the outer aspect of God's true being. Man can neither see nor know God as he is in himself. But God graciously allows man to behold his glory as he passes man by and so remains beyond the range of human understanding (Exod. 33:22). In the parable of the last judgment (Matt. 25:31-46), we read how Israel is asked if she has remembered her calling, which is to open blind eyes and bring light to those who sit in the darkness of the prison house. That is what Israel is elected *for,* as DI has said. Only in Israel therefore can God's glory be made plain, and his name be revealed.

Most commentators suggest that it is to false gods that Yahweh *shall never give* his glory, such as to Marduk in all his lacquered magnificence. But in the light of 40:5 and 49:3, such an interpretation cannot stand, even though the parallel in the second half of this line might suggest that it should be adopted. *Pesilim* are certainly *graven images.* However, in this verse we are presented with the paradox that God, who does not allow man to make any image of himself (cf. Exod. 20:4; Deut. 5:8), has actually elected Israel to be his image. Originally God had made man, as such, in his image (Gen. 1:27). But that image the J historian believed had long since been marred by sin. DI however now speaks in terms of the re-created image of God that Israel—not all mankind at the moment—may yet become through the Spirit's settling upon her, and because of the fact that Yahweh delights in her; or in other words through grace. Accordingly, the straightforward way of expressing this truth is to declare, as DI does, that the glory of God is to be made manifest in and through Israel.

9.

God's glory had appeared to Israel in the days of Moses, says DI (Exod. 16:7, 10; 24:16). That manifestation of glory had thus represented the *first things* he mentions. But now, *before they spring forth*—a botanical metaphor, with emphasis upon the development of the plant out of the seed that has first to die—God will do *new things*, for he is about to reveal his glory in a new way. Yet these new things DI does not yet dare disclose. They are too astonishing just to be mentioned casually. DI will need several chapters still to allow him to work up to the point at which he can disclose what is in his mind. For what he is hinting here is nothing less than what we today would designate the death-and-resurrection motif as it becomes manifest in innocent suffering.

10 Sing to Yahweh a new song, (sing) his praise at the end of the earth:
Let the sea and what is in it roar [its joy], the seacoasts and their inhabitants too.
11 Let the wilderness with its settlements raise [a shout], the villages which Qedar inhabits.
Let the inhabitants of Petra shout for joy, let them yell from the top of the hills.
12 Let them offer glory to Yahweh, let them proclaim his praise around the coasts.
13 Yahweh is coming forth like a warrior, he is fanning his zeal like a man of war.
He is shouting, indeed he is yelling, as he displays his might to his enemies.

10.

The mention of the word "new" is sufficient for DI to invite all flesh to *sing to Yahweh a new song*. No old song is good enough to match the marvelous new things he is about to do (cf. Pss. 33:3; 40:3; 95; 96; 98). Miriam had sung a great song in praise of Yahweh when the former things, the Exodus and the crossing of the Red Sea, had taken place (Exod. 15:21). The Babylonians were accustomed to sing enthronement songs as each New Year came round—and DI must surely have heard these sung. How can *the end of the earth* refuse to sing when God does new things greater by far than just to bring in a New Year? Even inanimate nature is to join in the song. Here the word *sea* may even include the waters under the earth, the deeps of chaos that we have seen are the negative element in God's good and positive universe.

11, 12.

This interpretation is borne out by the next summons, which is to the desert to join in also. This is because the desert, where no grass grows, was another manifestation of the chaos concept to the Hebrew mind. Up to this point we have heard the call to join in the song go forth to (1) the end of the earth, (2) the waters of chaos, (3) the coasts of the ocean, (4) the wilderness. Now both (5) rural areas and (6) commercial cities are to contribute their meed of praise. *Qedar* was the home of those marauding Arabs who were Israel's ancestral enemies, and *Petra* was the capital city of Edom, Israel's brother nation, but also her ancestral enemy. Negative becoming positive indeed! *Shout for joy* is a verb expressing exultant, delirious happiness. It speaks of the battle cry of the excited warrior who knows that he is going to win. *Yell* is an unusual word which in Arabic means to bellow like a beast. And since these all are to shout from *the top of the hills*, and are to offer glory around the whole Mediterranean Sea, the passage seems to speak of that eschatological joy of which the NT has so much to say. For example, at Pentecost, Peter has to deny that his particular remnant is drunk (Acts 2:15). They are in fact, as we can now see, experiencing that hilarity (II Cor. 9:7) which is the mark of the redeemed at all times.

13.

But Israel is not alone in her odd behavior. Yahweh too is *shouting* and *yelling* as he rejoices in rescuing his people from the powers of evil. His *zeal* is his burning purpose of love. The root of the word means to be red or black with dye. Yet it is often expounded in the OT in terms of fire and heat (cf. Exod. 19:18; 24:17; Deut. 4:24; Isa. 33:14; Mal. 3:2).[3]

[3] See "Our God Is a Consuming Fire," in my *Christian Theology of the OT*.

And so it is but a short step to understand it as passion when it is used of God. The Gentle Shepherd of 40:11 is also the *warrior*, the heat of whose *zeal* or passion is able to destroy his *enemies*. This is similar to the language of 63:1 *ff*., a passage which is paraphrased in Julia Ward Howe's famous hymn:

> Mine eyes have seen the glory of the coming of the Lord;
> He is trampling out the vintage where the grapes of wrath are stored.
> He hath loosed the fateful lightning of His terrible swift sword.
> . . . .
> Our God is marching on.

God the warrior then is marching on. Cyrus the warrior is marching on (41:1-3). But Israel also is marching on (40:31); yet only in the strength of him who, while marching *in* Cyrus (41:4), also grants all needed strength—or Spirit—to this same weary and exhausted army, viz., his chosen people and Servant Israel.

14 Ever since eternity I have kept silent, I have kept still and held myself in;
But now like an expectant mother I am groaning and grasping and panting at once.
15 I am about to lay waste mountains and hills; I am about to dry up all their vegetation;
Rivers I am going to turn into sandbanks, pools I shall render dry.
16 I have been leading the blind along a way they did not recognize,
and have made them go along unknown paths.
I have been turning darkness into light, and crooked places I have been making straight before them.
These are the things I have merely begun to do—I shall never leave off now!
17 Let those who trust in idols be thrust back; let those be utterly ashamed who say to molten images, "You are our gods."

14.

The new thing to come will not be new in the sense of the Greek word *neos*, but new in the sense of *kainos*, i.e., it will represent an emergent newness.[4] On the one hand, the new thing is to be something astonishing to Israel, for it will appear to her to be different. Yet on the other hand, it will be based on the consistency of Israel's trustworthy God and on the actions which he has already performed in the days of Moses.

Without warning now come quotation marks, as it were. God himself is speaking. "The exodus events were but the conception in the womb of my mighty plan. Now the time of delivery has come. Through the whole long period of gestation I uttered never a word, even when Israel was going constantly astray. I could well have burst out with zeal, but instead I continually *held myself in.*"

What a daring metaphor this is to use. DI actually puts into the mouth of God the idea that God is an expectant mother. The three verbs in the sentence describing the pains of childbirth represent those pains as they climax at the time of delivery. At 66:7 the figure is used of Israel. Here it is used of God. By such language, DI shocks his readers into recognizing that God is not beyond the pain which his people is even then suffering, but must be one with them as they meet the judgment which he himself has caused. This theme of DI actually contributes to the message of comfort with which he began his sermon (40:1). DI teaches Israel here that his people can be grateful even for pain, for pain puts them in touch with the living God. God himself has chosen that it is to be out of pain that new life is to spring just like the birth of a baby boy. What then may not the ghastly pains of the Exile bring forth in the providence of God?

15.

The coming new thing that is about to be born will actually produce a cosmic effect. We who are wise after the event know how this happened, and how the historical event of the "death and resurrection" of exiled Israel actually formed the mold into which God poured the final historical revelation of his redeeming, loving self in action. But such words as "cosmic" and "effect" the Hebrews could never have employed. Instead, in the mythological manner of the nations of the Fertile Crescent in DI's day, they pictorialized the significance of God's actions in poetic language.

16.

Two significant truths seem to be emerging: (1) Inanimate nature is actually one with the humanity that dwells along with it. It knows the effects of human sin only too well (Gen. 3:17-18; and cf. vs. 11 above).

[4] See my *Law and Grace* (Philadelphia: Westminster Press, 1962), pp. 57, 64.

(2) What God has begun to do for the redemption of man in the days of Moses he will continue to do; so *I shall never leave off now.*

All nature then is to be shaken to the core by the birth pangs of—a cosmic redemption? No. It will be an insignificant event, lost in the sweep of world history, that is to begin with the opening of the eyes of a poor blind people when the Light falls on their darkened sight. Yet such an act is truly representative of Israel's God. For all along he had been leading poor blind Israel on the strange paths of Babylonia, and *making straight* the *crooked places* on which she had had to walk. And he had been doing so even while Israel was either cursing her bitter fate or was giving up all faith and hope in the God of her fathers.

17.

After hearing that Yahweh is really like that, how utterly foolish it is to trust in handmade divinities. The subtlety of DI's sarcasm is observable only when we realize that the word for *molten images* is singular and that *our gods* is plural. For the plural form of the latter noun, employed as a singular concept, is that which is also employed for Yahweh, the God whom DI knows has created the heavens and the earth (40:12 *ff.*).

18 Hear, you deaf, look and see, you blind!
19 Who is it that is blind, if it is not my Servant, and deaf,
like this messenger of mine whom I am sending?
Who is as blind as my hired Servant, or as deaf as the Servant
of Yahweh?
20 Though (able to) see many things, thou dost not pay any
attention; though possessing ears that have been
opened, they hear nothing at all.

18, 19.

Who but God could invite the deaf to hear and the blind to see? Only God knows that it is possible for the blind and the deaf to respond. For only God can perform that miracle. Moreover we are now explicitly informed that the blind mentioned at vs. 16 above are really exiled Israel (cf. also 43:8 and Ezek. 12:2). Although Israel had been chosen of God to become his *messenger,* Israel had never realized what the years of the exile in Babylon could mean in relation to God's plan. The word for *messenger* represents the Hebrew word which may also be translated by "angel." That is to say, the Hebrews used the one word for both heavenly and earthly messengers. We have noted before (at 40:5) that the prophets drew no hard and fast line, as the modern world does, between heaven and earth or matter and spirit. Gideon, for example, is not sure whether he has seen an angel or a man (Judg. 6:11 *ff*.). So too in the case of Manoah (Judg. 13:6, 8, 13, 22) or the women at the open grave (Mark 16:5). Again, Elijah and Jesus are both fed by "messengers" (I Kings 19:5; Matt. 4:11). In this way we are given to understand that just because Israel is God's messenger, she is caught up, in some sense, into God's cosmic plan.

Yet there is no suggestion that Israel is herself mission. God alone is such. Israel is but the vehicle of God's mission. As such she is witness to the Sender (43:10, 12). In and by herself she is not able to prove the existence of God to the heathen bystander. It is only those who are within the covenant fellowship of God who find that witnessing can create that proof in their own hearts. Yet Israel, the covenant people, is called to witness that in fact the blind receive their sight (42:7; cf. Matt. 11:5); if however she does that faithfully in the hearing of the Babylonians, she can then leave the outcome of her witnessing with assurance to God.

However, the shocking reality is that the *hired servant* unfortunately cannot understand the majesty of such a calling. This word *hired servant* is difficult. It may come from the root concept of "completion," *sh-l-m*, just as the name Solomon was supposed to do (I Chr. 28:9; I Kings 11:4; the man with the "whole heart"). So here it may mean "perfected." Others have translated it as "devoted," for the noun may be voweled to be similar to the Arabic word *muslim*, "he who is devoted to God," though the word is unlikely to have carried that connotation in DI's day. In like manner it may mean "one who is in a covenant of peace" with another, and would then form another manifestation of the root from which we get the word "perfected." Yet "rewarded" or "paid" and so "hired" servant is the likeliest meaning to give it. We are now presented with the strong contrast: (1) that Israel is committed to be God's messenger, (2) that Israel is blind. The resolution of that paradox can obviously come about by grace alone.

20.

Israel's blindness consists in her being (*able to*) *see many things*, yet recognizing no significance in them; and her deafness in *possessing ears* yet not understanding what God was doing through historical movements and events. Israel had thus committed the greatest of all sins, virtually that which the NT calls the sin against the Holy Ghost. For Israel had called white black and black white. And so we are left with the ridiculous position that God chooses to accomplish his mission through an Israel that has sinned against him to a degree that none of the pagan nations could ever possibly do. Israel by herself is not merely impotent to obey; she is actually damned. And yet God insists upon using her for the salvation of the world.

21 Yahweh has planned, for his saving purpose' sake,
to enhance and glorify the Torah.

21.

Torah is the revelation that has already been given to Israel through Moses. Torah was not the work of Israel but of God. All that Israel had done was just to receive it. Once again now *Yahweh has planned . . . to enhance* this Word that he has already spoken, and *glorify* it. This action of his is, of course, part of *his* saving purpose, saving meaning both victorious and righteous because it contains both God's power and his love. Torah is not a static collection of laws or even of divine instructions; far less is it a moral code. It is the Word of God, even when that Word is necessarily expressed in the forms of legal enactments. Now the Word of God endures (40:8). Of that fact DI is sure; thus Torah must in some sense be alive, for the God who first uttered it is alive (cf. 51:4). Consequently, as a living entity and like any human person, it continually develops and unfolds so as to meet with potency every possible new situation that may arise. Jeremiah certainly held this view of Torah; it was part of his faith that new things were still to come (31:33). And DI would undoubtedly know these views of Jeremiah. Part of the outcome of the living, evolving nature of Torah were the utterances of the great prophets (cf. Isa. 8:16), even when they themselves recognized that they were what they were, viz., prophets raised up within the people of God just because they had inherited the Torah that had created their people. The vitality of Torah is such, as DI understood it at this juncture in history, that it can witness to the action of God in destroying his own people and in exiling them in Babylon. Torah, as represented by the first commandment, had declared: "Thou shalt have no other gods before me." Israel had not heeded this Word of God. The centrality of this commandment Israel had therefore still to learn, even if it meant the hard way of destruction and the death of the nation. Only thus could the Word of God stand forever.

The whole verse is a surprising statement. It means that Torah is to flower especially at that point where Israel had failed God most, and therefore where she needs him most. Paul met opposition at a particular place in his travels; *therefore* a great opportunity for spreading the gospel was presented to him (Acts 14:3). Opposition is here seen as God's footstool. By stepping on it he attains greater ends than if there had been no footstool available. Thus DI in his parenthetical verse is in reality declaring a basic truth of the whole Bible, viz., that God uses even the sin of man for the achievement of his purpose. In this case the sin is embodied in the Servant Israel, despite the fact that the Servant is called to be the instrument of God's purpose for the world. Therefore, by himself Israel cannot meet God's needs in the development of God's plan. Israel as such is not the instrument by which God attains his ends. That instrument is the Word. It alone can effect God's plan of redemption. But it uses as its locus to that end the sinful body of the Servant people of God.

22 But they are a plundered and exploited people, they are
all ensnared in pits and hidden in prisons;
They have been plundered without anyone to rescue them,
they have been deserted without anyone to say,
"Set them free!"
23 Which of you gives ear to this, or pays attention or
hearkens to its significance?
24 Who turned Jacob over to despoiling and Israel to be
plundered?
Was it not Yahweh against whom we sinned? In whose ways
they had refused to walk, and whose Torah they would
not obey.
25 So he poured upon them the heat of his anger [which
showed itself as] defeat in war.
It inflamed upon them from all sides, but they never
realized why;
And it burned them, but they did not understand its
significance.

22.

Torah is God's gracious gift to this missionary instrument that Israel is called to be. Israel must therefore necessarily pass it on to others (cf. 51:7, where Israel is called the people who has my Torah in their heart). But she believed that she was not in the position to do so. She is *a plundered and exploited people,* imprisoned in the Babylonian political and economic machine—DI consistently uses an historical situation to illustrate an inner state of mind. Israel is in reality prisoner of her own unbeliefs and folly and is now in consequence robbed of all initiative, *without anyone to say "Set them free!"* Instead of seeking others with a missionary purpose, Israel is actually waiting for others to seek her out and set her free.

23, 24.

In fact the *significance* or ultimate outcome of such unbelief no one seems to care about. Then suddenly DI identifies himself with his sinful people as Isaiah had done before him (6:5); he now asks questions of Israel, using the pronoun "we" to include himself with his people. Had Israel not realized that our present plight was God's doing? God had been compelled to act through his servant Nebuchadrezzar to destroy his own temple and city, to give his elect people over to *despoiling*—this is an abstract noun—and *to be plundered,* as in fact had happened in 587 B.C. Yet he had done so only after repeated warnings from the lips of the preexilic prophets, who had declared that if Israel was to remain God's people, then they must obey God's voice; and God had acted in this way only after several hundred years of postponement of his judgment, and after Jerusalem had been given the chance to see that judgment first fall on the Northern Kingdom in 722 B.C. Finally, God had acted, for *was it not Yahweh against whom we sinned?* Israel had not obeyed God, who had commanded her to keep his Torah and walk in his revealed *ways.*

25.

And so when God acted in the end, the burning *heat* of his zeal for Israel's good had *inflamed* upon his own beloved people, through the flames of the torches of Nebuchadrezzar's soldiers as they set fire to the homes and temple and walls of Jerusalem (cf. II Kings 25:9). *From all sides* this had happened, for Israel could not escape the judgment by flight in any direction. Yet even that terrible event had not spoken home to Israel's conscience, for she had gone off into exile merely bewailing her fate, and without even confessing her folly.

Das Verstockungsproblem, the problem of the hardening of the heart, is one which the Bible never resolves, yet it fully acknowledges it as a reality in God's dealings with men (cf. Matt. 13:14-15; Mark 4:12; Luke 8:10; John 12:40; Acts 28:26; Rom. 11:8). God had warned Isaiah more than a century before that the more he should preach to his people, the deafer Israel would become (6:9-12); what is more, his preaching would actually create that deafness of which God spoke, and would produce a refusal to convert and be healed. That is to say, God's Word would in itself produce unbelief. Moses had seen this happen in the case of Pharaoh, as Pharaoh's heart grew harder at each evidence of Yahweh's power, to the point that the writer could say: "The Lord hardened the heart of Pharaoh" (Exod. 9:12). But then Pharaoh had not belonged in the chosen people of God, nor did Pharaoh know what it meant to be one with a nation bound to the living God by an eternal covenant. Nor could he know that such a covenant relationship was the container that gave locus to the most wonderful revelation of God ever yet made, God's covenant love and loyalty (*ḥesedh*) to Israel. Israel's apostasy therefore was a far greater sin than anything Pharaoh could ever have committed. For Israel had actually been chosen to be the means of God's grace to all the pharaohs of this world.

How necessary it was therefore for Israel in DI's day to learn that "our God is [still] a consuming fire, even a jealous God" (Deut. 4:24). Jealous is more nearly our word zealous. Thus the pictorial imagery of fire represents here the white heat of God's judgment of love. So greatly does this loving God loathe the sin of Israel that he must necessarily consume it. Before DI's time Isaiah too had seen the significance of the zeal of God. He had said: "The sinners in Zion are afraid; fearfulness hath surprised the hypocrites. Who among us shall dwell with the devouring fire? Who among us shall dwell with everlasting burnings?" (33:14). No one can, and yet—herein lies the mystery of Israel's election—Israel does in fact survive the judgment of love that she has rightly brought upon herself, but only by God's grace. The mystery of the hardening of Israel's heart DI is not able to resolve, even when he sees what God actually does with the hardened heart of Israel, and how he uses that hardened heart to display his grace. But this mystery becomes the passionate theological interest of our writer as his chapters unfold.

At the present juncture, however, even as DI questions his people in this pointed way, the hardening process is complete. Israel's heart has become so hardened that she is no longer able to make any response at all to the judgments of God upon her. Even when the zeal of God was burning into her bones, she *never realized why,* and *did not understand its significance.* Because of course a corpse (see commentary at 41:14) cannot feel the pain of the flames of the cremation ceremony. Yet, here is the unique new thing which DI has come to realize is basic to God's entire plan of action as he uses his people—in and through the fires God might possibly, and by grace alone, give new life even to the dead body of this his chosen and still-beloved instrument. And if he should do so, then would not such an act resolve forever the yet unresolved mystery of why God's Word should create, in the first place, a heart that had grown too hard to listen to him of its own warped and sinful volition? DI will return to this theme later.

CHAPTER 43

1 But now! Thus says Yahweh, who created thee, Jacob,
and formed thee, Israel,
Do not be afraid! for I have redeemed thee;
I have called thee by thy name; thou art mine!
2 When thou hast to go through waters, I shall be with thee,
and through rivers, they will not go over thy head.
When thou hast to go through fire, thou shalt not be
burned, and the flames shall not consume thee.
3 For I, Yahweh, am thy God; the Holy One of Israel is
thy Savior.
I have [already] given Egypt to be thy ransom,
the Sudan and Ethiopia instead of thee.
4 This is because thou art precious in my sight, and
worth my loving thee.
So I gave mankind instead of thee, and the nations
in place of thy person.

1.

Theologically speaking, this is another highly significant chapter. It contains the roots of much of our Christian theology. For we are consistently to keep in mind that while DI addresses his contemporaries in and through a historical situation of pain and sorrow, he is also preaching about the meaning and significance of those same events. Thus he is here declaring the mind of God upon them—and that is theology.

He continues with an exclamation in order to force his readers to think. The first point of significance arising from God's rousing of Cyrus from the north is that Israel has no grounds whatsoever for lack of faith. *Do not be afraid* resounds again, as it does throughout the Bible, and in DI's work again at 43:5; 44:2; 54:4. Think, Israel! First I *created* you by uttering the Word (*says Yahweh*), just as I spoke the Word about the heavens.[1] Next I *formed* you; after that, because in Adam you had fallen into sin, I *redeemed* you. Is that not sufficient reason to know no fear, even in the dungeons of Babylon? Your case is like that of a slave girl for whom her master has paid the necessary price in the first place, but who has run away from home, and has turned up eventually in the slave market. There the Master has recognized his Servant in all her misery, and has called out to her: *Israel, . . . thou art mine!* even as she stands shivering in her nakedness. Thereupon he pays for her a second time in order to be able to take her home where she belongs. It is true that Israel had paid double for all her sins (40:2), but now it is apparent that God too has paid double, so to speak, in order to bring Israel back home to himself once more. More than that—*I have called thee by thy name: thou art mine!* The divine Lover has now proceeded to call Israel by her "Christian" name, and in this way has claimed her as his own beloved.

In Israel's early days, if a man knew another's name, he believed that he knew his friend's personality intimately. This was because the name, ideally speaking, was the true description of its owner. So God knew Israel through and through. She need therefore have no fear in committing her heart to him, since he already knew everything that was in her heart. Moreover, God calls "Moses!" "Elijah!" "Saul, Saul!" in such a manner that the individual hearer learns that he possesses an individual identity in the sight of God. He learns that he exists in his own right by the Word of God addressed to him. It is in accordance with this biblical way of thinking that the ordained minister today proclaims in God's name: "John, I baptize thee" and John thereby becomes the individual child of God within the divine family that God has already named as Israel.

2.

God does not promise, however, to remove his beloved from a world of floods and diseases and trials and tribulations. What he does promise is that when Israel passes through these things, he will walk beside her. This is a most interesting development of the argument set forth previously at 42:25. The story of the three representative Israelites walking in the fires of the exile in Babylon without being burned, and finding a Fourth walking beside them (Dan. 3), may well be a midrash upon the verse

[1] Cf. 42:5. The idea is explicit in Ps. 33:6, a passage which was traditional in DI's day.

that is before us now. Moreover, this is a constant theme in the OT, as we see from such passages as Deut. 31:6-8; Pss. 66:12; 91.

Again, the *waters* symbolize several ideas for Israel, ever since God rescued her from the waters of the Red Sea. For example, the waters referred to may be the waters of judgment, as the Red Sea undoubtedly was for Egypt. Or again, the theological significance of waters is frequently linked in prophetic thought with the waters of chaos that rage continually both above the sky and underneath the earth (cf. Exod. 20:4; Isa. 51:9-10). So the *rivers* were the streams of the river of chaos that flowed underneath the foundations of the earth. Israel always sits precariously on the verge of chaos. Yet she is held back from falling into the abyss of chaos only by the might and the grace of God, for he has promised never again to allow the floods to overwhelm and destroy the earth as would be the proper expression of his righteous judgment (Gen. 8:21-22). DI, like the author of Ps. 46, is absolutely confident that God is in control of the floods, because they are in effect his floods. That is why his people will not be saved from the floods, but rather, when they must necessarily pass through the floods, these will not overwhelm them. For *in* God's floods they will find that God is beside them, and that he is sharing with them all the tribulations that man must face when passing through a situation of that nature.

We have seen that God's glory was envisaged under the form of fire (Exod. 24:16-17). A natural development of this second theological picture therefore was to speak of God's radiant, burning glory as capable of burning up both sin and evil as fire can burn up chaff. Thus fire represents the holy and dreadful presence of God, present like a refiner's fire. It is interesting to realize that the prophets of the OT drew no line between God's living, guiding presence with Israel in the burning zeal of his love, and his judgment upon Israel's sin made evident in the trials and troubles of life which, as here, were constantly pictured in terms of burning fire. This is because they believed that God is responsible for all that happens in human life. Thus trials and vexations are his holy presence. That significant fact, as we can see, DI has accepted in full from those who have gone before him. Thus he can exclaim with confidence that *when thou hast to go through fire, thou shalt not be burned*.

3.

This guarantee is expressed by God's declaration or virtual oath that he really is who he is. The declaration is opened by the word *ki,* a particle which can be used to follow an unspoken phrase like "I declare" or "I swear," and so it precedes a strong asseveration. In the days of Moses God had made himself known under the name of Yahweh (Exod. 3:14; 6:3; 33:19), and in doing so he had coupled his name of self-revelation with overt acts of salvation. In this way he had shown himself to be Israel's *Savior. The Sudan and Ethiopia* may mean the then little-known southern area of Egypt rather than the areas covered by these names today. What DI is declaring then is that little Israel is worth more than the whole of greater Egypt. Yet the phrase is a Semitic hyperbole of the same genre as similar expressions used by our Lord, such as, "If thy right eye offend thee, pluck it out." On the other hand, the pharaoh of Egypt, or the pharaoh's son, was regarded in DI's day as the representative figure who could sum up in himself the meaning of Egypt. In the light of this are the words of God at Exod. 4:22-23: "Thus shalt thou say unto Pharaoh, Thus saith the Lord, Israel is my son, even my firstborn. And I say unto thee, Let my son go, that he may serve me: and if thou refuse to let him go, behold, I will slay thy son, even thy firstborn." Israel then was the son of God. As a fact of history this son had escaped disaster, yet only at the expense of the life of the pharaoh's son. Such a thing could happen again, therefore, as Deutero-Zechariah was also to affirm some generations later (Zech. 10:11).

The above may seem to represent a strange theology. But in this world love can be known only as a personal experience. It can never be understood as a mere concept. Therefore, in the providence of his wisdom God chose to draw near to all men by entering into a bond of love with one particular people. Through his relationship of love with his people he purposed to let all men see his glory. Israel's calling was to become a kingdom of priests vis-à-vis the rest of the world (Gen. 19:6). Yet the other nations were ipso facto excluded from being the chosen nation of priests. They had thus to pay the cost of Israel's election. The rich countries of the West today are obviously chosen to have a very fortunate standard of living. But it is also a fact that they maintain that standard only at the cost, at least in part, of the underprivileged masses of the East. However, this situation must only be one of temporary advantage to the West. For along with privileges, responsibility always goes. The West is therefore bound before God to pass on her good fortune to those who were not chosen to begin with, or else to suffer the fate that Israel suffered when her own God had to destroy her as a national entity for not accepting her priestly calling.

4.

Reverting to the thought of DI, we see that he is sure that the turn of the gentiles will come. For if Israel is faithful to her calling—and even if she is not—then they too will know Yahweh and in the end will bring their riches to his feet (cf. Isa. 19:23-25; 44:5; 45:14; 61; 66:19). Meanwhile Israel must never forget her position of responsibility to *mankind* (cf. Amos 3:1-2) and so must never cease to walk delicately. She dare not judge her neighbors in their unbelief, for their unbelief has been necessary in the first place for her belief. God alone is judge of all the earth. This is sufficient answer for the modern Western sophisticate who rejects the Christian faith in favor of some form of syncretism, declaring that he could not selfishly accept salvation when the masses in China—or the Sudan—have not had the chance to hear of Christ.

Meanwhile, the *person, nephesh,* of Israel is *precious* in God's *sight.* Israel here is clearly depicted as one corporate entity, one personality sprung from the loins of Jacob-Israel. As such, of course, he is a child of promise—Israel is masculine in this strophe. So he must possess value in himself. Though a worm, a louse, he is yet *worth my loving thee.* This is not because, ontologically speaking, he is valuable in himself, as DI has already said. Israel is valuable to God on the ground that he is the object of God's election-love and the instrument of the revelation of God's glory to all men. It would be well at this point to note how rarely the love of God is spoken of in the OT. This is because God's love is not a concept to philosophize upon. Love is something that happens to those at whom God's saving activity is directed even as they live in a particular historical situation. The OT is full of such actions and situations; these reveal God's loving purpose when they are seen with the eyes of faith, as God willed that they should.

5 Do not be afraid! I am really with thee.
I shall fetch thy seed from the east, and
gather thee in from the west;
6 Saying to the north, "Hand over!" and to the south,
"Do not hold in prison!"
But fetch my sons from far away, and my daughters
from the end of the earth,

7 All those who are called by my name, whom I have created, and then formed for my glory.

5.

But the significance of the idea that Israel has been chosen at the expense, in the first place, of *adam, mankind,* is so disturbing that God has to repeat the comforting words: *Do not be afraid!* And then he adds: I swear that I am with thee," or *I am really with thee,* in this form of close relationship that the prophets knew of as covenant loyalty and love (cf. Exod. 3:12; Isa. 7:14; "God is with us"). For if God is not *with* his people, then he can only be *against* them. There can be no third way. Not that the covenant with Israel was a new thing in the world. Far from it. Covenants between a god and his people through the medium of the king were known long before the day of Moses. It is the peculiar content of the OT covenant which is so challenging, strange, and new. For despite the fact that the Northern Kingdom seemed to have been cut to pieces and its people scattered to the winds as much as a century and a half before the destruction of the Southern Kingdom, the prophets were certain that the reality of the covenant still held Israel together as one people in the sight of God. This kind of covenant therefore forms the framework of the revelation of God's unchanging *ḥesedh,* his loyal love. Thus Israel cannot finally perish; God's people are destined to return home where they belong—all of them, even those who are presently scattered to the ends of the earth. Jer. 40:11 and 41:17 tell us that Israelite exiles had fled to Moab, Edom, and Ammon in the East, and to Egypt in the West, and many other passages speak of their wide dispersion ever since the fall of the Northern Kingdom in 721 B.C. But God is Lord of all the forces that at present militate against the working of his purpose through Israel for the saving of the world.

6.

So he has but to say, *Hand over!* and these forces will no longer be able to keep this people in the *prison* darkness of night and unbelief.

7.

Also, says DI, this people possesses two names. What he means is that Israel is (1) the corporate son of God. (2) But God knows each individual member of this people by his Christian name. In the light of (1), this people possesses a surname or family name as well as their individual Christian names. And that family name is actually Yahweh.

As his sons and daughters—note how women have an equal place with men in DI's thought—live within the mysterious intimacy of the covenant, their raison d'être is to show to all the world the glory of Yahweh their Father, for he created them for this end. Now no man can see God himself and live. Yet God's glory may be known through human flesh. It has been the signal privilege and awesome responsibility of Israel to be God's choice of human flesh for that end.

8 Bring out (that) blind people who yet possess eyes! that
deaf people who yet possess ears!
9 Let all the nations congregate as one, let the peoples
be gathered together.
Which of them could report this? Let them tell us about
the first things.
Let them produce their witnesses, and see if they are right,
and let people hear if they speak the truth.

8.

What a tragedy for God that the flesh, the *eyes,* which should have revealed his glory, were *blind!* Now whom does God here summon to act for him? For God's commands are in the imperative, singular, masculine, and the form of the verb is rare and unusual. The prophet himself seems to be the only one who can fit the situation. But the DSI reads DI's verbs as a plural. If the latter is the original reading, then it may be God's angelic hosts who are here summoned to do God's bidding once again (cf. 40:1).

9.

Deaf and dumb Israel is to be led into court in the presence of all the nations. By this means Israel may possibly be shamed into recognizing how deaf and dumb she really is. God will then ask any nation that volunteers to do so to step forward and recount how Yahweh has acted in that nation's history, in the manner that Yahweh has already acted in Israel's history since the days of Moses. Of course none of them will be able to produce any witnesses at all to any such mighty events, for they have no one in their midst to interpret what God has been doing. Their history has not been *Heilsgeschichte,* nor have they prophets to interpret it.

Of course it is easy to be wise after the event and critical of the point of view of the Hebrew exiles as they listen to the summons of God when this court is in session. More than a generation has now gone by since the fall of Jerusalem in 587 B.C. This means that the great majority of DI's hearers have been born in this strange land of Babylonia, which is therefore their country as truly as Australia is the native land of the sons of immigrants, no matter from where they come. It was thus quite natural for DI's hearers to dismiss as irrelevant the seemingly rather comical interpretation that DI had been giving them of the past history of a land they had never known, and which now seemed so very far away from the civilized life they had come to regard as the only possible life that man could live. Much better, as we would say, to do in Rome as the Romans do and recognize that Bel (see 46:1) was the real god of all, not this Yahweh of DI, this God merely of a little hill tribe that had been conquered anyway by gods obviously more powerful than he.

10 "You are my witnesses," is the oracular utterance of
Yahweh, "and my Servant whom I have chosen,
In order that you may know me and believe in me, and
realize that I am He.
No god was formed before me, nor shall there be any
after me."

10.

Then God turns dramatically to Israel and exclaims to this people that is quite satisfied to do in Rome as the Romans do: *You are my witnesses,* for you were there when I brought Israel through the waters of the Red Sea and gave you my covenant by the hand of Moses, and then led you into a land that was not yours to possess but was a gift from me to my people. This all happened in order that *you may know me and believe in me*. Later in his thesis DI will show of course that the world is to have the opportunity to believe as well. At the moment, however, in the double capacity as *witness*—some scholars suggest voweling this word in the singular—and as *Servant,* Israel has become the one proof of the existence of God that cannot be gainsaid by formal reasoning.

The word *know* can of course be used in ordinary ways. The Hebrew verb *y-d-ʿ* according to circumstances may have to be translated by perceive, learn, understand, have skill. But it can also speak of existential knowledge. For example, we read that "Adam knew his wife, and she conceived" (Gen. 4:1). Obviously intellectual understanding is here only a part of what is involved. In the same way, when Adam in the Garden of Eden story ate of the forbidden fruit, he expected, like Julian Huxley with drugs, that his whole experience of existence would be raised to a new dimension, to that in fact of the gods. It is this act of experiencing, entering into a heightened awareness, that the J writer describes by this verb *y-d-ʿ*. The translation of one word into another in a different language can obviously be controlled only by a strict examination of its relation to the sentence in which it stands.[2] Here, at vs. 10, to *know* God is qualified by the idea of believing in him. Consequently, the verb to *know* as it occurs here has that fuller and deeper sense which it can convey. So as Jeremiah says: "And no longer shall each man teach his neighbor and each his brother, saying, 'Know the Lord,' for they shall all know me." (31:34 RSV.) Possibly the reason why DI does not elaborate on Jeremiah's words is that there was no need to do so. Jeremiah's hope may well have been the common property of the exiles.

Israel then is to *believe in* Yahweh. This verb means "to take a firm stand upon," from the original root which meant "to be firm." DI was not a philologist and is unlikely to have known this fact; the content of the idea of "believing in" that he offers is another thing. He would be acquainted with the common figure of speech where the God of Israel is described by the epithet of rock (cf. Deut. 32:18; Isa. 17:10; Ps. 18:2). The following suggestion may not be wholly fanciful then. To *believe in* God, as DI sees it, is not to demand any special activity on Israel's part. All that Israel has to do is to place her feet on the Rock which is already there; then she will discover that she too is as "sure," *ne'eman,* as the Rock beneath her feet. To believe in God is to make the existential discovery that God is faithful and reliable; it is not to make an act of belief oneself, nor is it to attempt anything which one does not have the strength to do. It means to discover for oneself the reality of God's actions in history, even in one's own personal history (cf. Rom. 8:28). It means to recognize that God himself is historical, that is, that he works in the realm of space and time and thus in the area of scientifically observable data. This does not mean that God is searchable and provable,

[2] See James Barr, *The Semantics of Biblical Language* (New York: Oxford University Press, 1961), pp. 161 *ff*.

for God must always remain inconceivable. Yet he can be *known,* in this new biblical sense of the word, within the covenant relationship.

11 I, Yahweh, only I am; apart from me there is no Savior.
12 It was I who declared (and spoke the word) of salvation,
and let you know of it: it was no alien [god] in
your midst.
While you are my witnesses, is the oracular utterance of Yahweh,
I am God!
13 As day succeeds day I [remain] He; thus no one can snatch
thee out of my hand. When I act,
who can reverse it?

11, 12, 13.

Now, no other god ever produced a saving purpose like Yahweh's for no god is saving love as such except Yahweh alone. And so he says: I had but to speak the word: "Let there be deliverance from Egypt," and there was deliverance. It was I who did it, he might go on to say, not the gods of Egypt, for I, Yahweh, am God! I am He, not It, the living One, active, creative, purposive; in fact mine is the only purpose. This means that there is no power that can *snatch thee,* Israel, *out of my hand;* there is no power to deflect, far less to *reverse,* my purpose when I have begun to act. This is because the Word of salvation, once uttered, cannot return unto me void (see 55:11). Why in heaven's name, therefore, should Israel have to be called blind, when she has already witnessed God's mighty acts?

This is an important passage. It suggests the ultimate victory of God over all opposition. It declares that God's essential purpose is that all men should know him and believe in him. And it also reveals that Israel will definitely be used by God to this end, since God has chosen her for this and will not change his mind.

The passage also suggests, however, the extraordinary freedom that God has given to Israel. Israel is free to witness against God as well as for him. On the other hand, if Israel is rebellious and witnesses against her Lord, then it is her very rebelliousness which becomes the medium through which God reveals his grace. Incidentally, God chose a whole nation as one entity to be his witness; individuals could easily be lost in those turbulent days. It is interesting to read, for example, that the Philistines knew about the Exodus tradition that was the heritage of the entire people of Israel, their neighbor (I Sam. 4:8). Thus it was all Israel that became Yahweh's *ʿedhim,* witnesses. From the same root comes the feminine form, *ʿedhuth,* which was used for the testimony of the Decalogue (Exod. 31:18, etc.), and the *mishkan ha-ʿedhuth* was the tabernacle of the testimony (Exod. 38:21, etc.). In later writings even the whole code of law was called the testimony of Yahweh (Ps. 19:7). But Israel's cult and cultic objects were *witnesses* in this sense, only because Israel as a body, as a congregation (Josh. 24:22), was such. Israel's raison d'être, we recall (42:1-7), was to be the instrument of God's mission. Now it was also to be God's witness. Curiously enough, here again this can come about only in the strength of Yahweh, since he is the only true and faithful witness himself (Jer. 42:5). For example, it is only Yahweh who can swear by himself alone (Ps. 89:35; and cf. Gen. 31:50). Thus once again comes the proposition that while Israel may indeed exist in the ontological sense, in reality she is of no value in her own right; the real ground of her existence is the Word of God.

14 Thus says Yahweh, your Redeemer, the Holy One of Israel:
It is for your sake I have sent (him) to Babylon,
and shall bring low (their) fugitives, all of them,
even the Chaldeans in their masted ships.
15 I am Yahweh, your Holy One, Israel's Creator, your King.

14, 15.

This fact is now thoroughly emphasized. Israel's existence over against God rests entirely upon her having been redeemed by her *Redeemer.* DI calls Yahweh Israel's Redeemer more often than all the other OT writers put together. He is also *the Holy One of Israel.* But this last name of God is now rendered in the form of an even more disconcerting juxtaposition, viz., *your Holy One,* or, the Holy-One-of-you. English uses five words to translate what is one word in Hebrew. That one word unites in solemn bond the unspeakable difference and distance between the wholly other God and you, Israel, living only by grace and quite capable of witnessing against this Holy One, who has bound himself to this people in a unique relationship, for in Israel's flesh God's glory is to be made manifest to all the world.

16 Thus says Yahweh, who lays a route through the sea,
a path through the mighty waters,

17 Who calls out [in pursuit] chariot and horse,
army and forces together:
("They're lying down!" "They can't get up!" "They've expired!" "They're quenched like a wick!")

16.

The second scene in this new act of the drama is now about to open. The first scene was God's rousing up of Cyrus from the east and north. Now (vs. 14) Cyrus is nearly at the gate of Babylon, the capital city of the empire, and this too is God's doing. The text of the next line is difficult. But when we remember that the whole city was cut in two by the river Euphrates, we are able to build a picture from the few words that we have. While the city had admirable defenses on its walls, the weak link was where the river entered and left through the walls. For at those gates there was no possibility of erecting bars, although there was some kind of bridge-of-boats defense boom. In DI's day Babylon also had long lines of wharves within the city where ships could tie up before cavernous warehouses; for Babylon could trade with the Eastern world via the Persian Gulf. The Greek historian Herodotus moreover tells us that the city surrendered to Cyrus almost without a blow. For Cyrus' troops entered the city where the river entered between the walls. They had succeeded in temporarily diverting the main stream by leading it off into a depression. Therefore, while the other translations noted above are all possible, those which best fit the facts are selected. Cyrus then *lays a route, . . . a path,* through the waters of the Euphrates, but he will do so only at the Word of him who is Lord of all the seas and oceans. When he reaches the city, Cyrus will meet masted and oared ships, now lying high and dry, with slaves lashed to their oars. Remember that all oarsmen were slaves even as late as the Hellenistic period.

17.

This coming act of Cyrus will naturally be an effortless activity for Yahweh, who has already laid a route through the Red Sea, and destroyed the Egyptian army therein; yet that was but Act I in God's continuing *Heilsgeschichte*. It was at the Red Sea that man's hubris had met its judgment, only to find that Yahweh's is infused with a saving purpose. That saving purpose Isaiah had been aware of once again two centuries before DI's day (19:23-24). For Isaiah had recognized that although Egypt had passed under judgment in the days of Moses, she was still to be blessed in the days to come. Yet this would happen only if Israel's faith could rise to meet the descent of the purpose of God, and if she let herself become the medium of that purpose as it had dealings with Israel's ancient enemy Egypt. DI makes his picture of the reaction of the Babylonians to the triumphal entry of Cyrus into the city all the more vivid by putting his words in the present tense, as if they were being uttered by an excited onlooker.

18 Do not even recall those former things, do not even
ruminate on those previous events.
19 Behold, I am about to do something new.
It is just about to spring into being—do you
not understand that?
I am going to lay a route through the wilderness,
and roads through the desert.
20 Even the wild beasts will honor me,
such as the jackals and the ostriches,
For I am about to put water in the wilderness, and
streams in the desert,
To give my chosen people drink.
21 That is, the people whom I fashioned for myself,
that they might tell forth my praise.

18, 19.

What Cyrus is going to do under God is something far greater than the events at the Red Sea of old. And so Act II is now about to open. To emphasize it, DI makes God forbid Israel even to think back to those mighty events of old. Look at me in action now, he says. What I am about to do is something which, though new, will not be a surprise; for it will spring organically out of the old, as the butterfly develops from the caterpillar. Thus I am going to *lay a route,* not this time in the sea, but over *the wilderness* that separates Babylonia from Palestine.

20, 21.

"No ravening beasts will be there" (35:9). My action is to have cosmic significance; even the brute beasts will cooperate. Then "in the wilderness shall waters break out, *and streams in the desert*" (35:6). Observe how close our verse is to Isa. 35 and other similar passages, one of which we shall meet later at 55:12-13. But this is not the place to discuss the authorship or provenance of Isa. 35. *Streams in the desert* are of course fundamental for the preservation of any form of life in the wilderness.

The whole of the above section is obviously to be understood metaphorically and not literally, even though the declaration is based upon the literal emancipation of the exiles by Cyrus and their literal return to their homeland in Palestine. Several factors should be noted before making an interpretation. The wild animals are here to serve God's purpose as it becomes embodied in returning Israel. Behind ravenous beasts lie the figures of desert and waste which these creatures inhabit. As we have seen, these are figures for all the forces that militate against the creative and loving purpose of God. Yet God's plan is to continue to work out through sickness and pain, and even through death itself, so that life may blossom therefrom. Other passages that deal with this theme seem to us even to confound the healing of the sick with crossing the desert (35:5-10; 61:1-6). But sickness and death are but manifestations of chaos or of desert, as DI believed. In fact, in the Hebrew language one can refer to "being deserted" as an experience built on the usage of one of the Hebrew nouns for desert. *Yeshimon, desert* (vs. 19), was the name of an area so completely barren that no sheep could graze on it at all. Deut. 32:10, a verse in the song of Moses which DI quotes so frequently, declares that "he found him in a desert land, and in the waste howling wilderness." That is both literal fact and at the same time a picture of what life is like without God. Moreover it is what life could become once again for Israel should she rebel against God's good guidance and stray from the straight and narrow road. Once again she would be lost in the desert. Yet, as DI declares, if this happens, in his grace God will not immediately lift her out of the desert and set her back on the road. He will lay new roads for her *in* the desert, and open pools of water for her to drink *in the desert* just as he had done before at that time when he gave Israel water from the rock that Moses struck (Num. 20:7-11). And he will do so in order that, walking beside her as the Good Shepherd, he may gently lead her back to where she belongs.

Thus Israel will retain her free will even in the desert, for God never forces his people to return home to his care when they do not wish to do so. The whole eschatological picture is virtually theological teaching drawn from an existential situation. Here we have the second or third indication of DI's important thesis still to follow, viz., that God is able to bring salvation to others out of the suffering and even death of his chosen people.

22 Yet Jacob, thou hast not called upon me; in fact,
Israel, thou hast grown tired of me.
23 Thou didst not have to bring me any sheep as thy
burnt offerings, nor didst thou have to honor
me with thy sacrifices.
I have not been making thee serve me with meal offerings,
nor been putting thee to trouble with frankincense.
24 Thou hast not had to buy me sweet cane with money,
nor saturate me with thy fatty sacrifices;
On the contrary, thou hast turned me into the Servant
[who has had to deal] with thy sins, and it is
I whom thou hast made weary at the cost of
thine iniquities.

22.

How tragic it is that for the fifty long years now that Israel has been in exile she has been blind to this underlying purpose of God. Israel was that people whom God had originally fashioned to be his own necessary instrument, and in creating Israel God had known the joy of the Father who rightly demands his own eternal praise (Ps. 102:18; Luke 1:74-75; Eph. 1:5-6). But now the ideal is suddenly confronted with the actual. With six verbs in the negative, God points out how Israel has *not* declared the praise of the Father. Israel has actually *grown tired* of God. What an admission this is that God has to make! And not for the first time, either. We read with astonishment God's question of Israel two centuries before: "Wherein have *I* wearied *you?*" (Mic. 6:3). DI knew that Israel was not in Babylon by chance. God had put her there to be his Servant in that particular situation, in fact, to be the means of offering to the gentiles the full life he wanted them to live. But now the eternal plan and purpose of God had failed. And it had failed through Israel's growing tired of God.

23.

And so the curtain is here drawn back on the pain in the Father's heart. For he is united in covenantal bond with this ridiculous people as the Holy-One-of-you, a people that chose of its own free will to turn its back on God's cosmic purpose.

The next lines are not easy to translate. They must almost be paraphrased at times rather than translated, and no two expositors have produced exactly the same rendering in English. Yet two points should guide in translating the equivocal Hebrew. (1) The words are addressed to a historical situation such as we can envisage, insofar as we know the details of the exiles' life about 540 B.C. (2) The words come in sequence as part of the sustained theological disputation that we call Isa. 40–55, and are therefore to be understood not as an isolated utterance, but as the link in the argument that now introduces DI's coming exposition of God's saving method of suffering love.

DI makes God point out that ever since the temple had fallen in 587, Israel in exile had not been able to offer sacrifice. This was a great deprivation for her, for sacrifices were God's own choice of the means of grace for Israel.

24.

But the Exile had put an end to those daily and expensive offerings. So the opportunity had arisen for Israel to realize that she could now hold intimate communion with her chosen God without the instrumentality of the sacrificial cult. Her prophets had sought to teach her so: "Hath the Lord as great delight in burnt offerings and sacrifices, as in obeying the voice of the Lord?" (I Sam. 15:22). "Will the Lord be pleased with thousands of rams? . . . What doth the Lord require of thee, but to do justly, and to love loyalty [the covenant fellowship with himself], and to walk humbly with thy God?" (Mic. 6:7-8.) Yet that glorious opportunity, arising out of the discipline of the Exile, had been missed. Throughout the years of exile God had not looked for Israel to serve him with what it was now impossible for her to offer. On the other hand, Israel might have shown an astonished Babylon how it is possible to live in faith without the props of established religious practices. For one immediate outcome of God's action in destroying Jerusalem could have been that Israel would learn the possibility of this kind of fellowship with God. But God had foreknown that Israel would not behave in this way, because it was he himself who had hardened Israel's heart (Isa. 6:9 *ff.*). In consequence, Israel, who had been called by God to be his Servant, had insolently forced God to be her Servant.[3] God

[3] For this translation, see Wilhelm Vischer, *Das Kerugma des Alten Testaments* (Zurich: Zwingli Verlag, 1955), p. 21; and Vischer, *Valeur de l'Ancien Testament* (Geneva: Labor et Fides, n.d.), p. 150.

had actually had to carry Israel's burden when she, throwing off all constraint and restraint and believing that the covenant bond was now virtually annulled, had given herself over to wallowing in self-pity and despair.

There is no discussion here on the origin of sacrifices, or as to whether God had originally demanded them or not. On the other hand, sacrifice is obviously an instrument in the covenantal plan of God. Sacrifice is a concept therefore that must not be discarded because circumstances now prohibit the actual slaying of beasts upon an altar. Israel ought therefore to have been making the discovery that, since the sacrifice of beasts was no longer possible and since the principle of sacrifice must still hold, it was she herself who had to become the beast that must now be sacrificed. But Israel had not made that forward step. Israel, however, had given up her obligations to the covenant when she broke her word to keep it. On the other hand, God had not broken his. In consequence it was he alone who was now bearing the sacrificial cost of the union, this union which the Holy-One-of-you had forged and laid upon Israel his chosen Servant. God thus necessarily experienced and bore upon his own flesh—for in DI's day the glory of God was regarded as the spiritual counterpart of flesh—the pain that Israel had refused to bear, and which was concomitant with being the Servant of God to the world. It is God himself then who is thus in an ultimate sense *the Servant* that Israel had been called and chosen to be. Just as it is the devoted husband who feels the pain of his wife's folly and lack of social conscience, and who thus takes on himself the burden that she refuses to carry, so too in the case of Israel's God. We shall discover that DI actually uses this metaphor of marriage in a later chapter to exemplify the reality that God must necessarily undertake for Israel what Israel cannot do for herself.

The above words are not theological speculation. No human mind could have invented the thoughts contained in vs. 24. These can be no less therefore than revelation, revelation into the very heart of the living and loving God, who in his condescension has stooped to unite himself with this intolerably insolent people that he now calls his own. Theological discussion of revelation should always be secondary to a recognition of that revelation in one's own experience. This is just what DI does. Hereafter he has to think deeply before he dares return to this extraordinary theme, which he does only ten chapters further on in his thesis. But the above passage is so iconoclastic of all man's preconceived notions about what is proper for the divine Being and what is not that it has been passed over in silence by the great majority of scholars. The traditional theological view about God in the works of the fathers of the early Christian centuries, and even at the Reformation period, is that God must necessarily be impassible. The conception of God's impassibility might be acceptable if it arose in face of the idea that man's sin can thwart and frustrate the Almighty. But the work of DI reveals to us the sufferings of a God who wills to suffer. In his capacity as Creator and Redeemer of his world he sees that his ends can be met only in, through, and by means of the sufferings that the sins of the men he has chosen in love have caused him. On the other hand, DI's God is he who knows the end from the beginning. Therefore his sufferings cannot efface the joy he carries in his heart. He knows that in the end he will win his whole world to glad acceptance of his proffered love.

25 I, I am He, who for my own sake wipes away thy rebellions,
and thy sins I will call to mind no more.
26 But do thou recall me to mind. Let us argue the thing
out together.
Do thou tell [thy side of the argument] to show if thou
art in the right.
27 Even thy first ancestor was a sinner, even thine
interpreters have been rebellious against me.
28 [So that was why] I had to defile the sanctuary officials,
and hand over Jacob to be extirpated,
and Israel to blasphemers.

25.

Behind the action which *wipes away* Israel's rebellions lies the pathos and the passion of a God who does this wiping away at an unspeakable cost to himself. The word *rebellions* is chosen to represent the typical sin of a people that is bound to God in a personal covenant. Hebrew has many words for sin, each of them presenting its ugliness from a different point of view. But ultimately sin is not to be understood as if it were an object at all, for sin is the breaking off of relations between persons who are committed to each other in some degree of bond. Divorce, for example, is a far harder thing to forgive than a series of sinful acts on the part of the couple in question. "It is I," however, the one and only and real and living God who so forgives that he forgets. The All-Knowing thus forgets. And he does so on the ground that it is the very essence of his nature so to do—*for my own sake.* This is a doctrine that goes beyond anything that even Isaiah or Hosea had declared before the Exile.

26.

But while God may forget, Israel dares not. Israel must keep her covenant relationship to God constantly in mind. For it is when she *re*-calls, *zachar,* God's saving acts of old that Israel actualizes them in the present, that is to say, even in the Exile, where she does not have the cult to aid her in this act of recall. But when she does this, she can become existentially involved once again in the saving power of God's redeeming acts, and find that the significance of the chronological moment of long ago is as real now as it was in the days of Moses.

27.

Once again, therefore, God gives Israel the chance to present her own selfish case, for he is the kind of God who will not browbeat his blind Servant into acquiescence to his will. But God solemnly reminds Israel that even Abraham was a sinner—recall how he lied to Abimelech (Gen. 20:2). Or if we regard Jacob as Israel's *first ancestor,* as more than one tradition asserts, then the evidence is stronger still of his despicable nature, as we saw at 41:8. Even the prophets, *thine interpreters* as they are called here, were sinners all, from Moses to those of the Exile (cf. Isa. 6:5), for all were involved in the corporate sin of that corporate entity known as the people of Yahweh. The hardening of Israel's heart was such that Israel had reached a point when a "slight healing" of her wound (Jer. 6:14; 8:11) would have been worse than useless. This is because the means of grace that were available in Jeremiah's day through the temple services and the sacrifices of the cult could be of no possible advantage to a people that was no longer in the moral position to use them. Even for a century before Jeremiah's day Israel had been wholly sick, sick all over from head to foot, as Isaiah had put it clearly (1:6). But now, a whole two centuries after Isaiah had said those words, Israel was not even to be considered a sick man.

28.

Israel was now in reality a dead corpse, as we saw at 41:14. There is only one thing you can decently do for a corpse and that is to bury it.

Yet the only undertakers available to God are *blasphemers* themselves.

Is it not a blasphemous idea itself that the Holy One should hand over his beloved *to be extirpated?* The word is "put to the ban" or totally destroy, as Joshua did to Jericho (Josh. 6:17) on the ground that Jericho—apart from Rahab—was wholly evil and was imbued with the spirit of a god of nonbeing. This reference to extirpation looks even more horrible when we meet the words *sanctuary officials.* For while this title covered the whole priestly class, it also included the king, for he was in reality the chief priest and intermediary between Yahweh and Israel. And the king in Judah at least, we should remember, was of the dynasty of David. And to David God had promised through the lips of Nathan that he would be his Father forever (II Sam. 7:14; Ps. 89:20-29). Yet this specially chosen line of David was included in the extirpation order, even though God had promised to uphold it forever. The *blasphemers* were those gentiles who did not know Yahweh, such as Nebuchadrezzar and his soldiers who were the instruments of the destruction of Jerusalem. But Holiness can do nothing else than this awful act. Holiness cannot remain bound up in the Holy-One-of-you relationship with a people that has become a corpse (cf. commentary at 41:14; Ezek. 6:5; 37:11). Holiness must necessarily loathe and hate the corpse to which it is tied, for a corpse renders him who even touches it unclean, or unholy, according to the priestly laws that were being codified in DI's day. It was therefore essential that Israel should suffer the curse that goes with being bound to the living and utterly pure and holy God (Dan. 9:11). For God is not one to be mocked.

But while Holiness must react in what may seem to us a negative manner when it comes in contact with what is foul and evil, yet since Holiness is God himself, this negative reaction must be part of God's positive and creative or even re-creative purpose as it works out to its ultimate victory. Although it may now be anticipating DI's argument, it would help to note at this point what DI reveals to be God's final answer to the impasse into which the covenant fellowship has fallen. His answer, as the remaining chapters of DI's book unfold step by step, is to reveal the only possible course left to the Holy-One-of-you if he is to continue in faithfulness and loyalty in contact with the corpse to which he has bound himself in covenant. That course is to resuscitate it.

DI must have been acquainted with Ezekiel's great vision in ch. 37 of the book that bears his name, as it describes in pictorial form his certainty that God will do just this very thing with the dry bones of his people Israel. Yet DI must have known that even God could not perform this act of resuscitating a corpse—stinking as it now was after almost fifty years, buried as it was said to be in the soil of this strange grave of Babylon, to use Ezekiel's tremendous imagery in that seminal chapter of his—merely by uttering an arbitrary divine fiat like a powerful dictator. This is because God would violate his own freedom should he behave in this manner, and violate too the freedom of those very Israelites whom his action was intended to save. God must proceed to this action, which is basic and central in the history of the world, only if that action remains in conformity with his chosen method of self-giving, and with his promise to be with his people forever (cf. Exod. 3:12; Isa. 7:14).

It was manifest by now that the one partner in the covenant, Israel, who had been called to be the Servant, was not in the position to raise herself out of the state of death she had now reached. Therefore it must be God alone, the other partner in the covenant, who would do this thing for her. Accordingly, in the freedom that only perfect love knows and expresses, God himself stoops to share with this stiff-necked Servant people the experience of being damned *(ḥerem)* and dead. In doing so, he is of course serving them within the bonds of the covenant in the only way possible for the Lord of the covenant to do. Since the wages of sin has been death at all times since the fall of Adam, the living God—what an unspeakable paradox—now takes those wages to himself. In so doing, he himself becomes the Servant of the people whom he has bound himself to love and to cherish in a bond that can never under any circumstances be broken or annulled. In this way he removes from Israel's heart the curse that she has necessarily brought upon herself, and is able to set her free, helpless as she is to do it for herself, from the law of sin and death. The promised deliverance from the death of the Exile—the theme which DI leads to in a later chapter—is a deliverance whose significance continues to unfold as the years go by in the history of this covenant people. The deliverance is an historical incident which we can date accurately just as we can date the resurrection of Christ. This historical incident becomes the sign and seal of the power of God, that he will be able to act in a like manner when he comes to redeem not only his firstborn Son (Exod. 4:22), but now all his sons of every nation of men. DI sees that the resurrection of the people of God must follow upon their "crucifixion," when they "suffered under Nebuchadrezzar" in 587 B.C., and so his mind becomes for us the channel of the revelation of the pattern of God's redemptive work at all times. We can understand how Paul can use for this decisive moment in the world's history the words "according to the scriptures" (I Cor. 15:3-4), for it is the same God who acts with infinite compassion and absolute loyalty to his covenant in the days of DI as in the days of Christ. Since God is faithful, it is only to be expected that the revelation he gives us of his love and holy purpose in 539 B.C. should be one with that which he makes of himself *ephhapax,* once and for all, when "in Christ" he both reveals himself and acts to reconcile the world unto himself (II Cor. 5:19).

CHAPTER

44

1 **Now then listen, Jacob my Servant, Israel**
whom I have chosen;
2 **Thus says Yahweh thy maker and fashioner, who has been**
helping thee ever since thou wast born;
Do not be afraid, my Servant Jacob, Jeshurun whom I
have chosen.
3 **For I am going to pour out water on the thirsty [soil],**
And streams on the dry ground;
I am going to pour out my Spirit upon thy seed,
and my blessing upon thine offspring.
4 **They shall spring up like a green bay tree,**
like willows along irrigation channels.
5 **One will then say: "I belong to Yahweh," and another**
will call himself by the name "Jacob."
While a third will inscribe "Yahweh's" upon his hand,
and a fourth will entitle himself by the name
"Israel."

1.

The grace of God is nowhere more clearly seen than in this section. One would think that 43:28 had related the end of the story, so to speak, and that *Heilsgeschichte* had come to a full stop on account of the intransigence, disloyalty, and rebellion of God's covenant partner, his Servant Israel. But God now takes up the theme of his purpose through his chosen instrument without any pause, and as if the extirpation order were no hindrance to his plan. God is of course almighty. DI therefore sees that he cannot be thwarted even by the sin of man, even by the deliberate defalcation of the essential instrument he had planned to use.

But in this verse God seems to bypass the whole problem he now faces, for he insouciantly continues to call Israel his Servant even as she declines the honor.

2.

He just reminds her that she was created for that end, and that he has been helping, forming, fashioning, and training her for her office ever since she was born. Then instead of scolding, which would only have produced resentment, he repeats his call, one that can melt the hardest of human hearts—"Do not be afraid."

It is interesting how frequently DI refers to the song of Moses in Deut. 32; it is also interesting that DI's hearers must have been well acquainted with the song to have understood his references. For the name *Jeshurun* is used for Israel at only two places, at Deut. 32:15 and 33:5, 26. Both of those chapters are in verse and are very ancient.[1] In both of them the word Jeshurun appears as a poetic name for Israel. The root of the word seems to be the word for "upright." If such is the case, then the poetic writers employed the name to designate Israel under her ideal character, in the light of what God her Lord saw she could and might yet be. Moreover, Jeshurun occurs here in parallel with the ideal description of Israel's God that is found under the term "Rock," a name for God which has already been noted as characteristic of Deut. 32. If the above reasoning is correct, that DI is drawing his material from the ancient poetic sagas of his people, we have in our hands a clue to his choice of the name Jeshurun. He evidently wishes to declare that Israel is not to be dismissed out of hand as God's failure, in that she cannot keep her bond. The noun Jeshurun may be built linguistically like the tribal name Zebulun. If so, it is in the form of an endearing diminutive. This, is what the LXX has had in mind in translating Jeshurun by the Greek word for "beloved."

3, 4.

However we understand this strange word though, one thing is clear. God is determined to resuscitate Israel's faith and to raise her from the death of her corpse-like state to a new life of responsibility. The symbolism has appeared before. The desert and dry ground have been representative of the nonbeing of chaos that militates against the Light. Israel

[1] William Albright, *From the Stone Age to Christianity* (2nd ed., Baltimore: Johns Hopkins Press, 1957), dates it in the tenth century. Otto Eissfeldt, *Einleitung in Das Alte Testament* (Tübingen: J. C. B. Mohr, 1956), between 1070 and 1020 B.C.

is at present actually in that state of chaos. But Jacob's seed, that is, those whom DI is now addressing, are soon to know the power of the *Spirit* coming upon them again (cf. Ezek. 37:1-14). Remember that God's Spirit is none other than God himself. The Spirit is God manifest in action. Similarly his *blessing* is his will, uttered from the heart through the lips in the form of the Word; and since it is God's will that is uttered, then it must be effective. The very life of God is to enter into the corpse Israel as she lies in her grave in the broad valley of the Tigris-Euphrates Rivers (Ezek. 37:12).

God's original promise to Abraham was couched in the form of a blessing whose potency would enable the seed of Abraham to multiply and be as the stars of the sky for number. But now that that seed had fallen into the ground and died, it did not mean that the promise too had died. God was once again about to pour out his Spirit upon Israel's seed, and the promise would then be one step nearer to its final fulfillment. The combination of water and spirit, which is so important in NT thought, forms an imagery as ancient as the Tammuz ideology of Babylon, which DI would know and whose ideas he could copy. Another important vision of Ezekiel (47), which DI would probably know, outlines the close relationship between the water of life as it pours into a desert and this language that DI uses here. But unlike Ezekiel, DI draws his metaphor from a Babylonian geographical background with its artificial irrigation channels such as were unknown to the inhabitants of hilly Palestine.

5.

The water of life converts. The Spirit changes the human heart. There is no suggestion here that only Israelites are to experience this new birth. Thus, says DI, a pagan will one day declare, *I belong to Yahweh.* Another proselyte will enter the family of God by calling himself by the family name of Jacob, the Father of Israel. Still another proselyte will tattoo his hand in the manner that a slave had to do to show to whom he belonged, or even as a jar was marked when it bore the name of its owner. The fourth proselyte mentioned here will, so to speak, be baptized into the people of God with a new name to show his new condition. However, the verb *entitle* is doubtful. It may come from the noun for a standard used in battle, one which could bear the emblem of the tribe or group. Some would alter the verb to read "honors himself with the name Israel." But there is no need to change the text to get good sense, for the phrase is the last in a series of four similar declarations, any one of which suffices to reveal DI's mind.

Theologically speaking, this passage is interesting. The children of Israel are born into and claim their heritage by right; pagans are to enter the people of God by profession of faith, just as they do today on the mission field. The people of Israel is thus ideally more than an enlarged family group of men and women bound together by the ties of blood. Israel is *Jeshurun,* the Israel that is the ideal of God. So DI now portrays her as a supranational idea (cf. Rom. 8:14-17; 11:13-24) or even, to use present-day language, as the Church as she exists in the mind and purpose of God.

6 Thus says the King and Redeemer of Israel, Yahweh of
hosts:
I am the beginning and I am the end; apart from me
there are no gods.
7 Then who is there like me? Let him [stand and] proclaim;
let him tell it and set forth [his argument] before me!
Ever since with outward signs I established a people for-
ever,
They should have been able to foretell the future.
8 So be neither scared, nor alarmed; have I not been informing
thee ever since that time, and been
telling thee?
You are my witnesses as to whether there is any god other
than me. There is no other Rock. (At least) I know
of none.

6.

Who is this *Yahweh* to whom the heathen will turn in longing? *For the whole world is longing for his revelation.* (42:4.) The answer comes foursquare. (1) He is *the King and Redeemer of Israel,* that is, of his chosen people here on earth below. (2) He is Lord *of hosts,* and so is king of all the powers in the realms above. (3) He is also the beginning of all things. (4) And he is the end of all things. No other four corners could contain the whole purpose of creation and redemption as do these. It is that foursquare God then who has a missionary purpose to work out through Israel, and that God is *Yahweh,* the covenant God of Israel.

7a.

Yahweh is utterly unique. There are two words for "one" in Hebrew. One is *yaḥidh,* used for example of an only or unique son (cf. Gen. 22:2; Amos 8:10) or of an isolated person (cf. Pss. 25:16; 68:6). Here Yahweh is clearly declared to be one or unique in this sense, for he is Lord of all and wholly other than his creation. But he is also one-with his hosts, for amazingly enough he stoops to share his redemptive purpose with them. They are his messengers, as we have seen, and convey his will in shared delight and joy. More astonishingly still, as DI will show later in detail, Yahweh is actually one-with recalcitrant Israel, even as a good husband is one with his erring wife. "Therefore shall a man leave his father and his mother, and shall cleave unto his wife: and they shall be one flesh." (Gen. 2:24.) This second word for "one," *'eḥadh,* that is used here in Genesis cannot therefore be understood merely in a mathematical sense. Yet it lies at the basis of the biblical conception of the nature of God. Remember that this same word for "one" occurs in the so-called *shema',* not the other word which has been translated as "unique": "Hear, O Israel: The Lord our God is *one* Lord" (Deut. 6:4). The Holy-One-of-you is therefore one-with the you whom he addresses, even though he is the beginning and the end.

7b.

The book of Exodus speaks of the *signs* which accompanied the election of Israel—the pillar of cloud by day and the pillar of fire by night, of the fire upon the mountain, of the water from the rock, and so on. The need for these outward signs was interpreted to Moses in his own original experience of the call of God. Not only did he hear a voice speaking in his heart; he also saw a burning bush (Exod. 3). The rod which Moses cast to the ground and the leprosy of his hand (Exod. 4) were also each a sign, or *'oth*—the word used here—given him by God. Each of these was the outward and visible sign and seal of an inward and invisible reality. We recall that in the view of the Old Testament prophets the universe that God has made is one, for God himself is one. One realm of this universe, however, that which we call the world of the spirit, we cannot see. That is why God gives—to the eye of faith only—physical signs that exhibit the spiritual reality whose significance God wills to bring home to the human heart. Throughout the Bible God acts in this manner. He offers as sign a tabernacle, a sabbath day, a people, a cross, and even bread and wine. With these he conveys to and seals in our hearts what those signs signify in the beyond. Israel had been granted a knowledge of God beyond that of any other nation, at that time when under Moses God had redeemed her from the power of Pharaoh. God had declared the meaning of his actions then by means of sacramental signs that conveyed in themselves their own interpretation of what he was doing. In turn therefore Israel ought to have been able to understand what God would do next. For on the basis of the signs which she had been given in the past, she should have been able to interpret the future. God's nature was consistent with that revealed in Moses' day; and Israel was still the object of his love, since he had created her to be his *people forever*.

8.

Moreover, possessing this saving knowledge, it was ridiculous that Israel should be afraid. God's revelation of his saving love in her history had been consistent. *Have I not been informing thee ever since that time*, that is, since the time of redemption in the days of Moses; and have I not been *telling thee* what my will is for thee, Israel? What DI means is that everything which has happened in Israel's history is interpretable on the basis of what God did at *that time,* that is, at the time of the Exodus. This is astonishing, but DI believed it to be the truth. But what is still more astonishing is that Yahweh permits his own uniqueness to be evidenced by the unique *witnesses* of Israel.

9 All those who make idols are themselves "negative," and their favorite gods are no use to them. As for their (the gods') witnesses, they neither see nor understand
10 enough even to feel ashamed. What man, in fashioning a divine being, would pour a graven image that he did
11 not expect to be of use to him? See how all his fellow guildsmen and craftsmen are so ashamed, because their god turns out to be even less than human. They hold a meeting and all stand around in fear and shame together.
12 An ironworker, for example, first cuts one out, then works it in hot charcoal, then fashions it with hammers, forging it with his strong arm. But when he gets hungry, he loses strength, and if he has not drunk water, he grows tired.
13 Or take a woodworker: he sets his rule, designs one with a stylus, works at it, and makes it into the shape of a man with the features of a cultured townsman.

14 **A third type cuts down cedars for himself, or takes a holm oak, or**
another kind of oak which he has tended by himself till it has grown
mighty amongst the trees of the forest; or a cedar which he has planted
and which the rain
15 **has made to grow. People use it for firewood. He takes some of it**
then and makes himself warm with it; and as he burns it he bakes
himself some bread; and then he fashions a divine being and pros-
trates himself before it, or a
16 **graven image and grovels down in front of it! Thus half of it he**
burns in the fire; with this half he eats meat, roasting it, and feels
full. Then he warms himself again and
17 **says: "Ah! How warm I am, looking into the fire." But the rest of it**
he makes into the graven image of a god. Then he grovels before it,
prostrating himself and praying to it with the words: "Save me, for
thou art my god!"
18 **They do not know, they do not understand, for he has smeared over**
their eyes so that they cannot see nor discern their own
19 **hearts. So no one takes it to heart, nor has understanding nor dis-**
cernment enough to say: "One half I burned in the fire, and actually
cooked bread on its charred embers, roasting meat for a meal; the
rest of it I have been making into an abomination, and I have been
groveling before what comes out
20 **of a tree!" This is just feeding on ashes; a befooled mind has led such**
a man astray. It cannot save his soul; he cannot even ask, "Is it not
a deception I am holding in my right hand?"

9.

This passage, vss. 9-20, is a brilliant piece of writing. It contains sarcasm to a degree. Unlike the rest of DI's work, it is preserved for us in prose. Possibly he felt that the subject was in fact too prosaic to make verse of. Here DI subjects the idol-making of the Babylonians to scorn. The sound of that laughter has resounded down the ages. There are translation difficulties in the passage, however, owing to the fact that we are not now in the position to know all the technical processes that craftsmen employed in Babylon. The day may well come when we shall be able to translate more exactly some of the specialized words that occur here. But of course their exact translation does not affect the religious issue, nor do any of these doubtful words have theological overtones.

DI's previous lofty passage had ended asking *whether there is any god other than me. There is no other Rock.* (*At least*) *I know of none.* (Vs.

8.) But the Babylonians knew of many others. And so DI has to take up this point and deal with it finally and thoroughly before he can proceed with his main argument. The Babylonians may indeed possess idols, he says, but these are nonbeings; they belong in the realm of negation. Even their favorite gods are helpless to succor them just at that point where gods are needed most, viz., when their worshipers are in trouble.

10, 11.

Imagine a *man* fashioning a *divine being, 'el,* in the hope that the thing he has made with his hands will aid him in life! What we have in vs. 11 is merely the few words "are so ashamed, than *adam.*" No one would wish to assert that one translation of this cryptic phrase is definitive. This can be only an approximation. Again, *they hold a meeting* is also a paraphrase of a Hebrew verb meaning "to congregate."

12.

DI first speaks generally of craftsmen and guildsmen. Then he takes a specific example from an ironworker. His example is meant to lay open the argument once and for all that idols can be of help to man. So he portrays a smith in action. Having swung his hammer vigorously with his strong arm, this smith being only human soon grows tired and weary and very thirsty in the heat of the smithy. How on earth, DI implies, could a man who grows weary produce a god who does not grow weary and could even give health and strength to his worshipers? DI must surely have had in mind here what he has already said about Yahweh, how Yahweh never grows weary, and how he alone gives strength to *his* weary worshipers (40:28-31). As someone has said, idolatry is an ontological deception (cf. Jer. 10:14; Mic. 5:13; Hos. 14:3), and this is so even when idolatry assumes the form, not of a wrought-iron divinity, but of an idea in the human mind (Ezek. 14:3, 7; Deut. 27:15; Rom. 1:25; I Cor. 8:4). DI would agree with Karl Marx that religion is the opiate of the people. DI's concern is not with religion, which is man's thoughts on the divine, which are always false, but with revelation from God to man.

13.

DI's next example is the work of a carpenter. Here especially we are not sure of some of the technical terms. But what is important is the emphasis DI places on the highest form of humanity that the carpenter can imagine. How uncouth and pockmarked most peasants and slaves must have looked. But a young man who lived in a house, one of the royal court perhaps, could have been as attractive and wholesome as one of those young athletes of Athens who at this very time were drawing the admiration of Greece's greatest sculptors. We can wonder whether when DI wrote this line, he had in mind the awesome words of Gen. 1:27, which both he and his hearers seem to have known: "So God created man in his own image." But here the carpenter creates his god in the image of man—even though man as he is at his best. Even that is the reverse of the faith of the Bible.

14.

The carpenter is shown working with all reverence at his task and choosing the very best materials available. The *cedar* tree did not grow in Babylon. It had to be fetched—at a price—from the Lebanon mountains. The various kinds of *oak* trees were probably evergreens, and thus were endued with a special divine essence, for they did not die at the end of the season. Once they had grown *mighty amongst the trees of the forest,* the king or chief forester would allow them to be selected for felling only by special permission. Finally we read with astonishment that our woodworker was skilled enough to try to acclimatize cedars, probably doing so in the royal estates near the city of Babylon. On the other hand, the subject of *planted* may be "he," God, nature, what you will, and could be translated by the passive voice, such as "got planted" or "planted itself."

15, 16, 17.

Now follows a picture both humorous and pathetic, and one which speaks for itself. The translation of *'el,* "god," is here *divine being,* since DI surely meant us to be shocked by the contrast he was drawing. Here a man grovels before a divinity, half of which he has used to fill his stomach! Notice the simple pleasure at the sense of well-being that a full stomach gives a man when he has leisure after a good meal to sit and gaze into a fire. Like his smith brother, our woodworker too needs to rest. The word for *fire* used here is a rare word. In 50:11 DI chooses it again to refer to false worship. Evidently he does this to draw a contrast with the faith of the prophets. They believed that Yahweh is the sole fire (*'ur*), for he alone is light (*'or*). These two words employ the same consonants in Hebrew and so lend themselves to punning. But finally our craftsman in his human weakness seeks deliverance and strength from his own creation (cf. Hos. 4:12; Rom. 1:21).

18, 19.

Here is a clear statement that Yahweh has blinded the eyes and hearts of the heathen, so it is beyond their competence even to become aware of the falsity of their notions (cf. II Thess. 2:11). Thus DI points to a fact that the Church must constantly take into account, that people are born into a religious heritage, whether it be in the Congo or in Afghanistan, which to them makes a complete and logical system of belief.

20.

But that does not alter the fact that these beliefs may be so wrong that for him who holds them it is a case of feeding *on ashes*, and *a befooled mind has led such a man astray*. His faith *cannot save his soul; he cannot even ask, "Is it not a deception I am holding in my right hand?"*

Let us note two issues in passing. First, *soul* here means the whole personality, the body included; for the Hebrews knew that man is primarily a body (Gen. 2:7) into which God has breathed life. Man needs his flesh (Ps. 63:1), even his kidneys to praise God (Prov. 23:16-17) just as much as his heart. And so the salvation that man needs is in the competence only of a God who has created both matter and spirit. Second, the last phrase may be a proverb which DI's hearers would know already and which he would thus be quoting with telling force.

21 Keep these things in mind, then, Jacob, especially
that thou art my Servant, Israel.
I fashioned thee that thou (alone) shouldst become my Servant;
so then, Israel, thou shalt never be forgotten by me.
22 I have wiped away thy rebellions like a cloud,
and thy sins like mist.
Come back to me, for I have already redeemed thee!
23 Exult, ye heavens, for Yahweh has done it;
shout aloud, ye regions under the earth;
Burst into song, ye mountains,
ye forests and every tree therein.
For Yahweh has redeemed Jacob and is glorifying
himself in Israel.

21.

Once again DI leads forward logically in his argument. He both answers the problem he has raised in vss. 9-20 and at the same time connects the solution with the point he had reached in his previous argument at vs. 8, before the insertion of the long prose description of idol making. If it is God who has blinded the hearts of the heathen, as he has just said, and if it is God who has rendered them logically satisfied with their particular *Weltanschauung*, or world of belief, then how are they ever to know the true God as he really is, and gain that true or whole way to life which DI has spoken of before? The answer to that is now clear—it is to come about through Israel's wholehearted service to Yahweh, for it is she who has to take this whole way of life to the ends of the earth (42:4). But DI is not satisfied with such an easy answer to this fundamental problem. One does not convert to a new way of life a people convinced of the validity of their beliefs simply by preaching to them. History has proved that a hundredfold. Something much more fundamental is needed than mere words to reach home to the hearts of a sinful and prejudiced world.

At this point we are made aware of the depth of DI's theological grasp. He sees that Israel's God cannot be postulated as the mere object of human thought. He does not speak of God as Supreme Being, the Absolute, that Power which controls all things in heaven and earth. Such a "thing in itself" as a Supreme Being would be—and this is how modern man is apt to understand the God of Israel—has nothing at all in common with DI's God. For man is able to think this Being whom he thus defines. But if man can even think his God, then that God is merely an idol, noticed like a log by the workings of man's mind. DI's God, however, is apprehended by man's mind solely by virtue of his own freedom and decision and by virtue of his saving activity. It is the nature of Israel's witness to that freedom and that activity, that becomes the all-important factor in the matter of the divine revelation to the world.

So DI slowly, gradually, and logically moves forward in his argument from now until he can make clear what the new factor in witnessing to such a God must be. Meanwhile Yahweh promises Israel he will not forget her. The Hebrew for *thou shalt never be forgotten by me* is a curious composite form. It seems to be a pun, a mixture of two possible meanings. First, it contains the above translation; and second, it can mean, "Thou mayest not forget." The LXX favors the second meaning. But DI has the ability thus to create a vital double meaning of a word that he is handling in his own native tongue.

22.

The position of Israel in God's scheme is central. God must necessarily woo her back to himself if he is to go forward with his plan that through her his glory might be revealed to all nations. Yet this mighty act of revelation has already begun, DI declares—begun with Israel's redemption in the days of Moses, at a moment in history before Israel even knew she was being called to become the true Servant. So DI repeats that vitally important evangelical truth which he has already uttered and discussed. It is that God forgives us *before* we repent, not when and *if* we repent, as many imagine the content of the gospel to be. Perhaps the metaphor of the cloud here is copied from Hosea, who used it three times, for it is a striking one. When one is walking in fog or cloud there seems to be no end to it, and one can be wholly depressed. But the warmth of the sun can in a matter of minutes completely dissipate the fog and leave not a wrack behind. Sin is an action filled with potency. A man's evil word can initiate a chain reaction which soon gets quite out of the speaker's control. Thereafter it is only God who is able to stop the reaction from progressing further. Thus God's action is actually twofold. Negatively speaking, he can control Israel's iniquity, and so we become aware that Israel's sin cannot thwart his plan. But positively speaking, we see how his forgiveness can utterly transform Israel and render her as clean as the clear blue sky that lies behind the cloud and fog.

23.

There is nothing in heaven or earth that man desires or needs more than this total forgiveness of God. It is here shown to be the one factor that permits Israel's life to proceed at all. Were there no forgiveness, then her communal apostasy would have landed her in the *tohu*, the negation or chaos, in which, morally speaking, Babylon was even then wallowing without knowing it. No wonder DI uses such extraordinary language at this point in his argument. For it is an extraordinary thing that he is talking about, something that is almost too good to be true. What he is saying is that *Yahweh has redeemed Jacob* already in the days of Moses. Why will Jacob not grasp that mighty fact? Moreover, just because of this objective and incontrovertible reality, God is now going on to do something else, for he is now *glorifying himself in Israel*. This is the tremendous theme that DI will now continue to unfold as his chapters proceed. At the moment, however, note that this root employed here, *p-'-r*, hardly means "glory" as in the KJV. But DI has more to say before he ventures to apply the root *k-b-d* with all the fullness of meaning that the term conveys to this situation; for *k-b-d* does mean "glory"; *p-'-r* means something like "splendor."

It is possible that this is the verse of a hymn that was sung by the exiles when they met together in Babylon for the worship of God. Possibly too we can trace here the first beginnings of the synagogue of later years. We do not know. But DI was painstakingly making the exiles aware that they were sinners all. He was also now helping them to make the still more wonderful discovery that while sinners they were also redeemed sinners, and that God loved and cared for them despite their apostasies and hardness of heart, as we saw at 41:14. The very heavens must have begun to appear bluer for those forlorn exiles once they took this good news to their hearts; and since salvation in the experience of many Old Testament witnesses produced in them transports of gladness and joy, it is no wonder that the redeemed here should expect the heavens to join them in their joy. They had now learned that *Yahweh has done it,* not man. The hills are therefore invited to *burst into song.* What is more, even the chaos that undergirds all life is ordered to join in. Remember that chaos, *ye regions under the earth,* was linked in the imagination of OT man with Sheol, the underworld of departed spirits; Sheol thus partook of the negative qualities of chaos. If man should ever descend into Sheol—and OT man certainly believed he could taste its horrors even in this life (cf. Pss. 130:1; 139:15)—then he was descending into *tohu.* But even *tohu* must obey the command of God.

This vital passage is surely evidence once again of the seminal value of the thought in that ancient poem to which DI seems to be so indebted. For he must have read the words at Deut. 32:39:

> See now that I, even I, am He, and there is no God with me:
> I kill and I make alive; I wound and I heal:
> Neither is there any that can deliver out of my hand.

No wonder that joy is to be found at the heart of the biblical faith.

24 Thus says Yahweh, thy Redeemer, he who has molded thee since the womb,
I am Yahweh who makes everything, who alone stretches out the sky,
Who spreads out the earth. (Who is with me?)

25 Who nullifies the omens of prognosticators, and
makes diviners look foolish,
Who upsets the arguments of philosophers, and makes their
knowledge look silly.
26 Who upholds the word of his Servant, and fulfills the
counsel of his messengers;
Who says of Jerusalem: "She shall be inhabited again"
(and of the townships of Judah: "They shall be rebuilt");
"For I shall reerect their ruins."
27 Who can say to the ocean deep: "Be bone dry! For I am
going to dry up thy streams."
28 Who says of Cyrus: "My shepherd. For he is fulfilling all
my purpose";
Who says of Jerusalem: "She shall be rebuilt, and let
the temple be refounded."

24.

Ch. 44 comes to a climax with a series of magnificent utterances expressing the nature and purpose of God in terms unsurpassed anywhere in the OT. By following his order of thought, we can note the emphasis that DI makes. *Thus says Yahweh,* that is, the covenant God, who is alive and utters his will by word of mouth, Israel's *Redeemer,* for to love and to forgive is the essence of Yahweh's nature. Yahweh's plan was predetermined before Israel came into existence. This of course is easy for a God who is the creator and author of all things. Hebrew has no word for the Greek idea of cosmos; instead it just uses "all" or *everything.* Here then we have the concept of "God in creation" united with that of "God in history."

With a touch of genius DI now interjects here a question he puts on God's lips, viz., *Who is with me?* Up to this point he has led us to believe that no one can possibly be *with* the Lord God Almighty. But he is now approaching in his argument the most amazing volte-face imaginable. For he will soon be saying that while no god could ever be with Yahweh, yet paradoxically Yahweh is *with* Israel, to the extent that Yahweh is even *in* Israel. This argument is developed fully in ch. 45.

25.

Remember that for the whole ancient world the word spoken with intent had power. The curse and the blessing were each like arrows sent flying through the air and were bound to hit their target. Once shot off, these arrows could not be recalled. We would be foolish to suppose that this concept has no reality in our day. The modern psychiatrist knows better than to try. For he might have to dig deep into the mind of a neurotic patient to discover what barbed words were shot into his childish mind by a cruel parent thirty years before, or what shocking incident scarred his soul while he was still a little boy, only to be buried deep in his subconscious mind. And so once the arrow is shot the damage is done. Nothing can recall the arrow once it is sped. That looks like common sense.

Yet DI did not believe that this was so, even though it appeared to be a fact of nature. He maintained that an aspect of God's almightiness is that he is able to deflect the arrow in its flight and make it reach the target that *he* wills, not the speaker. God, he believed, does more than just war against evil. As Creator of all he is also Re-creator of all. In other words, God is able to bring good out of evil. *Omens,* words spoken with intent and packed with power to affect the lives of men, flying through the air like atomic warheads, God *nullifies* or diverts. For DI the foolishness of God is indeed wiser than men. DI not only sweeps away the wisdom of the complicated and integrated hierarchy of Babylonian priests and philosophers and discounts their whole system of astrology, as we have seen before; he also offers a positive philosophy of history in place of their ideas. He can do so because for him faith is not a form of gnosis but living by the Word of God. He declares that the Babylonian magi could not explain the horrors that resulted from the onward march of the conqueror from the east, so they saw it as disaster and ruin. But then neither could faithless Israel see any good in the exile she was in, far from home as she was, and living without hope and purpose. DI on the other hand knew that God can bring good out of evil, even life out of death. And so he declared to Israel what she did not recognize, that she already possessed the divine Word in her midst, the Word that is therefore divinely and not merely humanly potent.

26.

He also declared that she had been given a glimpse of the divine counsel, *'etsah,* whose fulfillment nothing can deflect (40:8; 45:23; 46:10; 48:14; 55:11; 53:10; cf. Ezra 6:14). Thus if Israel would only act in faith and obedience—if in other words she would just let herself be the Servant and the vehicle of mission in one—then God would guide her arrows to their target. Even as she utters her human word, probably through the mouth of one of his representatives such as DI himself, God gives it the potency and direction that not only she wills but which he himself wills for the attainment of his plan.

Recalling that *messengers* can equally well be translated by "angels," we get a vision of the great purpose of God working out both in heaven and on earth at once. God fulfills his plan as it is brought into action by principalities and powers in the heavenly places within the realm of history. Here again, as at 42:19, we find that the prophetic mind draws no line between God's messengers in heaven and those on earth; for the hosts of Yahweh were to be found both in heaven and on earth (cf. Ps. 33:6 with Exod. 12:41; I Sam. 17:45).

Right at the center of God's cosmic plan there stands a city. This particularism of the biblical faith is strange to the wisdom of the Greeks. In the days of David, God had chosen Jerusalem to be that spot on earth where all things must be fulfilled (cf. Luke 9:51; 18:31). The Chronicler is very interested in this theme, following upon the Deuteronomist before him; and many psalms sing of its reality (cf. Pss. 78; 68; 87:2; 132:13). Before the Exile, Jerusalem had been that one place in all God's creation where God had put his name to dwell, so that he could be present in the sanctuary in Jerusalem in a special way (I Kings 8:13, 27-30). Nebuchadrezzar had destroyed that sanctuary, however, and for fifty years now it had seemed as if the arrow he had shot had continued to speed on to bring about the final ruin of the people of God. But God could deflect Nebuchadrezzar's arrow even after fifty years of flight. God, says DI, needs Jerusalem for his purpose now just as truly as ever before. So Jerusalem *shall be rebuilt* along with the whole area of depopulated and ruined Judah.

27.

Such a mighty project, as it must have seemed to the exiles who knew that Jerusalem was lying in ruins, was obviously a small thing, declares DI, for a God who can command the *deep* of chaos and dry up its rivers and *streams* to the bare rocks below.

This of course is mythological language. Interpreted theologically however, what DI would have us understand is that in the beginning there was order, for order is of God. But God permitted chaos, *tohu,* to exist as an entity over against his order, *shalom,* for his own inscrutable ends. *Tohu* is to be found even in the deeps of the subconscious of the human mind, and is certainly to be found also in the depth consciousness of that corporate human society, that body which the Bible knows as Israel (Ps. 139:

15-16; Jer. 50:38; 51:36). Yet even out of the depths an individual can cry to God and be saved (Pss. 69:1-2; 88:6-7; 130:1). Out of the depths of the sea of chaos, historicized as the Red Sea, Israel did in fact call upon God and was saved (Exod. 15:5-13; Isa. 51:10). What God has done before he can certainly do again. In the end he will surely bring back order and conquer chaos forever (Ps. 104:3-9). Sin and evil belong together in this realm of chaos. In redeeming Israel from the waters of chaos therefore, God was also redeeming her from the potency of her own sin. For example, and to quote another prophet who took the same view of the significance of the Exile as did DI, no matter to what depths sinful Israel might sink, God could command the mythological monster that personalizes the waters of chaos to vomit up Jonah—the picture of representative Israel—even as he seeks to escape from his mission to the gentiles; and so God can give Israel a second chance.[2] The exiling of Israel far from home is thus an action of God in which he historicizes for her the ever-present realities of chaos and the deep. But God's care and loving purpose are not cut off once Israel is actually overwhelmed by the Flood. For God's rule extends right to the bottom of those deeps, and when he but utters the word, the monster must vomit back its victim to the shore.[3]

28.

Exactly at the right moment therefore God has raised up an instrument to perform his will in this regard. DI now proclaims Cyrus is just that instrument whom God is about to use to create renewal out of disorder and bring rebirth, re-creation, redemption, even life, out of what appeared to be the death of his chosen people. And so the cosmic plan will continue on its way serene and unimpeded by the sin of man. Once again God will set his name to dwell in the chosen city of Jerusalem, and once again the temple will be standing to receive that name as its dwelling place on earth. Once again Israel will become conscious of her mission as the people of God, yet now as a people that lives by grace alone, because she has been redeemed from the death into which her apostasy had ultimately led her. DI shows us that the creative word, the re-creative word, and the divine fiat that controls the whole of human history are all really one, and he

[2] Notice in the poem that comprises the second chapter of Jonah that Jonah cries to God from the belly of the underworld of chaos: "For thou hadst cast me into the deep" (2:3). This last word is that which DI uses here for the waters of chaos, though historicized once again as the *ocean deep*. See also discussion at 51:10.

[3] See my *Ruth and Jonah* (Torch Bible Commentary; London: SCM Press, 1950), p. 65.

shows us how the reality of that oneness has become plain in that historical situation which we who stand on the sidelines of events regard merely as the fall of Babylon.

So at last Cyrus is named, in the very last line of the chapter. This is the genius of DI, who knows how to pursue his argument step by step as he moves from theme to theme. At this point he shows us how Cyrus is actually the particularizing, the historicizing of the cosmic purpose at that moment in history. Yet that same Cyrus never knew that he was being used by Israel's God. Moreover DI tells us nothing at all about the character and nature of this powerful man. Obviously neither the faith nor the nature of Cyrus is important in itself. Yet if we turn to a pagan source to learn of the wars of Cyrus, the historian Xenophon can give us graphic word sketches of Cyrus and show us how he was indeed a character who impressed himself greatly on his generation. In DI's eyes this mighty warrior has value solely as the instrument of the purposes of God.

A corollary of this fact is also of great interest. It is that the pagan state can evidently be used as God's instrument of mission, just as much as can the church. For Cyrus—the state—is the instrument of the re-creative Word of the living God in action in a historical situation. On the other hand, while God used Cyrus for the rebuilding of Jerusalem, it was not he but Israel, the people of God, whose hands in the final event actually did the rebuilding of the city.

Cyrus is called *my shepherd*. This one word in Hebrew can also be voweled to mean "my friend." At 48:14 Cyrus is known as he whom Yahweh loves. DI means that Yahweh chose Cyrus from all other possible alternatives to be his instrument. In this way God has continued to choose the unlikeliest of persons to be his instruments down the arches of the years. He chose the writings of his servant Nietzsche, for example, to prevent the Christian religion from becoming a mere system of ethics. Because of his servant Hitler, a new biblical theology arose to give vitality to the Church in Europe at the very juncture when the latter was about to lose its thrust in the perplexing new world that was initiated by the atomic age. It might be said that because of his servant Karl Marx, the Church awoke to the social implications of its own Gospel to a degree that it might never have done if he had never penned *Das Kapital*.

DI now presents a combination of concepts. First, in the Tammuz ideology of the Babylonians the king was regarded as the shepherd of his people (cf. Jer. 3:15; Zech. 13:7), but also in Israel many hailed the

Davidic line in similar terms (cf. Ezek. 34). The people of Israel now in exile would naturally make this association of ideas, even though at this point DI himself is making no reference to the line of David. But secondly, as the instrument of Yahweh, Cyrus is to act even as the Shepherd of Israel acts. All unwittingly Cyrus is to become the instrument of him who, as DI has already proclaimed, is about to carry the lambs in his bosom home to the ruins of that Jerusalem which figures centrally in God's cosmic plan (cf. Matt. 16:21; Mark 10:33; Luke 9:31; Rev. 21:2).

CHAPTER 45

1 Thus says Yahweh to Cyrus his anointed, whose right hand
I have gripped,
To subdue nations before him,
and the loins of kings I will ungird;
To open doors before him, that gates should no
longer be shut:
2 I myself will go before thee, I shall make level the mountains;
I shall shatter the gates of brass, and smash the
bars of iron.
3 I shall give thee the treasures of darkness and
[open to thee] the hidden hoards of mammon,
In order that thou mayest know that it is I, Yahweh,
the God of Israel, who have called thee by thy name;
4 For the sake of my Servant Jacob, Israel my chosen one.
[That was why] I gave thee thy name and surnamed thee,
though thou wast not cognizant of me.
5 I am Yahweh; there is no other; apart from me there are
no gods.
I have been girding thee, though thou hast not been
aware of me;
6 In order that men might become aware,
from the rising of the sun and from the west,
that apart from me there is only nonbeing.
I am Yahweh, and there is nothing else.
7 I fashion the light, and I create the darkness;
I make order and I create evil.
It is I, Yahweh, who do all these things.

1.

Sidney Smith writes: "It was an Assyrian, and therefore, probably a Babylonian, custom that client kings who had revolted and then been captured, might be punished by being fastened to the bolts of the city gates with chains in such a way that, bound round the middle, they were forced to adopt a sitting posture; this gave rise to ridicule, for they looked like squatting bears." [1] This may be the background of DI's vigorous statement by God, *the loins of kings I will ungird,* but it is not necessary to elaborate. The words are a poetic exaggeration typical of the Eastern mind. Yet the phrase is a plain statement. It means to render the kings helpless, for one had to buckle up the outer robe before it was possible to move freely.

2.

Now follows a still more vivid Eastern hyperbole. Says DI, God is about to *level the mountains* before the feet of Cyrus.[2] He will do so, of course, because Cyrus is God's instrument; in fact he is actually God's anointed. But the Babylonian king was also the anointed of Marduk. "Whose right hand I, Marduk, have grasped" are words to be found on a clay cylinder unearthed in Babylon. DI was obviously a man of education. We have seen before that he knew court etiquette and the liturgical language of his captors. But what is amazing is that he dared to seize upon expressions embedded in an alien mythology and a pagan ritual and apply them to the God who repeatedly declares: "Apart from me there is no other god."

In Israel's heritage several types of persons were anointed to office. For example, according to Ps. 105:15 the patriarchs were anointed to their task, whatever the words meant in this case. Most important was the fact that the king was anointed (II Sam. 19:21; Pss. 2:2; 18:50), as was the king's cultic successor in the days after the return from Exile, viz., the high priest (Lev. 4:3). By inference, as we have it at Isa. 61:6, the whole corporate body of redeemed Israel—whom Hosea (4:6) had declared God had threatened to reject as his corporate priest to the nations—will yet be anointed as one body of priests to Yahweh (cf. Exod. 19:6). So it is important to recognize that the word *anointed* represents the Hebrew word for "messiah" as it is rendered elsewhere in the English versions. At this

[1] *Isaiah, Chapters XL-LV: Literary Criticism and History* (London: Oxford University Press, 1944), p. 73.

[2] See what is known as the "Cyrus cylinder" in James Pritchard's ANET, p. 315; D. W. Thomas, ed., *Documents from Old Testament Times* (London: Thos. Nelson & Sons, 1958), pp. 92-94.

point one should be watchful about reading into it any technical meaning along this line; for as DI uses it, it is the pagan king Cyrus who is here entitled Yahweh's anointed. Could it then be said that no tyrant who ever reached his throne or created an empire by wading through the blood of the conquered has thus placed himself outside the care of the God of Israel? For God is able to weave that tyrant's wickedness and follies into the grand unfolding purpose which he has continually in mind.

The wording used here by DI reminds us of themes of the Magnificat: "He hath shown strength with his arm; . . . he hath put down the mighty from their thrones, and exalted those of low degree." (Luke 1:51-52 RSV.) None could be mightier than King Croesus or the king of Babylon; none could be of lower degree than exiled and imprisoned Israel.

3.

So also with the words: "He has filled the hungry with good things." For Cyrus had by now looted the vaults of this same Croesus at Lydian Sardis, and these contained *treasures of darkness,* indeed *hidden hoards of mammon.*[3] This last word is usually translated as "hidden treasure," but it is quite probably the basis of the NT word "mammon." Finally the Magnificat declares: "He has helped his Servant Israel." How he will do so DI will tell soon.

Why then had God used Cyrus in this extraordinary manner? The word *lᵉmaʿan, in order that,* now occurs three times in rapid succession to show us.

The first occurrence runs, *that thou mayest know that it is I, Yahweh, . . . who have called thee by thy name.* It is doubtful whether Cyrus ever did come to acknowledge Yahweh. In fact we are almost sure that he never did. Yet Cyrus is merely representative of the great powers of the earth, whom Yahweh intended should one day acknowledge him as Lord. Implicitly, from DI's point of view, Cyrus did in fact acknowledge Yahweh later when he encouraged the rebuilding of the Jerusalem Temple.

4.

Yet DI explicitly admits that God could say of Cyrus, *though thou wast not cognizant of me.* The second *lᵉmaʿan* reads: *For the sake of my Servant Jacob, Israel my chosen one.* [*That was why*] *I gave thee thy name.* Just as at Christian baptism the child is given a name, a Christian name,

[3] J. Skinner, ed., *The Book of the Prophet Isaiah, Chs. XL–XLVI* (rev. ed., Cambridge Bible; Cambridge: Cambridge University Press, 1951), p. 65.

so that in God's sight he becomes unique and beloved for his own sake, so it is here; and this is what DI meant when he added *though thou wast not cognizant of me,* for no child is aware of God when he is brought as a babe to the font. The emphasis here is that it is *God* who chooses Israel for his own good (cf. Ps. 18:39), and not Israel who chooses God. This means that God's action in election and adoption is one of grace alone.

5.

Moreover, we observe this grace even more clearly when we notice the deliberate parallel in language between 45:1, where it is Cyrus who is the chosen one whom Yahweh has been girding, and here where the chosen one is Israel. For with this parallelism it becomes clear that the instrument which God chooses for himself is not chosen for any intrinsic value. Neither Cyrus nor Israel by themselves were ever in the position to bring in the kingdom. The election of each of them therefore is one of grace alone, and has obviously nothing to do with moral worthiness, quality of life, or any other factor.

6.

The third *l^ema'an* says in effect, "So that men—all men everywhere—might become aware that Yahweh alone is God." Once again, DI turns back to the underlying missionary purpose reposing in God's choice of Israel and in his employment of Cyrus. These actions of Yahweh are evidently not just ends in themselves. Both of them are means to the end that the whole world should know Yahweh as God.

7.

Election for DI is therefore election *for* an end beyond itself. Finally, to crown the whole climactic expression of God's purpose, DI makes use of the finest religious concepts that Cyrus' Persian world had ever produced. The controversy has not yet ended as to whether King Cyrus was a Zoroastrian by faith or not. Probably he was not, for Zoroaster seems to have been born after Cyrus' day. But Zoroaster did not introduce into Persia a wholly new set of concepts; what he did was to develop the dualism native to the early Persian *Weltanschauung*. In that world view the gods Ahriman and Ormuzd issued originally out of time, Zurvan; yet Zurvan was nothing more than the starry hosts on high. Thus the hosts, about which both Isaiah of Jerusalem and our prophet have so much to say when they declare that these serve Yahweh and obey him as his minister, in ancient Persian thought were actually exalted to the highest place of all. Zoroaster took over the ideas that were native to the Persian view of reality. He deified the concepts of both light and darkness. Ormuzd, the god of light, he designated the apotheosis of the good, and Ahriman he called the god of evil. The two powers are obviously always struggling with each other for mastery in this mysterious universe. The important addition that Zoroaster made to this basic view of things, however, was to assure his followers that the good would in the end prevail over the evil.

But to DI any form of dualism is merely ridiculous, in the light of Yahweh's continued declaration that he alone is God and that apart from him *there is nothing else* (vs. 6). So now he makes one of the great categorical declarations of the Bible: He says of Yahweh, *I fashion the light, and I create the darkness.* In both the Old and the New Testaments light is regularly employed as a symbol of God's creative and saving purpose (cf. Gen. 1:3-4; Pss. 19; 27:1; 37:6; 104:2; Isa. 2:5; 42:6; John 1:5; II Cor. 4:6). Equally, darkness is symbolic of all that is negative and contrary to the divine will (cf. Gen. 1:2; Eccl. 2:14; Isa. 9:2; Joel 2:2). Throughout the whole OT, God is in control of darkness even as he is in control of light (cf. Gen. 1:4-5; Deut. 5:23; Job 12:22; Pss. 18:28; 104:20; 139:11). Both light and darkness are therefore instruments of his will. They are neither twins nor mutually exclusive divine powers that will keep warring to the end. So DI's next line, in parallel with vs. *7a,* proceeds to explain the concepts of light and darkness in theological rather than in mythological language. *I make order,* he says of God. "Order" represents the seminal Hebrew word *shalom,* commonly rendered by "peace." But here it occurs as the opposite of *ra'*, *evil*—a thing which Yahweh actually creates. Conversely, since *shalom* is regarded as the opposite of *ra',* the concept of good must materialize before the mind's eye in the form of integration or perfect harmony. Evil too is comprehensible to the eye of the mind in terms of disintegration; for *ra'* is closely related to DI's favorite concept of chaos, a concept which he holds in common with the priestly writer of the first chapter of Genesis.

So Yahweh forms *light* and *order,* which are integral to his nature as the living God, but he has to *create the darkness* and *evil,* for they are not of his essence as God. Here we have a reference to why God created evil in the first place. God uses evil to subserve his total plan so it can work out to its triumphant conclusion. Without darkness the concept of light is unthinkable. Without evil, the goodness of God is incomprehensible. The OT of course has no conception of goodness as such. Goodness is not a static quality that can be observed and measured. Nor is it an object that can be packaged for the mail. DI understands goodness in terms of God's actively creative, saving love. He sees it in terms of concern, of compassion, and of the pouring out of the self that others may be saved. This reality becomes ever more clear as we continue our study of DI's thesis.

But if saving love is indeed the great reality behind all things, then there must exist some other entity from which man requires to be saved. Moreover, that entity must be part of the creation of God, even though it is not to be classified as an object any more than goodness. For God is of course *all,* and there is nothing else but *He.* Thus if concern and compassion are radical expressions of the nature of the living God, then something else must have enslaved those for whom his compassion is displayed, even though that something else must also have been created by God.

God's essential purpose is that the light should reach all men (42:6), and that all men should know his name (45:6). If they should thus come to know him, they would be saved from the powers of evil, of *tohu,* of negation, of self-destruction and pride. The transitive (Hiphil) form of the verb *yasha'* can be used for the action of bringing men out of chaos and evil into that which is normal. That is why the Hiphil active participle can be applied to God and to the divine activity. For God is no less than *Moshia',* or Savior (43:3), of Israel. The new state of being into which God saves Israel can then be known as peace—as *shalom* is usually translated—yet not as peace in the modern connotation of the word. Here the word signifies not just the opposite of *tohu,* negation, but everything that *tohu* is not; for that which is wholly good can never be described in terms of evil, nor even in terms of evil's opposite. *Shalom* speaks of that perfect *order,* wholesomeness, wholeness of being, which is present as the norm in God's loving purpose for man and for his universe. And since that norm already exists in heaven and God offers it to Israel on earth—as DI had learned from the works of Isaiah before him—then it will be *on earth* that God must eventually triumph over evil in all its many manifestations, and must establish the reality of *shalom.* Finally DI declares, *It is I, Yahweh, who do all these things.*

8 Let the sky pour down from above, and let the clouds
rain down saving activity!
Let the earth be opened, that salvation may sprout forth,

And that (human) righteousness may spring up as well; I, Yahweh have created it.

8.

The genius of DI is like that of Shakespeare, who knew how to relieve the tension in a drama by the unexpected insertion of light relief. DI here inserts a little poem of only one verse, containing a great declaration of faith. From it we learn again how he himself regarded the historical events through which he was living. He knew them to be truly God's events, and so he saw them in an eschatological light. One or two words in the poem need comment. The word *righteousness,* as we have now frequently seen, means "saving activity" to DI, and so it occurs here in parallel with salvation (cf. also Rom. 3; see the discussion at vs. 7 above). The emphasis of the LXX version is on God's pity for man. But the Hebrew is different. In it the word *righteousness* occurs in two forms. First, in line 1 it appears in the masculine—*saving activity.* This form evidently represents *God's* righteous or saving purpose, even when it is manifested in human institutions and human activities. In line 3, however, the word is found in its feminine form. This form is normally used for *man's* actions, even as he obtains from God the strength to perform them. Yet occasionally this feminine form is also used of God. Since the root meaning of *salvation* is "width," it can be used to represent the opposite of narrow, straitened circumstances. Hence the idea of security and ease. So then, DI declares, *I, Yahweh, have created it. It,* being masculine, must refer to the whole process of God's saving activity, which is to burst up from below as well as pour down from above.

Some scholars suggest that the word for *earth* here may hold the meaning which the Babylonians would put into it, that of "underworld," much the same as the Hebrew Sheol (cf. Gen. 37:35; Deut. 32:22; I Sam. 2:6; Job 7:9; Amos 9:2; Ps. 22:5; Matt. 27:52-53). If it does, then this picture rests upon two assumptions of the ancient world: first, that the sky is masculine and the earth feminine, and second, that the waters of chaos are to be found both above the sky and beneath the earth. Now, declares DI, it is saving love that is to overwhelm the earth—not condemnation, as one would suppose. And so in the unity of a cosmos redeemed by one all-embracing divine action (cf. Hos. 2:21-22; Pss. 72:6; 85:11-12*b*), man will learn to exhibit righteousness or compassionate love for his fellows.

He will derive the power to do so from God, just as plants *spring up* toward the sun that gives them life.

9 Woe to him who takes his Potter to court, a potsherd
just like other potsherds made of earth!
Does the clay say to its potter, "What art thou making?"
or, "Thy work, there's nothing to it?"
10 Woe to him who says to a father: "What art thou doing
in begetting?" or to a woman, "What art thou
doing in travailing?"

9.

DI now shows a degree of anger and impatience with the exiles who are so slow to believe his good news. We can only surmise that he has to meet all kinds of objections to his thesis. For example, some would surely object to his interpretation of Cyrus' advance on Babylon. Others would certainly challenge him on the question of the providential care of God for those exiles who could see simply no evidence of it in their present fate. Perhaps some of them, loyalists and conservatives by nature, brushed aside his teaching because it contained no reference to a messiah of the line of David. Certainly the exiles would be split into parties and factions, as happens to all exiled groups in the strange atmosphere of a foreign land. Yet to all of them DI offers the one reply: We and our little plans and preoccupations do not count at all. It is to God and his plan alone that we must hearken and obey, and nothing else.

10.

The insolence of Israel's attitude toward God is borne out by such questions as, "*What art thou doing in begetting* at all?" rather than, "What art thou begetting?" DI reminds them that Yahweh, as both father and mother of his people at once, has given them birth for a purpose that reaches the stars (cf. Rom. 9:20 *ff.*). So DI blasts this fifth column, whatever its policy was, as he does again later at 49:15; for it represents a display of that ultimate lack of faith which, almost identifiable with the sin against the Holy Ghost of the NT, is a form of virtual suicide. Not to accept life as God has decreed it is in a sense to take one's own life. If Israel persists in this attitude, then she is sinning to a far greater degree than the Babylonians, for they know nothing of a life planned and given to his loved ones by the Almighty, to be lived out in trust and obedience.

11 Thus says Yahweh, the Holy One and Potter of Israel,
"Should men ask me for evidences in regard to my children, or give me instructions in connection with my handiwork?
12 I made the earth, and created man upon it;
It was my hands that stretched out the sky, and it was I who gave instructions to all their host.
13 It is I, then, who roused him up, for a saving purpose;
and all his paths I have been leveling.
He will rebuild my city
and set the exiles of my people free;
Yet not for payment nor for reward," says Yahweh of hosts.

11.

It is now God's turn to take up the questioning of the exiles. DI is obviously being careful to clear up every possible objection to Israel's calling as a Servant before he comes to explain the nature of the office. The word *evidences* is doubtful; it is "things to come," less the interrogative particle. Of the half-dozen emendations suggested, this translation here does least violence to the Hebrew text, although that of the RSV is a good alternative. *Give me instructions* is more nearly "commend to the care of." Isaiah of Jerusalem long before this had referred to the Israelites as God's *children,* or sons (1:2). In Exod. 4:22 God had addressed Israel in the singular, as one collective entity, under the title of "my son." If Israel is such, God has the right to do with him as he wills.

12.

Today, for example, we take it to be the right of parents to give their children the education of their choice. So God has the power as well as the right to educate his children as he chooses (49:2; Jer. 27:5). The verb *created* used of man is very emphatic here, and means so much more than the previous *made* of physical matter. It draws attention to the fact that God the Almighty has total rights over his creature man.

13.

So then which of his creatures dares question Almighty God about his use of Cyrus? Even more significant is God's action in rousing up Cyrus, for by the use of that strongly anthropomorphic verb DI is emphasizing that God has the right to smooth the path of Cyrus even as he has already promised (40:3) to smooth the path of Israel. God has *roused* [*Cyrus*] *up for a saving purpose,* even as he has long since roused up Israel also for such an end. Which of the exiles without the enlightenment of the Holy Spirit would ever have thought out that startling equation? For on the face of it, and in view of Israel's knowledge to date of the ways of God, the equation sounds little less than blasphemy. However, its two parallel lines converge not at infinity but at a particular moment in time and at a particular spot on earth. This convergence actually happened in the year 538 B.C. It was then that Cyrus issued his famous decree, which included permission for all displaced persons to return to their homes; as the book of Ezra informs us, permission was also granted to the Hebrew exiles to rebuild their ruined city of Jerusalem, and this they did actually with the aid of a grant from the royal treasury. These things happened just a couple of years or so after DI spoke these words. Two parallel lines did meet, but not in infinity as would be expected. They met at that very material spot known as Jerusalem and at a time which can accurately be dated. That is to say, a miracle, the impossible, did in fact happen. Cyrus enabled the rebuilding of Jerusalem, *yet not for payment nor for reward;* for that enlightened monarch knew nothing of the significance of the moment that he was living through in the sacred history of Israel.

14 Thus says Yahweh: "The toilsome produce of Egypt, and
the traffic of the Sudan, and the Sabeans (tall men
that they are),
To thee will all these pass over and they will be thine;
They will come up behind thee, and pass
[before thee] in fetters.
They will bow down unto thee, and make supplication
to thee,
'Truly God is in thee [they will say], and there are
no other gods at all.
15 Verily it is in thee that God hides himself, the God
of Israel, the Savior.' "
16 They are all put to shame and confounded together; those
who have fabricated idols have walked in confusion.
17 But Israel is saved in Yahweh with an everlasting salvation.
You will never be ashamed; you will never be confounded
to all eternity.

14.

This verse is difficult to interpret. It is closely related to 43:3. First, a few word studies will help towards the interpretation of the whole. *Toilsome produce* is one word, but an example of the pregnant power of so many Hebrew concepts. The root means "toil," but the noun emphasizes the result of the toil. Does this word refer to the pyramids of Egypt, built as they were on the backs of countless sweating slaves? *The Sudan,* as in 43:3, would be what we call Upper Egypt; *the Sabeans,* some taller people in the south, perhaps even the Ethiopians. *Traffic* is both traffic in the sense of caravans, and that which is handled by the merchants—merchandise. Such traffic is often referred to in the OT and must have been a well-known feature of trade in the ancient world (cf. Pss. 68:31; 72:10-11).

Now comes the question, is it Cyrus the conqueror of the known world that these peoples are to pass before, as at a later Roman triumph? Many expositors think that this is the case. But the pronoun—or suffix in Hebrew—*thee* occurs in the feminine, and is repeated as such five times in this short and self-contained strophe. *Thee* must therefore refer to Jerusalem, the mother of Israel, the feminine city that has been referred to already in vs. 13. Again, are these peoples regarded as coming in fetters, as conquered nations, as transports of prisoners of war? Surely not, for this is not a historical statement that is presented, but rather a vision. It thus conforms with the hopes of the many other prophets, both before and after DI's day, who believed that the whole world of men will come eventually and bow down before Israel and bring their gifts with them (cf. 49:23; 60:9, 10, 14, 16; Zech. 6:15; Rev. 21:26). Notice that it is not before God that they are to bow, as Isa. 2:1-5 and other passages declare. It is to be before that Israel whom God has already addressed as worm, or louse. At first impression the picture seems to offer a very dangerous, man-centered and unbiblical notion of the ways of God. It is true that Israel did at times fall into the temptation of imagining that the day would come when the nations would bow before her. Yet such a reading of this verse is corrected by its last words. Note that they are uttered by the heathen nations who stand and watch: *Truly God is in thee.* Thus from the lips of the heathen world comes the dramatic statement: "God was in Israel, reconciling the world unto himself," paraphrasing with reverence the words of Paul (cf. II Cor. 5:19; also I Cor. 12:12 *ff.*; Rev. 1:9). Israel in herself is nothing but a worm, a louse. How then could the nations bow down before her in adoration? But if God is *in* her, that makes all the difference. It is God who is all in all. Israel remains as nothing. *There are no other gods at all,* the heathen actually declare at this point. Thus it is preposterous even to suggest that apostate Israel could compete with Almighty God for one moment as he uses her to reveal his glory to the nations.

15.

One of the pitfalls into which biblical interpreters can fall is to isolate a verse and seek to expound it out of its context. For centuries, theologians have sought to relate Isa. 7:14 ("Behold, a virgin shall conceive") to the birth of Christ, without relation to the two verses that follow it and with which it forms an integral whole. Such a course is virtually dishonest exegesis. All exegetes can make mistakes, but all ought to deal resolutely with the text both as part of its context and in respect to its historical setting. Our vs. 15 is another verse that theologians have frequently handled in isolation. Taken out of its context and removed from its strophe, the verse speaks of the *Deus Absconditus,* of whom much has been written in semiphilosophical terms. Theologians have discussed him as if he were an abstraction, as we sometimes blame the Greek element in our heritage for teaching us to do. But this verse obviously follows directly from the previous line. There we read that the God who is in Israel is also the *God of Israel,* and as such he is Israel's Savior. But that reality does not leap to the eyes of men without the help of faith. In fact, to say that Yahweh is *in* Israel, reconciling, might appear to be merely another scandal or stumbling block or even blasphemy, when one sees her lying helpless in the darkness of Babylon. For God is light and power; he is the creator of the ends of the earth; how ridiculous even to suggest that he is even now *in* Israel. If he is indeed in her, then he is hidden by that ridculous situation rather than revealed to the eyes of men. Yet DI makes the lips of the heathen witness to the reality that God is truly present in his self-emptying, when he is *in* a people that is both louse and prisoner in the dark. In such an Israel he *hides himself,* yet that act of hiding is his revelation of himself. For it is just such an incarnation that reveals him to be no less than Savior.

16, 17.

There is nothing that the unbelieving nations can do when the truth of this extraordinary reality is made manifest but hide their faces in shame for even imagining that divinity in any form could ever be found in an idol. But once Israel herself becomes the flesh in which God Almighty hides his Godhead, she becomes caught up herself in God's *everlasting salvation,*[4] and thus naturally she *will never be confounded.* The essence of God's hiddenness is here declared to be actually the mystery of his incarnation in the body of the corpse Israel; yet even his very hiddenness then becomes an activity and must not be understood as a state of being. That activity is in the one particular historical situation with which Cyrus is involved.

18 For thus says Yahweh, the creator of the heavens
(He is the Godhead!)
The Potter and maker of the earth—he it is
who founded it.
He did not create it to be negation; he fashioned
it for civilized life.
"I am Yahweh, there is no other.
19 I have never spoken in secret, nor in dark places
of the earth;
I did not say to Jacob's seed: 'Seek for me in
negation.'
I am Yahweh, who utters a saving purpose and
announces what is true."

18.

There now follow three "Words" of revelation, at vss. 18, 20, and 22. The first of the three Words bears upon it the divine signature. Its content follows in natural sequence from the previous strophe. It is that, whether we call him creator or potter, God will not rest till his world becomes once again what it was created to be. It was not created to become *negation,* that is to say, for the continuance of the reign of sin, disease, and war. It was created for *civilized life,* literally "for dwelling." We saw at vs. 7 that the opposite of evil is order or peace (*shalom*). *Shalom* includes inter alia the concept of ordered community life. But it does so only when men who possess *shalom* in their hearts put it into effect in their community life. And so this first word reveals that God's purpose is one of peace in the widest sense of the term. It is a peace which *he* gives, not one which man tries to produce (2:3-4); and once this peace is given, man is able to

[4] *'Olamim* is here used for the first time in the OT to represent endless time or eternity.

know God intimately (Jer. 31:34), and will want to love his neighbor as himself.

19.

Now, this Word that DI mentions is neither new nor unexpected; it was not suddenly revealed as an afterthought on God's part, nor was it once uttered long ago and then kept *secret* till DI's day. This *saving purpose* God actually revealed as far back as when he promised *Jacob's* grandfather that through his seed the whole world would be blessed (Gen. 12:3). So we are back once again to our prophet's central theme, that Israel is God's chosen instrument. God's purpose cannot therefore remain hidden in darkness, nor can it remain a mere unspoken Word. For his Word has in fact been uttered long ago and is now hidden in Israel. To begin with, God had acted *for* Israel; now, once his acted Word has gone forth, he is also working in Israel. That Word is even now becoming flesh or event, in the manner that every word spoken with intent behaves (cf. 55:11; John 1:1 *ff*.; Matt. 12:36). However, DI develops this theme more fully in ch. 55, so at the moment he leaves us to meditate on it. He ends the strophe with what is a highly pregnant phrase: *who . . . announces what is true*. "What is true" is a single word that could equally well be translated by "reality" or "truth." It occurs in poetic parallel with *saving purpose*, and is in this instance probably a synonym for it. On the other hand, it means that God's Word, being alive, must by its very nature resolve itself someday—an explosive situation—in a *living* form.

20 Assemble yourselves together and come close; draw near,
you survivors from amongst the gentiles!
Those who carry [in procession] their wooden idols,
or who pray to a god who cannot save, do not know
[the truth].
21 Declare and present [your case], let them in fact
take counsel together.
Who foretold this from the days of old, who announced
it ever since that time?
Is it not I, Yahweh? (and there are no other gods
apart from me);
The God of creative goodness, the Savior—nor does
anything exist apart from me.
22 So turn to me and be saved, all ye ends of the earth,
For I am the divine Being, and there is none other.

23 By myself have I sworn; from my mouth a Word has gone forth
with saving purpose; it will not come back—
"That unto me every knee shall bend, every tongue shall swear."
24 Only in Yahweh, he said to me, are [man's]
righteous, saving actions and strength [to be found].
But all those who are incensed at him will come before
him—to be shamed.
25 But in Yahweh shall all the seed of Israel be made righteous,
that they may make their boast [in him].

20.

The second Word is a command. It is based upon the first Word which is one of revelation. *Assemble yourselves together,* Israel, for mighty things are just about to happen. God declares the urgency of the situation by calling the exiles even now, proleptically, *survivors,* escapees. Note they have not yet started to escape. But if God has now said the word, "escape," then of course they shall. One important result of their escape, one element in the total redemption that is about to come, will be the sounding of the death knell of heathenism. The reference in vs. 20*b* is probably to the annual New Year festival in Babylon when the gods were carried in procession through the streets. But in total contrast to that sorry rite, Yahweh, declares DI, is about to carry Israel away (cf. 40:11; 63:9).

21.

DI will return to this theme in the next chapter. But to produce the cumulative effect which he is so good at creating, he feels compelled to return first to his refrain of the greatness and uniqueness of Yahweh, who has been revealing himself ever since the days of the Exodus in Israel's life. None of the gods is as alive and full of *creative goodness* as is Yahweh, who announced his saving plan for his whole cosmos at that point in history which DI calls *that time.*

22.

On the basis of God's saving nature, and on that of his uniqueness as God alone, the third Word becomes one of loving invitation. "Come unto me, all ye that . . . *and be saved.*" For it is the good will and blessed purpose of the one and only God that *all ends of the earth* should *be saved* (cf. Pss. 22:27; 65:5).

23.

This truth is expressed now in clear and vivid terms prefaced once again by God's own signature, one that he has actually made on oath, so to speak. For his part, man must always swear by something greater than himself. "By heaven, I'll," he is ready to say (cf. Heb. 6:13). But God can swear only by himself, for nothing exists apart from him (cf. Gen. 22:16; Jer. 22:5; 49:13; Amos 6:8; also Deut. 32:40). Here God does this very thing. Moreover his oath precedes a word of universalistic hope. This word is so striking and so exciting that many of the early Church theologians regarded it as a clear promise from the lips of the living God expressed in living words. For living words, like arrows shot from the bow, must hit their target in the end, since it is God Almighty who has sent them forth, and since the Word of our God must stand forever (40:8; cf. Rom. 14:11, which quotes from the LXX version; Phil. 2:10).

The Targum on this verse translates, "He said to me that by the Word of Yahweh he [Yahweh] would bring righteousness," and the previous verse, "Look unto my Word and be ye saved." The Targum on Isaiah was the interpretation of the book that was made in the vernacular of the Jews in the early Christian centuries, but only assumed written form about the seventh century A.D. Yet the tradition effectively conveyed the accepted interpretation that had been offered at least ever since the first century before Christ. The various Targums preserve the concept of the vitality and essentially creative nature of God's Word, as does the prologue to John's Gospel. In this later Jewish Targum, we are given an interpretation of the text of DI which goes beyond what the Hebrew text actually says. Its authors have understood that DI was putting together two fundamental concepts. One is contained in the sentence, *Apart from me there is no Savior,* to be found at 43:11 and elsewhere. The other is that God's saving activity will one day be found *in* Israel.

24.

As we reach the powerful climax of this profoundly important chapter, it is indeed a pity to have to pause to question the integrity of the text. For the words *he said to me,* though obviously meaningful enough, are not in conformity with what DI says elsewhere. The significance of DI's great asseverations however is not affected by this minor textual difficulty. *Righteous, saving actions* is here the word *tsᵉdhaqoth.* That is the plural of the noun which DI normally employs for *man's* righteousness as he learns it from Yahweh. *ʿOz, strength,* on the other hand is essentially an aspect of God's divine nature. For DI's unique God is power itself. As such he cannot "do nothing," nor can he produce chaos again; nor can he do everything, even though the possibility is there. For unlike the gods that man invents, Yahweh is able to do only what he wills to do. His will, DI declares, is known to man as this, *that unto me every knee shall bend.* Therefore Yahweh's strength is to accomplish this, his declared will. Therefore, in his turn man becomes real man—and not merely man's philosophical idea of what a man should be—when he lives by that strength and expresses it toward his fellows in the way that God expresses it to him, in the form of compassionate, loving activity.

Thus DI sums up this section of his argument by declaring that the saving acts, which Israel is to deploy when as the Servant she seeks to win the gentiles, are fused into the strength that God alone supplies. On the other hand, the nations *who are incensed* at Yahweh *will come before him,* obviously for judgment. Although DI does not speak of any punishment for these gentiles at this point in the development of his thesis, he seems to suggest, because of his universalistic view, that the nations will be so *shamed* that they will be moved to repent and turn to Yahweh.

25.

But there is no doubt about the salvation of Israel *in Yahweh* (cf. the NT phrase "in Christ," Eph. 1:1). Then it is not surprising that their salvation will be marked by boasting aloud *in* Yahweh; that is to say, when Israel enters into the joy of her Lord, she will confess that he alone is all in all, and that her salvation as power to save others comes from him alone.

CHAPTER 46

1 **"Bel's knees are giving way!" "Nebo's toppling over!"**
"They've actually put their graven images on beasts
and cattle!"
"What loads your bundles are!" "They're only burdens
for weary beasts!"
2 **"The men have stumbled and their knees have given way too!"**
"They can't rescue their load!"
"[The gods] themselves have gone off into exile!"

1.

In the city of Babylon DI and his countrymen watched each year at the Akitu festival the annual procession of gods through the streets to the great E-Sagila shrine.[1] Marduk was the most important of those gods. He was known also by the name of *Bel,* which is just the Hebrew *Baal,* a generic title for any god. Marduk was the tutelary god of the city of Babylon. *Nebo* is from the same root as the Hebrew *nabhi,* a prophet. Nebo was Bel's son, and was known as the speaker of the gods, like Mercury or Hermes in later centuries (Acts 14:12). Nebo was worshiped at Borsippa in a magnificent temple called E-Zida. Many kings were called by his name, such as Nebuchadrezzar (Nabu-protect-the-boundary). Nebo was Babylon's savior god (cf. Jer. 50:2).

The conversation overheard in this verse is almost certainly apocryphal. No displaced persons, aliens, foreigners would dare make sarcastic remarks such as these as they elbowed their way on the sidewalk when the procession of gods was going by. The Israelites would more probably have been numbed by the magnificence of Babylon's gods, and would keep re-

[1] See ANET, pp. 315-16.

calling how their own God had been defeated fifty years before. Even more certainly they would be numbed by the magnificence of the city of Babylon as their thoughts strayed to the heap of ruins on Zion's hill. But DI at least kept his sense of humor, as we see here. First it is the gods who are nearly *toppling* as the cart carrying them hits a rut or a cobblestone.

2.

Then DI's sarcasm swings to the human beings as they stumble and try to *rescue* their precious *load*. For effect he reverses the order of the verbs, identical as they are, which he uses for tottering gods and stumbling men. And then a ludicrous thought strikes him—the gods are fleeing the city. Cyrus is at the gate! All that those poor human beings are trying to save are their gods' shells; the gods themselves have already fled and are in exile from their home city. And Nebo was the savior god! Yet he couldn't save himself. When Cyrus did actually enter Babylon, he took the city by surprise, and the gods did not have time to escape. However, Cyrus respected the beliefs of the Babylonians and at once offered worship to the ancient gods he had conquered. But DI's purpose here is to preach, and this he does by means of sarcasm. He is not concerned to try to be a foreteller of the future like a Babylonian stargazer. He knows that that is not what a prophet of Yahweh is called to do.

3 Listen to me, you household of Jacob, all you remnant
of the house of Israel!
You who have been carried from your birth, and borne
since the womb—
4 Till (your) old age I shall still be He;
Till (your) gray hairs I shall [continue to] carry you.
I have done so already, and I shall carry you [again];
I shall go on carrying you and saving you.

3.

What DI does is to make the procession an object lesson. He addresses the exiles by the title of *remnant,* for that is a description of Israel which conveyed to them overtones of love and compassion. The preexilic prophets had used it: Amos (5:15), Micah (2:12), and Jeremiah with reference to Judah when the Northern Kingdom fell. DI's hero Isaiah (37:32) had used the term for the survivors of the Exile. This overtone of love is now carried forward by the figure of mother love and of the word *womb,* which has the same consonants as the verb meaning to show compassion. There go the gods, carried by their devotees. But you *have been carried* by your God ever since your birth, as a mother carries her child (cf. Deut. 1:31; Isa. 63:9).

4.

What is true of the past is therefore certain to be in the future. Yahweh will continue to *carry* Israel all her days. This is because God will not have changed. He will still be: "I am He." Here are set down two great affirmations of our biblical faith: (1) Man-made religions are a burden to those who hold them, but the God of the Bible upholds those who trust in him. (2) One need use only the present tense when speaking of Israel's God, for in both the past and the infinite future, God is always the same: "I am."

5 Whom would you liken me to or equate me with?
Whom would you compare me with, that we should
be equaled?
6 Take those who lightly squander gold from a purse,
Or weigh out silver in scales;
Who hire a goldsmith to make them a divinity,
To which they bow down and prostrate themselves!
7 They hoist it on their shoulders and carry it;
Then set it down in its place for it to stand.
But it does not move from its place!
Supposing a man cries to it, it does not answer,
Nor does it save him out of his distress.
8 So keep this in mind and place yourselves on a firm
foundation;
Take it to heart, you rebellious people.
9 Keep in mind the things that happened first,
at the beginning;
For it is I who am the divine Being, and there are no
other gods, nothing at all like me.
10 I keep revealing the significance of what happened at first,
And of things, beginning long ago, that have not yet
worked themselves out;
Saying, "My plan will stand, and I shall perform all my purpose."
11 Even now I am calling a vulture from the east, the man
in my plan from a distant land.

You see, I have spoken—so I must bring it to pass;
I have started fashioning, so I am bound to perform it.

5.

While it is a trifle wearisome that DI should return to this topic and should ask once again who can be compared to God, remember that the remnant must have needed much persuading. DI evidently felt that the occasion of the procession was too good an opportunity to let slip. Surely the exiles could now see with their own eyes what heathen gods looked like. There was an aura of mystery about Bel and Nebo so long as they remained hidden in a gaudy temple.

6, 7.

But here they were on the street, and anyone could see they were merely gilt-covered dolls. More of his sarcasm follows as he points out to the exiles, "Fancy, when *they set it down,* it stands!" But Nebo, the savior, is no savior, for he cannot rescue you from any kind of trouble when you cry to him.

8.

The moral of all this follows naturally. Not to believe in Yahweh's providential care is in reality being *rebellious* against the covenant relationship binding Israel to her God. Not to believe in Yahweh's plan means to have lost one's footing. Israel's God is her Rock, as DI has quoted before from Deut. 32:15. Yet there we read how Israel scoffed at her Rock. Now she has been doing so again. So he calls on her to *place yourselves on a firm foundation,* instead of standing upon her own interpretation of events, or copying the Babylonians, who were said to be mad about their idols (Jer. 50:38). The verb here is doubtful, however, and we are not able to determine precisely what root it comes from. Israel's firm foundation, on the other hand, is certainly God's covenant love for her.

9.

Within the bonds of that relationship God had long ago revealed himself in the mighty acts of the Exodus period. It had been the God of Moses who at that time had revealed himself as the "I am" (Exod. 3:14). Thus, explains DI, it could not have been Bel or Nebo who brought Israel out of Egypt, for these gods do not exist at all.

10.

Then DI goes on to declare that the Exodus revelation was only the first of God's mighty acts. What followed was that the *significance* of

God's actions slowly unfolded thereafter to the faith and consciousness of Israel. DI probably meant that it was the great prophets who expounded the developing significance of the covenant relationship. The Hebrew word for *significance* is usually translated as "end." But it means more than that for DI. The prophets saw God's world sacramentally, so to speak. They regarded any historical event through which they were living as if they were observing a coin. From where they stood they could of course see only one side of their coin. But that coin had an *'aḥarith* on the back—its meaning or, as we might say today, its eschatological significance. The meaning of all events, DI declares, God will therefore undoubtedly reveal in the end. Then the eyes of believing men will see how everything that has happened has fitted into the plan or purpose which has been working out all the time to its final solution.

11.

There was no reason to doubt that Cyrus, pagan *vulture*[2] as he was, could not fit into God's plan, that in fact he was actually *the man in* God's *plan* for the moment. How many pagan vultures there have been since Cyrus' day. If Cyrus belonged in the plan, then they must all belong in it too.

12 Listen to me, you stubborn-minded people,
Who are a long way off from righteous, saving activity.
13 This is why I have brought nigh my saving activity;
It is not far off now,
Nor is my salvation behindhand.
For I am about to set salvation within Zion,
And give it to Israel my glory.

12.

After Israel had seen with her own eyes how "in everything God works for good with those who love him, who are called according to his purpose" (Rom. 8:28 RSV), that she should express unbelief at this point was rebellion indeed. She was in fact a *stubborn-minded people*. No wonder she could perform no *righteous, saving activity* herself.

Stubborn-minded is a very strong word (cf. 48:4). It is actually a double pun. In the first place, the word *'abbir* is used of man. In the form

[2] The Greek historian Xenophon, in his *Cyropaedia* (VII, 1, 4) and his *Anabasis* (I, 10, 12) informs us that Cyrus' ensign was a golden eagle.

'abbir, however, it is used of God. Yet in DI's day the two words would be indistinguishable, for *bb* and *bh* both represent one Hebrew consonant. *'Abbir* is translated in English as Jacob's *Mighty One* (49:26). But here is the man Jacob—or Israel—thinking he himself is the mighty one, that he himself knows better than God. Yet what is the sin that DI says Jacob is committing at this point? Merely that he finds it difficult to believe in the providential rule of God. DI then declares surprisingly that such unbelief is a sin equal to blasphemy, one that is evidently worse than murder or stealing, of which DI never even suggests that the remnant is guilty. Secondly, the word is a pun on the Hebrew word *'ebher,* meaning "pinions." [3] The remnant was clearly now soaring on its own pinions (40:31), and thus was ignoring the pinions of the vulture whom God had decided to use.[4]

13.

Consequently God has now to act at this juncture in history despite his people Israel, and not by means of her cooperation, as he would have wished. He says: *That is why I have brought nigh my* salvation—for of course Cyrus was daily drawing nearer and nearer to the gates of Babylon. Finally we meet with a surprising statement. It is the simple yet profound declaration that God will now set *his* saving action within Israel, for Israel obviously cannot take even one step forward alone in her unbelief. When he does this thing, it will certainly not be with Israel's consent and cooperation, since she thinks herself wiser than God. God's action must therefore be one of grace alone. In poetic parallelism with the word for *saving activity,* there now follows a new and significant term, the word *glory.* It is possible to translate the second half of this line in two ways: either by "I will give my glory to Israel," or by *I will give it* [my saving action] *to Israel my glory.* Whichever way we take it, the statement comes to us as a great surprise. For it contains a dogmatic announcement which DI will develop only later in his argument. His statement is no less than this, that the glory of the Creator of the ends of the earth, the visible form of the invisible God, will be made manifest precisely through Israel's resistance to God's will, and through her rejection of God's plan, even as it was then working out in contemporary events and in the coming of Cyrus.

[3] See discussion on DI's use of homonyms, p. 17.

[4] In passing, note that the argument at Rom. 10:3 has been built up from words contained in this verse and could be regarded as a comment upon it.

Western man's delight in the Chinese allegory of the mountain reveals the total misconception of the biblical faith that is prevalent among those who have not encountered the God of the Bible. In the allegory men press upward from all sides of the mountain via the roads of all the religions of the world, finally to meet God and each other at the top. Thus all men, declares the allegory, will eventually clasp hands in their essential brotherhood, for every man will then have come to know what it means to reach the goal of life. DI would no doubt have been horrified at this allegory. He believed that God had come down to man, so that man did not need to search for God. At Sinai God had taken the initiative and revealed himself. However, and here is the particularism of the Bible, he had revealed himself not to the world at large but to one particular people. This people he had then elected to be the means whereby his glory might become evident to all men upon the face of the earth. Israel therefore had no need to go searching for God; for God had already found her, had chosen her, and had long been carrying her. Consequently it was pointless for Israel to try to carry in her mind the weight of a philosophical search for God.

Moreover, Israel's God is fully able to bring forth a perfect outcome from any possible concatenation of circumstances, whether those be the cruelties of Cyrus' armies or the stubborn unbelief of his own people Israel. No obstacles that man can place in God's path can prevent the fulfillment of God's incomparable cosmic plan of salvation. That is why God's glory without doubt will eventually be manifest to the eyes of men in his unique relationship to Israel, even though Israel herself will continue to resist his sovereign will and refuse to believe in his providential love. What a very different world of thought all this is from the philosophies of those who think in categories of "religion"!

CHAPTER 47

1 "Get down and sit in the dust, thou virgin daughter
of Babylon!
Sit down on the ground without thy throne, thou daughter
of the Chaldeans!
For thou shalt never again be called soft and voluptuous.
2 Pick up (those) millstones and grind (that) meal; pull off
thy veil!
Strip off thy long skirt! Bare thy thighs! Puddle
through those ditches!
3 Thy nakedness is about to be uncovered, thy shame
even is about to be exposed.
I am going to take vengeance and will not let myself
be entreated,"
4 Declares our Redeemer; Yahweh of hosts is his name,
the Holy One of Israel.

1.

This chapter belongs to a genre that occurs elsewhere in the OT, for example, at Isa. 13–14 and Jer. 50–51. It is an elegy on the coming overthrow of Babylon. As such it is a unity, a single poem in several strophes. But it is no insertion in the text of an otherwise unified whole. It follows naturally as the obverse of the promise which came at the last verse of the preceding chapter.

Cities in Hebrew are feminine, like ships in English. It is therefore easy for the poet to identify the queen at the Babylonian court with the city over which she is now preening herself in pride. Thus the verbs here are all in the feminine singular.

A queen is addressed as "thou." So here the queen city also is "thou," for she is a corporate personality or a unitary identity in the sight of God. Moreover, she is called a *virgin* even though she is married, on the ground that she has not yet been ravished by a conqueror and her *shame* has not yet been exposed (vs. 3). Note, by the way, that DI employs the word *Chaldeans* in parallel with the word Babylonians or *Babylon* (cf. 48:20), and so the two words describe the same people.

What kind of pampered and artificial existence did the queen lead in the royal quarters? Deut. 28:56 reads as follows of a lady: "The tender and delicate woman among you, which would not adventure to set the sole of her foot upon the ground for delicateness and tenderness." We can well imagine what this queen's small-minded and circumscribed life would be like. So the glittering civilization of Babylon was small-minded and artificial in the eyes of Israel's God. Although she was the greatest city in the world, the mighty emporium of Eastern trade, beautiful and adorned with the riches of empire, her culture was describable only in terms of *tohu* in respect to God's plan. Archaeology has revealed just a little of Babylon's former glory—her mighty temples, her exquisite palaces, the colonnaded streets of the sacred areas, the gate of Ishtar that pierced through the inner wall, the docks and warehouses along the river front, the homes of the nobles—but archaeology has produced not a trace of the slums of the rabble. Evidently Israel's God was more interested in Babylon's proletariat than was her queen, for she—and her court—provided the ordinary man with only a hovel to live in. It is evident that those homes of the poor must have collapsed just as soon as they were abandoned or disused.

Get down and sit in the dust. Man cannot help but pride himself in the miracle of his great cities with their mighty stores and warehouses, their lighted streets and temples. Yet as we look back through history we note how in reality few of the world's big cities survived for long. If they were lucky enough not to be sacked, then they gradually fell into decay; if in modern days they are not destroyed by fire, then they may be bombed or blasted sky-high. Now the people of God were only transient citizens of Babylon, but they supposed that the city itself would stand forever. Thus they still had much to learn about God's purpose for that other city which he had chosen in contrast to the impermanent and doomed city of Babylon. Under God, DI has to expound to his people how the chosen city, Jerusalem, is the type of a new kind of human society. This theme is taken up in chs. 49; 60; 62; 65:17 *ff*. The Babylonians, however, supposed that their city was an end in itself. It had owed its origin in the first place to the god

Marduk, and it would undoubtedly remain forever as queen of the nations, lording it over all the peoples of the earth.

This is a picture of human politics in all ages. But DI believes that the human city is, by virtue of its foundation, always under the judgment of God. DI's picture is quoted in the NT at Rev. 13. There the human polis, guided by the spirit of a god—e.g., Marduk—who is created by man to serve his ends and aims, becomes known as the beast from the abyss. Here it is to be the suffering of the Servant *within* that presumptuous city that God will use to unmask the spurious glory of the human city, as DI will proceed to show.

2.

DI must have watched with pity the simple peasant who formed the proletarian substructure of Babylonian society, as he or his womenfolk toiled in the filth of the suburban areas of the city. These areas were intersected by little irrigation canals, as in modern Egypt where the peasant women can be seen today on the banks with their skirts tucked up to the waist as they *puddle through those ditches* tramping on the family wash. *Bare thy thighs* was also the fate of the adulteress, as the earlier prophets tell us (cf. Hos. 2:10; Jer. 13:26). By using such a threat, DI was thus linking the false worship of Babylon with the lascivious cults that had attracted Israel's only too willing attention ever since she had entered the land of the Canaanites (see Hos. 1–3). DI's elegy can be regarded as the enunciation of an eternal principle which must eventually become flesh, on the ground that God has spoken it.

3.

DI here might almost be writing a commentary on his favorite source, the song of Moses: "To me belong the vengeance, and recompense; their foot shall slide in due time; for the day of their calamity is at hand, and the things that shall come upon them make haste" (Deut. 32:35)—words that may have been uttered as far back as the days of Solomon.[1] At the other end of the time scale, from the early Church's liturgy of worship, came the words: "He hath showed strength with his arm, he hath scattered the proud in the imagination of their hearts. He hath put down the mighty from their seats, and exalted them of low degree." (Luke 1:51-52.) Finally we have the words of Paul: "For it is written, 'Vengeance is mine, I will repay, saith the Lord,' " for at Rom. 12:19, Paul quotes from Deut. 32:35.

[1] According to Albright, *op. cit.;* and Eissfeldt, *op. cit.*

And now this same idea occurs as: *I am going to take vengeance and will not let myself be entreated* or persuaded to follow another course.

4.

Well might we ask the question—How could DI's God do otherwise? If he is indeed the *Holy One,* then sin must be anathema to him, and he must necessarily extirpate it from his presence, even when that sin is enfleshed in the corporate body of the queen city of the world. The beauty and majesty of this rich and mighty emporium must necessarily count for nothing in God's eyes if the civilization it embodies is riddled through with sin.

The rabble multitude in Scotland in the heady days of the Reformation never destroyed church buildings, even when they cleansed them of idolatrous images and Romish symbols. But they undoubtedly razed monasteries to the ground. They did so because they believed that the very stones of those buildings had become tainted with the wickedness of the men and women who lived within them. That is to say, in true biblical fashion, they felt that things must necessarily suffer along with humankind if they in their turn have become infected with human iniquity. For a man's things can express outwardly his inner purpose and nature. They may in fact be one with and represent the character of the man who handles and owns them. Trito-Isaiah puts this truth on a large canvas when he says, "For behold, the Lord will come with fire . . . to render his anger with fury, and his rebuke with flames of fire; for by fire and by his sword will the Lord plead with all flesh." (66:15-16.) "For behold, I create new heavens and a new earth: and the former shall not be remembered, nor come into mind." (65:17.) The present world, like the walls of those monasteries in Scotland of old, has become infected throughout by the disease of sin; and just as in the case of the total contents of the city of Jericho in the days of Joshua (6:17, 21), the present cosmos as a whole must be utterly destroyed. On the other hand, out of the death of the old and evil world a new one is yet to be born. And since the new world will contain within it no evil at all, those who dwell upon it will not even remember how different the old one had been. Trito-Isaiah thus carries on into the thinking of another generation this significant theme which he has learned from DI.

5 **Sit down in silence; enter the darkness, thou**
daughter of the Chaldeans!

For thou shalt never again be called queen of the nations!
6 I was wrathful at my people, I had to profane my heritage;
And so I gave them into thy power. But thou didst show them no pity;
Thou didst lay thy yoke very heavily on the aged.
7 Thou didst say: "I shall be queen eternally."
Thou didst not take these things to heart, nor call to mind their significance.

5.

The future holds a kind of poetic justice for Babylon. At the present time it is Israel that is sitting in silence and in the darkness of the dungeon (42:22; cf. Lam. 3:2). Paradoxically, however, it is Israel's calling to bring forth the prisoners from the same darkness and that very dungeon (42:7). Vs. 5 therefore is a highly instructive one about the ways of God with men, and about the good news of God as a whole.

At the present moment Babylon's heart is hardened, and so she cannot discern the good news that God is revealing to her through his Servant Israel. God must therefore act to break Babylon's pride, for pride is the root of all sin. It is the barrier to her reception of Israel's news. God will therefore bring Babylon down to the dust and overwhelm her in her turn with the darkness of the dungeon and despair. For in his wise providence, God has so ordained it—that only when a man is walking in darkness can the Light shine upon him. In other words, Babylon's eyes must first be blinded before God can use his instrument Israel to open the blind eyes, or *bring prisoners out of prison, and those living in darkness out of the dungeon* (42:7). Moreover, God is no respecter of persons. Even the queen of the nations must travel by this same terrible road if her soul is ever to be saved. God has been using her for fifty years now for his own purposes and ends.

6.

Israel refused her calling to be the Servant of the Lord, and so fifty years previously Yahweh had had to *profane my heritage,* and destroy the land and people of his choice. A man normally cherishes his heritage, of course, and finds it quite unnatural to have to pollute the land and people that he loves. So then with Yahweh. Yet Israel had had no right to presume upon her election when God had made her into his people, or to suppose that by it she was rendered exempt from the judgment of his holy zeal. That was why Yahweh had had to deal with Israel's pride in exactly the same manner as he was about to deal with the pride of Babylon. That was why Yahweh had used Nebuchadrezzar and the armies of the Babylonian power when he disciplined Israel at the beginning of the century. He reduced Israel to the level of a pariah nation and condemned her to mere existence in the "darkness of the dungeon." But now, DI said, Babylon had actually overstepped her duty as the instrument of God's righteous and saving wrath. Babylon had in fact overdone the punishing she had been called upon to administer, because she was naturally a cruel tyrant (cf. Jer. 50:17; 51:34; Lam. 4:16; 5:12). But DI had still more pointed and terrible things to say of Babylon's culpability and sin. Babylon, he believed, had actually chosen herself and made herself the measure of all things. She did not know or want to know that there already existed a chosen people, whom God intended to make the measure of all things. For the world can go only with Israel or against Israel—there is no third way.

7.

DI now declares that Babylon has actually committed the ultimate blasphemy of supposing that she herself is God. The Hebrew at this point for the words *I shall be* is *'ehyeh. 'Ehyeh* is the "I am" of God's self-revelation in Exod. 3:14. DI has used it about Yahweh more than once before, primarily in those cases where Yahweh has declared "*I am*, and there is no other, there is nothing else" (e.g., 43:11; 45:5, 6, 18, 22). Babylon here is virtually taking the Word of divine self-revelation out of the mouth of God and applying it to her own evil and proud self. In the light of the succeeding verse, this parallel can be drawn. Then again, the word *eternally* is part of the title of the living God as both prophets and psalmists in days both before and after DI's time employed it (cf. Isa. 9:6; Ps. 102:12).

The title "lady," or *queen*, is the personification or apotheosis of this created earth on which we stand, and which is shot through and through with the sin of sinful man. In all the ancient mythologies the sky god was presumed to be masculine in gender, but the earth below was always regarded as feminine. Even those words for earth that later became completely separated from their original mythological usage remained feminine in gender. This is true no matter where we look in the ancient world; and so we have *ge, terra, 'erets,* all of which are feminine. Thus Ishtar or Belit (lady), the Babylonian goddess of war and love, is ultimately the personification of the natural processes of earth, from whose womb there issues the life of nature, including both vegetation and the young of all the animals. Because men believed this way, all kinds of licentious orgies were associated with the worship of this goddess, at least so far as we know about her from the manifold information that the Canaanites have left us. For Ishtar is known in Hebrew under the name Asherah. The KJV sometimes euphemistically translates this name by the innocent English word "grove" (cf. Deut. 7:5; Judg. 6:30; I Kings 16:33; 18:19). In Canaan, Ashtoreth's consort was known as Baal, the god who rode the thunderclouds in the sky; and as we have seen at 46:1, the name Baal is to be identified with the word Bel that occurs as the name of Babylon's god. The interconnection of this fundamental cult throughout the whole Near East is evident, even when its details vary from land to land.

What the above discussion amounts to is this: DI was aware of the essential inner pride of the state of Babylon, and he regarded Babylon, mistress as she was of all the earth, as the apotheosis of the pride of the creature earth. This pride, he knew, was exemplified in a concept that was false—since earth gives birth to life, then earth must be mistress of all. On the other hand, DI has declared that it is Yahweh who is Lord of all, who is Lord of both heaven and *earth* (40:12). And DI has shown again and again in his argument that Babylon did not ever take Israel's extraordinary story *to heart, nor call to mind their significance*. If only she had done so, DI wishes us to understand as the climax to his argument, then Babylon would have acknowledged that Yahweh alone is Lord, and she herself was but dust and ashes in his sight.

8 So now, listen to this, thou voluptuous woman, sitting pretty
as thou art, and saying in thy heart:
"I am, and apart from me there is no one else!
I shall never sit [in the dust] as a widow; I shall never
know bereavement."
9 Yet those two very things will come upon thee,
suddenly, on one day;
Total bereavement of all thy children, and widowhood;
They will come upon thee despite thy many sorceries
and thy very powerful spells.

8.

Thou voluptuous woman is how DI conceives of the Babylonian idea, the zeitgeist or way of life, of the Fertile Crescent. For with the worship of the forces of nature there went an abominable practice. The lifeblood of the area has naturally been a peasant economy. The peasant has always lived a life very close to the soil. His virtual survival depends upon his annual crop. From earliest times he has been aware that the forces of nature seem to die in the great heat of summer. Rains do not fall at all in that part of the world until about October. The peasant therefore has always supposed that the personalized forces of nature have gone below the ground into the realm of death; thus he lives in the fear that nature might not return to life again should the autumn rains not return punctually.

Arising from the sympathetic rapport with nature which the landsman seems to feel, an understandable practice became woven into the cult. It rested upon the fact that to man is given the power to create life. By analogy man could, through sympathetic magic, create or procreate life even in inanimate nature. From earliest biblical times the high place was a feature of the peasant's cult. In it he worshiped Asherah, particularly at the end of the summer, by means of sacred prostitution. By means of this act he believed that Mother Earth would bring forth once again the plant life which had drooped and died in the summer heat. Such cultic actions were of course performed in all earnestness and sincerity of purpose. On the other hand, human nature being what it is, these festivals degenerated into licentious orgies. Here it is the apotheosis of this whole degenerate cult who exclaims: *I shall be queen eternally* (vs. 7). *I am, and apart from me there is no one else!* This is a parody of the words that the living God had used to manifest his nature to his chosen people (cf. Lam. 1:1, which is akin to this passage; and cf. Isa. 50:1; 54:1-17). No wonder the queen of Babylon believed that she would never be a widow, worshiped as she was in such sexual orgies; for she had at her command male consorts without number.

9.

DI saw the coming judgment of God upon the city of Babylon in answer to this all-pervading sex cult which so dominated the lives of men. For this cult, both in the ancient past and in the twentieth century, is bound up with that deeply primitive, felt need in man to worship the forces of nature and so to make libation to the very earth itself. Yet this queen of nature, this mere creature of the living God (cf. 45:9 *ff.*), actually declares that she will never be dethroned by her own Creator, even though he alone is the "I am," and he himself has created her in the beginning (cf. Dan. 4:28 *ff.*; Acts 12:23). The misuse of the fearful force of the sex instinct DI shows to be one of the chief means that man employs to hurl defiance at the God who made him in the beginning for himself.

10 Thou didst feel secure in thy wickedness:
Thou didst say: "No one sees me."
Thy philosophy and thy knowledge are what have led thee astray;
When thou saidst in thine heart: "I am, and apart from me there is no one else."
11 Evil then will come upon thee; thou shalt not know how to charm it away.
Disaster will fall upon thee; thou shalt not be able to expiate it.
Ruin will come upon thee, suddenly, when thou art not aware.
12 Stick to thy sorceries, then, and thy many spells,
Which thou hast toiled at since thy youth!
Perhaps thou mayest be able to effect something? Perhaps thou wilt inspire terror?
13 Hast thou grown weary of thy many plans? Let them stand forth
And save thee! Those astrologers, those stargazers,
Who make monthly prognostications of what is coming upon thee!
14 Behold! They're going to become like stubble; fire is going to devour them;
But they will never save themselves from the flame's power.
It will not be a [genial] glow at which to warm themselves, nor a fire for sitting in front of!
15 But this is what is going to happen to thee, who hast toiled at thy sorceries since thy youth;
Each one of you is going to stagger out straight in front of him,
But there will be no one to save thee!

10.

The Babylonians were no atheists—far from it. But in this sentence they implicitly admit the nonreality of their gods. *No one sees me,* says Babylon, just like the adulterer at all times. Let us take that particular sin as our example, since the LXX translates *knowledge* by *porneia,* "lasciviousness," "carnal knowledge." No wonder the author of Rev. 18 can build his picture of the scarlet woman from DI's incisive description of Babylon personified.

Moreover, as a concomitant of this practical atheism, there goes also a deep intellectual pride, pride in a kultur that is based upon a merely rational interpretation of life. Having ready an answer to all the problems of life, Babylon thus now felt secure in her wickedness. She believed that she could utter such a sentence as, "I am the captain of my soul." Moreover, she had the right to say so, for the whole ancient world knew of the wisdom of her wise men. Yet the more cultured the state of Babylon became, the less could her people realize how it was that *thy philosophy and thy knowledge are what have led thee astray.* The cult of sex, like the cult of blood, race, science, Marxism, democracy, or the absolutizing of any ideology which the living God himself has created, is bound to lead its devotees in a vicious spiral to the hardening of their hearts, and in the end to the expression of that ultimate blasphemy which declares with pride *I am, and apart from me there is no one else.* Now DI has revealed the heart of what idolatry really is, for it is not the worship of wood- and gilt-covered images; it is in reality a trusting not in God but in mammon or in human ideologies. Suddenly in the broad daylight of Babylon's exalted pride and glory the night of the soul can fall. God has many means at his disposal to bring this darkness near—an economic collapse, a plague, or a pagan king from Persia by the name of Cyrus.

11.

But whatever the means, DI is certain that for the clay arrogantly to rebel against the Potter is for the creature to call down upon itself the wrath of God. None of Babylon's wise men will be able to help her then, because no man can ever bribe the holy God. *Charm . . . away* and *expiate* present a striking assonance in the Hebrew.

12.

Some nations even as they fall have struck out in fury with all the sorceries of science at their command, still hoping thereby to *inspire terror* in their enemies. But neither the mathematics of the magi nor the atomic energy of the scientist can avail to avert the end, even when Babylon or Berlin cause in their fall as much ruin as they can.

13, 14.

Finally DI takes up the figure which Isaiah of Jerusalem had used so effectively before to declare the true nature of Israel's God. Isaiah had believed that God has a plan, or *'etsah,* for the redemption of the world. DI now declares that Babylon has *many plans,* but has grown weary of them all. At 10:17, Isaiah had declared that the Light of Israel would be a fire, and her Holy One a flame. At 30:30 he had likened once again the wrath of God to the flame of a devouring fire; and at 33:14 he had solemnly asked: "Who among us shall dwell with the devouring fire? Who among us shall dwell with everlasting burnings?" Isaiah thus agreed with Deut. 4:24: "The Lord thy God is a consuming fire." Let us note that this latter statement equates the concept of God as fire with his zeal, that is to say, with his burning, loving purpose, eager for the goal he has in view. We have already seen what DI believes that goal to be (45:23).

15.

He therefore is sure that Babylon must experience the fires of the zeal of God upon her flesh if the hardness of her heart is to be broken. And so in a final picture of a besieged city whose defendants are crazed with thirst and blood, he describes men surrendering to the attackers as they advance from opposite them, but finding no one to *save* them from the attacker's wrath.[2] Nebo, the savior god, now lets Babylon down just when she needs him most—but then Nebo is merely nonbeing, *tohu,* negation. So wisdom fails the philosopher; the study of economics and the practice of trade fails the merchant; even Babylon's religion fails her in the day of wrath. For it is only the power of Israel's God that can preserve a body from atomizing, and from splitting up into its component parts. So *each one of you is going to stagger out straight in front of him*—each man is seeking to save himself. The end of the story of Babylon is therefore a dreadful *sauve qui peut.* It is a representation of the elemental truth about ordinary, unredeemed human nature; for in the final debacle, whether it is to be in atomic warfare or in the face of disease or self-appointed ruin, sinful man finds himself utterly alone even as his little world tumbles about his ears, and as he recognizes that he has to face nemesis as a disintegrated soul.

[2] See again Rev. 18 for an interpretation of Isa. 47 made in the light of God's zeal toward all human institutions that say of themselves, "I am."

CHAPTER 48

1 **Hear this, O house of Jacob (though called by the name of Israel), you who have issued from Judah's semen;**
You who swear by Yahweh's name, and invoke the presence of Israel's God—yet neither truly nor rightfully.
2 **Who actually call yourselves after the Holy City, who lean upon Israel's God, whose name is Yahweh of hosts.**

1.

The previous chapter gives what might be called a typological exposition of retribution. The fall of Babylon still to come is there presented in the form of a theological truth—the zeal of God must necessarily show itself as wrath against sin and, in consequence, against sinners too. On the other hand, retribution alone does not effect redemption, so retribution cannot be the totality of God's action in the face of sin. Seeing this quite clearly, DI turns to the next problem. This is the problem that arises from the failure, not this time of pagan Babylon, but of God's own chosen people to be what God intended her to be. Has God not planned to use Israel as his instrument for the furtherance of his purpose, that his name might be known to the ends of the earth?

DI begins by emphasizing the privileged position that Israel holds in God's plan of redemption. The people of God are really "Jacobs," "heels" all—the root meaning of the word "Jacob"—although by grace they have been *called by the name of Israel*. For they too are a libidinous people. We have only to reread Gen. 38 to see what DI means, for there *Judah* behaves as any pagan might do who was not aware of his unique election and relationship to the all-holy God. Thus Israel practices her calling *neither truly nor rightfully* as the people of God should. It was her custom to call Yahweh's name to mind in order to invoke his real *presence* in a cultic act. But she was not giving any content to the meaning of his name or to the action she was performing when invoking him. Seven times in succession in this chapter therefore God solemnly addresses Israel with either the word "Hear" or "Listen," or with the clause, "You have heard" (vss. 1, 3, 6, 8, 12, 14, 16). At each summons the sternness of Yahweh becomes ever more vivid, and the judgment under which specially chosen Israel stands becomes ever more abundantly clear (cf. Amos. 3:2).

2.

The Holy One, we recall, named Jerusalem "my city" (45:13); in this way that city actually partook of God's holiness and could be called "the Holy City." Yet Israel imagined that she too must be automatically holy in this sense, because God had said to her that within the covenant relationship holiness was to be her calling (Exod. 19:6). Relying on her holiness therefore, she had come to *lean upon Israel's God* (cf. Mic. 3:11; Rom. 2:17). She had taken God for granted in other words, and had used him for her own ends, imagining him to be a kind of softhearted grandfather in the sky—when in reality he was the Lord *of hosts*. She might have thought *Dieu me pardonnera; c'est son métier,* as Heinrich Heine later said on his deathbed: "God will forgive me; for that's his job." What effrontery on Israel's part such an attitude was; what a misuse of her election it had become! It is possible that DI deliberately calls Jerusalem by the title of *Holy City* at this particular juncture in order to press his point more clearly, for this is the first time in history that Jerusalem has been so called by anyone. What he wants to bring home to her is this: how will the unholy people of Israel ever become the Servant of God in the unholy land of Babylon?

3 My primal actions I have declared ever since that time.
Out of my mouth they issued so that I could make them
(Israel) hear.
Suddenly I did them, and they came to pass.
4 For I foreknew that thou wouldst be stubborn, thy neck
an iron sinew, and thy forehead brazen.
5 So ever since then I have explained to thee,
before a thing happened I told thee of it,
Lest thou shouldst say: "It was my own toil that produced them,"
or, "It was my graven or molten image that ordered
these things."

6 **Thou didst hear: "Look at all that!"**
As for you then, should you not report it?
So I shall let thee hear new things from now on,
hidden things thou hast never known before.
7 **They are being created now; they are not from of old.**
Former days? No, thou hast never heard of them before,
Lest thou shouldst say: "Behold, I knew it all the time."
8 **For thou didst not listen, thou didst not even notice;**
Ever since that time thine ear has never even been open.
[I declare] I know that thou art utterly treacherous,
a rebel since birth canst thou be called.

3.

Israel has no excuse of course for the apostasy that is in her heart. For God is a God who speaks, who reveals both himself and his purpose by means of his Word. All he has to do is to speak, or do his Word, and then that Word becomes history. The redemption from Egypt, for example, was his Word *suddenly* proclaimed, and just as quickly it *came to pass*. Thus Israel all along has had the chance to know God's true nature as that of loving care for her and for the world.

4.

But now a strange statement follows. DI declares that God foreknew before his election of Israel that Israel would resist his will. For as Israel's Creator, he had given her a *stubborn* heart, a *forehead brazen*, and an *iron sinew* for a *neck*. In other words, God had actually created Israel able and determined to resist the purpose that he himself was planning to work out by his election of her.

5.

Despite that fact he had kept on giving her every chance, by telling her through the mouths of her prophets the significance of her choices even before she had to make them: *lest thou shouldst say: "It was my own toil that produced them."* DI is emphasizing here that the fact of the Exodus and all that accompanied it ought to have given Israel faith even though she was naturally stiff-necked. Israel should have realized that God would remain loyal to her, no matter what should happen. For God had done more than just complete the redemption of his people from Egypt; he had proceeded to give Israel a series of interpreters, the prophets, who had persistently sought to encourage her to understand the past and believe in the promises of God for the future. Incidentally, DI here vindicates the divine method of giving and withholding predictions according to Israel's readiness or not to receive them. Yet God knew that ultimately Israel would refuse the office of the Servant, and would not be willing to work in the world with and through her Lord.

6.

So we now reach DI's surprising conclusion to the argument. He declares that God had first let Israel hear the word: *Look at all that!* That was when, through the lips of his prophets, he had called upon her to ponder the mighty events through which she had passed, and thereupon to become witnesses of God's actions to her heathen neighbors (cf. 43:10). The swing from singular to plural will be discussed later. But Israel had not been willing to pay attention. Her heart had been too hard. Therefore God was now about to act once more. Unfortunately this could not be with Israel's cooperation; it had to be in and through her foolish resistance to his will. This whole conception of a God's winning his victory through the resistance of his people is surely completely new in the world's thought.

On this basis then, DI can declare that God is now about to show Israel *new things*. Some interpreters suggest that these new things refer to the new exodus which DI undoubtedly believed God was about to accomplish for his people, for God was certainly about to set his people free from Babylon and lead them home to Zion.

7.

But DI expounds the word *new* by saying that these things are *being created now*. That is to say, they are no mere repetition of God's previous mighty acts. *Thou hast never heard of them before*. They are *hidden things* (vs. 6), things that could come forth only from the mind of Israel's surprising God, or out of his peculiar involvement in the life of Israel (45:14). DI's choice of the verb *bara'*, create, is that found at Gen. 1:1, where it is used for God's original creative act. DI wants his hearers to understand that when they see it, men will not be able to say: *Behold, I knew it all the time.*[1]

8.

How tragic that the people of God should never have cooperated with God's plan to use them. Even their sufferings in the Exile and the loss of

[1] In passing, we should recognize that it would be ridiculous to ascribe these words to Isaiah of Jerusalem as those do who believe that Isaiah wrote all sixty-six chapters of the book. This line alone is evidence that he is not the author of this section, chs. 40-55. Anyone who lived in the centuries before DI could not say with honesty, "I knew it all the time," and then proceed to foretell events that were to take place two centuries later.

the Holy City had not opened *thine ear* to hear the Word of God as it was disclosed in events interpreted by the mouths of the prophets. Israel was completely deaf (cf. 42:19). This verse contains a terrible indictment—by the living God. Israel, the only nation given the chance to hear the Word, had been *a rebel since birth*. Her birth, by the way, is here equated in poetic parallelism with the Exodus events. Thus DI is laying particular emphasis upon the giving of the covenant at Sinai, for that was the moment when God both adopted Israel as his own, and married her as his bride (Exod. 19:1-8).

There are two possible conclusions from the above. First, it is obvious that Israel's birth is not enough for God to use. She still requires to be born again. But no one can be born again until his old self has first died. That therefore must be the *new* thing that Israel has never known before. If only Israel would recognize that the Exile was her death as the people of God, a death actually brought about by the God who loved her enough to do this thing that Hosea long before had declared that God must do: "I will devour them like a lion" (13:8 RSV); "he incurred guilt through Baal and died" (13:1 RSV). Secondly, God did not purpose to unite himself again with the *queen* of heaven, as might be expected of the King of heaven, for the people of Babylon was that totally self-sufficient creature who believed herself to be the "I am" that only God can be (47:7). God purposed to unite himself with that sinful yet newborn bride, the people of Israel. But this would happen only when she had emptied out her *nephesh*, her ego, unto death to give room for the Spirit of God to enter in and unite her with himself.

9 It was for my own sake that I kept postponing my wrath;
It was for the sake of the praise due to me that I kept holding myself in over thee,
So that I should not cut thee off.
10 Behold, I have had to refine thee, but got no silver out;
I have had to test thee in the oven of affliction.
11 For my own sake, for my own sake have I been doing this;
For how can [my name] continue to be profaned?
Yet I will never give my glory to any other [people].

9.

God's wrath is what we see of God when his love encounters sin. For the heat of his zeal must necessarily burn up and destroy that which essays to pollute his holy love. Yet the tension between God's mercy and his wrath is necessarily acute. For seven hundred years now, ever since the days of Moses, God has been *holding himself in,* not wanting to *cut thee off* (cf. Jer. 13:11; 33:9). This he had done so as to be true to himself—*for my own sake, . . . for the sake of the praise due to me;* for God's true nature is positive, creative, loving, merciful. And he had sworn to be faithful and loyal to Israel forever. That loyalty exhibits his true nature.

10.

But not even the chosen people can mock God forever. So finally God had to act, as happened at the historic moment of 587 B.C., when Nebuchadrezzar sacked the Holy City and took the cream of its population into exile. *Behold, I have had to refine thee, . . . to test thee* (cf. Ps. 66:10; Ezek. 22:20-22). God had never intended of course to exterminate his people. For God must remain true to his side of the covenant even though Israel should break hers. Long ago in the days of Egypt, however, he had already revealed what he would eventually have to do to Israel (Exod. 3:2), and he had also revealed how suffering is to be understood as a fiery furnace that must be endured (Deut. 4:20). Yet now in this new testing period of the exile in Babylon, even the heat of the fire of the wrath of God had not been able to smelt any *silver out* at all. DI is therefore declaring in this line that there existed nothing inherent in Israel herself that could be of use to God. There was in fact no vestige of intrinsic goodness in the chosen people, no silver at all. Herein we see the extraordinary paradox, that God has chosen a people to be his Servant who are in themselves intrinsically useless, and yet he is determined to use them.

11.

The resolution of such a paradox can obviously be discovered only in the faith which DI here sets forth, viz., that God's purpose and plan are to be understood in terms of grace alone. Or in the actual words of DI, repeated as they are for the sake of emphasis: *For my own sake, for my own sake have I been doing this.* Thus refining Israel in the fire is the only course left open for God to pursue; *for how can [my name] continue to be profaned?* Note Ezek. 36:19-23 for this theme. DI would probably know this passage. On the other hand, God will never let his worthless people go, for never under any circumstances can he be faithless to the covenant he has made with them. Consequently he does not even consider showing forth his glory by choosing and uniting himself with any other people on the face of the earth (cf. 42:8, where reference is made to this verse; 44:23; Ezek. 20:9).

12 Listen to me, Jacob, thou whom I called Israel,
I am He; I am the first; moreover I
shall be the last.
13 Note how it was my hand that founded the earth, how it
was my right hand that spread out the sky;
That it was I who gave them their names, so that they
should stay in place together.
14 Gather together, all of you, and listen! Which of you
[gods] ever announced these things?
Yahweh loves him; he will execute his will on
Babylon, and be his arm upon the Chaldeans.
15 I, I it is who spoke and then called him;
I fetched him and prospered his way.

12.

"O Love, that wilt not let me go" is as true a description of the God of the OT as it is of the God of the NT. DI now demonstrates that this is really what God is like by returning to his great theme of God as the self-revealing "I am" (Exod. 6:2-3; Deut. 32:39). Yet God sorrowfully acknowledges that his people is really rebellious *Jacob,* and is only *called Israel* by grace.

13.

Then DI reminds Israel that God can re-create simply on the ground that he has already created. God is still in command of the hosts of stars, and they obey his will absolutely. The RSV gives a good alternative translation of this line. DI's source book, the song of Moses, long before had suggested an identity between the hosts above and the hosts below (Deut. 32:8).

14.

The hosts below, in other words, the people of God, ought therefore to be continually aware that God is always in control. How silly to suppose that it was the angelic hosts, the sons of God (Deut. 32:8), or even the gods of the heathen nations, who had spoken the word of creation in the beginning, for the gods of the nations are themselves part of creation.

It is interesting to see how DI now leaps from creation to the contemporary scene. After all, we are more concerned about our present problems and distresses than about even the glorious moments of the past. DI therefore turns to the vital question of the moment: *Yahweh* actually *loves* Cyrus! We have seen that while "love" can also mean "choose," at the same time it can presuppose an intimate personal relationship, as in the case of Abraham at 41:8. Similarily Solomon was God's choice of king—"And the Lord loved him" (II Sam. 12:24)—for he was chosen to execute God's will in a decisive manner. Here is the next step in the plan that has been working out since the beginning.

15.

Cyrus is about to become God's *arm,* that is to say, the outward, tangible sign of God's invisible and divine *will* or purpose. Moreover, Cyrus is bound to accomplish that which pleases God; for it is the "I am" who has uttered his will, and who has been preparing for its eventual resolution in the paths of history. Yet before that moment of resolution can arrive, God sees fit to employ a period of preparation. We recall how God ordained that the Roman pax should prevail before the final act of redemption took place in the birth and death of Christ. Similarly DI regards Cyrus as God's instrument whom he is employing as he prepares the right conditions for the astonishing moments to follow. What these are we shall see later.

16 Draw ye near to me, and listen to this:
Since the beginning I have never spoken cryptically.
Ever since time began I have been immanent.
And now Lord Yahweh has sent me with his Spirit.

16.

DI reiterates that God's purpose will certainly work out. Then, in a line of verse where God plurally addresses the whole world of angels, gods, and men together, DI suddenly presents us with a striking sequence of thought. First, he declares that God has all the time been there in Israel's story, or *immanent,* as the verb is here translated. Second, he declares that that immanence is now being realized in a new way, even as God's Spirit uses DI's own mouth and mind. So we read: *And now Lord Yahweh has sent me with* [=and?] *his Spirit.* The speaker can be only DI himself. Only here, as well as at 40:6, does he ever make mention of himself; otherwise he is wholly subservient to the voice of God.

The word *now, 'attah,* is DI's choice of technical term for the contemporary moment. We have already seen that he selects the word *ro'sh,* head, or another noun built from it, to represent the concept of "beginning" or the first action of God in his handling of Israel in the days of Moses. DI believes that the period between has not been mere history. It has been *Heilsgeschichte,* for Yahweh has been immanent in it, working out his purpose for the world through his association with Israel. But DI is now keenly aware that at the very moment he is speaking, he is acting as the mouthpiece of God. He knows that it is God's Spirit alone and not his own human perspicacity which is enabling him to interpret events, and to be the instrument of the Word as it is even now becoming flesh in that vital moment of the world's history. Thus DI virtually equates the Spirit of God with the Word of God. In the OT the concept of Spirit normally contains the overtone of power. So when DI continues with his message we are to be sure he believed that the power of God's Word was now being uttered through him, and that his Word must necessarily be effective in the days to come. The Babylonians too believed in a reality they called the word of God. So also did the Egyptians. But both those nations understood the concept very differently from DI. They thought of it in terms of emanation. The Egyptians, for example, pictured the word as a fluid that issued materially from the mouth of the god who spoke it. DI, however, must have turned from this pagan conception with impatience. For to him the Word of Yahweh was no less than the creative, and consequently re-creative, power of the living God (cf. 42:1; 44:3).

17 Thus says Yahweh thy Redeemer, the Holy One of Israel,
"It is I, Yahweh, who am thy God, and who has been
teaching thee how to be effective,
Directing thee on the way thou shouldst walk.
18 If only thou hadst listened to my orders!
Then thy prosperity would have been like the Euphrates,
And thine own acts of compassion like the waves of
the sea.
19 Then would thy seed have been as the sand,
and the progeny of thy body [as many] as its grains.
Then thy name would neither have been cut off nor
destroyed from before my face."

17.

The Word of God, which he has uttered over the years to Israel, ought to have been effective in Israel's life. God's *tsedheq,* or saving activity (masculine; cf. 45:8), which he had poured down upon Israel, ought to have borne fruit in *tsᵉdhaqoth,* saving, righteous actions, or creative acts of compassion (feminine plural) on Israel's part (see discussion at 45:8).

But it had not done so thus far, because man cannot perform saving acts, or show creative compassion for others without accepting the *tsedheq* of God. Israel had not done so. It is only in fellowship with God that life can be lived effectively (cf. Pss. 32:8; 119:165).

This important point is not fully grasped unless we realize what DI meant by the word "effective." The prophets did not conceive of the good life as a mere static condition. In fact the idea of just being good is not to be found in the OT; it is not presupposed even of God himself. For goodness in OT usage means the desire to create such things as fellowship, trust, joy, and wholeness in the minds of others, not in oneself. Jesus later speaks of a goodness that is not the goodness of the scribes. Jesus speaks of one who sends—implying activity and not a state—his rain upon the just and upon the unjust alike, who turns (note the action) the other cheek to the smiter, not with the object of feeling a sense of self-satisfaction at his own self-control, but in order to win the sinner into creative fellowship. Effectiveness is the hallmark of divine goodness for DI also; and so we shall see later at 52:13 that it must be the hallmark of God's true Servant as well. DI's insistent indictment of idols was just that they were ineffective (cf. 44:10). Ineffectual saints have no place within the people of God. Yet Israel had committed just this very sin. She had rebelled against her calling to be effective, in other words to be holy even as God is holy (Exod. 19:6) and to love her neighbor even as God loved her (Lev. 19:18). Was there one thing in God's creation that was actually stronger than God himself—the rebellious free will of the creature Israel? If the words of Mark 6:5 may apply here, it is as if God could do no mighty works in her at all.

18.

How wonderful the world would have been by DI's day, *if only thou hadst listened to my orders*, says God (cf. Ps. 81:13). Then two good things would have eventuated. First, Israel herself, as the people of God, would have found her true *prosperity, shalom*. This word, usually translated "peace," as we saw at 45:7, means much more than that English word can convey. DI compares *shalom* to the influence of a river. The river Euphrates is perennial and is therefore reliable. But it owes its fructifying waters to God alone. It is not like a Palestinian wadi, which is a roaring watercourse for a week in winter and then a dry useless gorge the rest of the year. Moreover, because the waters of the Euphrates, like grace, are always there, they are of use to others; in other words, the Euphrates is *effective*. The

Mesopotamian plain in DI's day was interlaced with irrigation canals fed by the Tigris in the north of the plain and by the Euphrates in the area of the city of Babylon. This Euphrates water brought life to what would otherwise have been desert. Thus we have the peaceful picture of a gently flowing river, and we are shown how true joy comes from creating life and vitality where it has not been found before. Israel's life would then have been a concert of saving actions, of acts of compassionate concern *tsᵉdhaqoth* (cf. Isa. 11:9), just as all those little irrigation ditches which Queen Babylon was soon to puddle in (47:2) brought life to the peasants of the land.

19.

That would have been the first wonderful result. The second would have been this. The promises of God to the patriarchs would have been fulfilled by now, viz., that Israel would be as numerous as the grains of sand on the seashore (Gen. 22:17; 32:12; but also Isa. 10:22; Hos. 1:10). Whereas, the bitter reality was something wholly different. The sins of pride, apostasy, and disloyalty had now cut off Israel's *name*, or essential being, from before God's *face*, or presence, and consequently from happy fellowship and cooperation with him who had chosen her as his very own precious possession and the instrument of his saving purpose (Exod. 19:5).

20 Get out of Babylon! Flee from the Chaldeans!
Tell it with a shout of joy! Let this be known!
Send it forth to the end of the earth!
Say: "Yahweh has redeemed his Servant Jacob!"
21 They did not thirst when he led them through the deserts;
Water from the rock he made to flow for them,
when he clove the rock and out gushed water.

20.

There are scholars who remark that here we have a unique and individual oracle inserted in the text at this point for no obvious reason; for what it contains is DI's cry to the exiles at the exciting moment when Cyrus' armies reach the gates of Babylon (cf. Jer. 51:6). Yet these are not the words that anyone would use at such a moment. Even DI the theologian would have given more immediate and practical advice to his bewildered countrymen than the contents of vss. 20-21. Surely these words were spoken well in advance of Cyrus' arrival and in perfect sequence from vs. 19. Vs. 18 has just expressed what might have been. Vs. 19 has gone on to declare the awful reality of the situation as it is. But vs. 20 offers the kind of surprise that God delights to give throughout the biblical revelation. Our poem suddenly takes for granted that Yahweh will save his people after all. What DI now proclaims is that God will act, not *with* his people's cooperation, but *despite* their noncooperation. Surely this is grace abounding. This is indeed the love that will not let Israel go. This is surely God's opening a door of hope in the valley of Achor (Hos. 2:15). Here is the moment of Israel's greatest shame becoming a new beginning with all the possibilities that re-creation by the power of God implies. Israel's joy, when Cyrus should come pounding at the gate, is therefore to be no ordinary joy. *Rinnah* is a *shout of joy* issuing from a heart bubbling with excitement; in fact, it represents a joy that is virtually not of this world at all. The wonder of what God is doing at this crucial moment in the world's history—now, *'attah*—must in fact be shouted to the Hebrew exiles in every land and not just to those in Babylon. And what is to be the content of the shout? Is it to be: "Cyrus has set us free"? No. It is to be: *Yahweh has redeemed his Servant Jacob* (cf. Rev. 18:4).

21.

Getting out of the doomed city is thus to be understood in terms of what has already been done in the past when Israel fled from Egypt (Exod. 14). But the Exodus had been more than a physical deliverance; it was the beginning of a new life to be lived in covenant fellowship with God. At that time God had given his people water to drink; in fact, in the Wilderness *he clove the rock and out gushed water*. If God had done this before, then he could easily do it again, and do it for a people who would have to face the desert once again on the homeward road to Zion (cf. Exod. 17:6; Num. 20:11; Ps. 105:41; and already at Isa. 41:17-18).

Yet it is not likely that such practical issues were then uppermost in DI's mind. For DI regarded Yahweh himself as the Rock, as he is in DI's favorite sourcebook, Deut. 32:18, and as Ezekiel esteems him, if we can date Ezek. 47:1-12 as early as this, for Ezekiel envisaged the water flowing from the Rock as the eschatological river of life. That Rock, in symbolic language, is then identified with the rock on which the temple stood and the spot where the glory of God had been resident before 587 B.C. (Ezek. 10:4). DI evidently learned from Ezekiel that the glory departed from

Jerusalem after the siege (cf. Ezek. 9:3; 10:4; 10:18-19; 11:22-23), but that later on it became visible *with* the Israelites by the river Chebar in Babylonia (Ezek. 10:22) and thus was now immanent in the life of the exiled people (Ezek. 39:21-22). Speaking in the same metaphorical language as his immediate predecessor, DI draws a picture of the flood of grace that will follow the exiles, even as it followed their fathers in the days of Moses. We note that the Hebrew word for "rock" is one in origin with the Babylonian word for "mountain god." These can be compared with the metaphors in Ps. 18:2, a very ancient psalm whose expressions are similar to those used in early Canaanite cultic language. But if Israel had followed DI's argument to this point, she should have recognized that Yahweh alone is the Rock; for DI has the gift of making the Exodus so realistic that his recounting of events in those far-off days could sound like yesterday's happenings. His is the genius of the Negro spiritual singer who can ask with realism: "Were you there when they crucified my Lord?"

22 **"There is no prosperity," says Yahweh, "for the wicked."**

22\.

What does it mean to be wicked? It means to refuse the wholeness and fullness of life, the *shalom*, the *prosperity*, which it was Yahweh's will to give to his beloved Servant. It means in effect to refuse to be effective. It is therefore something negative, as refusal must be, and so it belongs in the realm of *tohu*. This chapter therefore concludes with a terrible utterance. We saw in ch. 47 what the end of Babylon was to be. Equally under judgment, however, stands the chosen people; and we listen in awe as we await the sentence of God upon them. But vs. 20 has just said that the sentence is to be one of grace and mercy. Vs. 22 is no editorial comment, as some would have us believe, written in by a pious scribe. Actually it is so important that it is quoted later by the writer of 57:21. It is a reiteration for great effect of the subject brought forward right at the beginning of the chapter in vs. 1. For DI wants us to recognize with awed surprise that God is determined to reveal his glory *in* Israel, *despite the fact that* she has broken the covenant and departed from him. God will, in fact, do so at that very point where Israel is farthest from him in thought, intention, and cooperative faith. We are now awaiting a revelation that can be accounted for in terms of nothing other than grace.

CHAPTER 49

1 Listen to me, O coastlands; hearken, you faraway peoples!
Yahweh has called me from the womb; he uttered my name even when I was still in my mother's body.
2 (First) he made my mouth like a sharp sword; then he hid me in the shadow of his hand.
Next he made me into a polished arrow, and hid me away in his quiver.
3 (Finally) he said to me: "Thou art my Servant, Israel; in thee shall I reveal my splendor!"

1.

If only thou hadst listened to my orders, God had said to his Servant Israel at 48:18, then thou wouldst have been *effective.* Yet effective to what end? We are obviously now drawing close to the heart of DI's remarkable exposition. He has eliminated more than one side issue by now. He has dealt with the question of the validity of idol worship; he has already vindicated God's action through his instrument, the Persian Cyrus; and he has more than once shown how the great "I am" has a purpose working through the events of the moment. So now he draws in his net and discloses what Israel has been meant to do and be ever since God called her to be his Servant, but a Servant very different from Cyrus. This fresh theme, however, has led some commentators to declare that ch. 49 introduces a new section of the book. Note that Cyrus is no longer mentioned in this section. Some commentators have therefore averred that we are now even reading the work of a different author. In reply it can be pointed out that ch. 40 offers a summary of material that appears in this second section of our document as well. Remember that DI is a theologian who is concerned with the *'aḥarith* of things, their eschatological outcome. While his method of exposition is to *begin* with history, as a good theologian must do, he then proceeds to expound its meaning in the light of God's plan; and this is just what chs. 49 *ff*. do.

First, we hear a voice addressing itself to the whole human race. Remember that *coastlands,* while meaning more specifically "islands," comes to mean "the whole earth" in DI's idiom. Interestingly enough, the LXX deliberately makes *faraway* refer to time and not to place. With no warrant from the Hebrew it reads: "For a long time it will stand, says the Lord." Then without warning, we find that it is the Servant who is speaking and not God, though we are not specifically told that the Servant is still considered to be the people of God. Let us now examine the text in order to establish his identity.

Yahweh has called me from the womb. At 49:15 DI will speak of a woman's beloved son as *the child of her womb.* It would seem that in some sense it is God's son who is spoken of here. Next we read that God *uttered my name* before birth, and for DI this phrase implies election in love. The speaker's first words are *Yahweh has called me;* Yahweh is the name of the covenant God. *Yahweh* is written at the head of the sentence, the Hebrew method of showing emphasis. This is Yahweh's act, not man's; it is the covenant God's, not the creator God's, or that of the Lord of hosts. The call is the call of election. It is the call to a specific individual who can be identified by name, and that name is Israel (cf. 43:1). God had chosen Israel from the days of Abraham (41:8), and it was his son Israel whom he had rescued from the hand of Pharaoh (Exod. 4:22). Moreover it was the covenant God, known to Moses as Yahweh (Exod. 6:3), who had thus called Israel to be his people, and it was with Israel alone that God had made his covenant in days of old. In light of this, von Baudissin has pointed out that in the LXX text of Isaiah the epithet meaning "the Lord" qualifies God as the Lord who is intimately bound up with his people Israel.

2.

What then does Israel confess that God has done for her? (*First*) *he made my mouth like a sharp sword*. DI himself has found that the Holy Spirit is using his mouth (48:16). But how could Israel, a whole people, comprising old and young, male and female, rich and poor, be said to possess one mouth?

This translation has carefully preserved in English the Hebrew singular number when the singular is used of Israel; for example, the words: *Thou art my Servant, O Israel.* It was noted in ch. 40 that God addresses his people as one individual personality or as one "thou." Moreover, this corporate personality that is Israel God has addressed by now more than once in the feminine singular. This feminine form cannot be rendered in English, nor has attention specifically been drawn to it as yet, though it is of prime importance as this chapter proceeds. The RSV has not preserved the singular number at all, for the sake of rendering a modern English translation. But when Israel is addressed as "thou" in the feminine, then in God's sight she is obviously the personification of Zion or Jerusalem, as we have seen before. In the same way the people of Babylon can be personified and typified in the singular entity of their queen, as discussed at 47:1. Later in this chapter, moreover, we shall note how DI uses the feminine singular in a very surprising and daring manner (vss. 13 *ff*.). While the conception is a difficult one for modern man to grasp, believing himself to be a strong individualist, remember that this corporate personality idea was a completely natural way of thought in biblical times. Moreover, it is carried forward into the NT. Jesus addresses Zion in the singular (Matt. 23:37), and Paul refers to the Church as the body of Christ (I Cor. 10:17; 12:12 *ff*., especially vs. 27). Paul was thus using language that was common to the whole OT. For Israel could say of a neighbor: "Woe to thee, Moab! thou art undone, O people of Chemosh" (Num. 21:29); or an Assyrian could say of Egypt: "Egypt is a broken reed" (Isa. 36:6).

When Eph. 6:17 (RSV) speaks of the "sword of the Spirit, which is the 13). The Babylonians used the adjective *sharp* with the royal word that pronounced judgment (cf. the figure at Isa. 11:4); so presumably DI, writing from within a Babylonian milieu, is implying that Yahweh had been teaching Israel his own word of judgment. So Israel had to learn to be the instrument of the Word, so that the Word might be effective in human life. The life of man, however, is one of dungeons and darkness; and it is into such areas that the Word must be carried by a willing Servant. DI is therefore hinting once again that he will soon be developing the question of what must happen when the Word is confronted with the darkness.

Then he hid me in the shadow of his hand must point to a period of quiet and undisturbed training, as does the phrase *hid me away in his quiver.* There was a long period after the establishment of the monarchy when Jerusalem, unlike Ephraim in the north, was undisturbed by war. *A polished arrow* is obviously an effective arrow (cf. Ps. 45:5). Israel was therefore being trained by God at the time to hit the target that he had chosen for her. Note that to miss the target is one of the many Hebrew words for "sin" (*ḥaṭa'*; cf. *hamartanein* in the NT). The word for *polished*, however, is composed of the same consonants as the word for pure or clean. DI would probably enjoy the pun that would spring to the mind of his Hebrew listeners. For he would want to emphasize the second truth too, that it is only "he that hath clean hands and a pure heart" (Ps. 24:4) whom God can use as his Servant.

3.

In thee shall I reveal my splendor. These words approach nearer to the heart of the matter to which DI is leading in thought. What he means is that while God is light indeed, his light cannot be reflected unless it strikes a polished surface. *Israel* has been created by God to be that surface, for to be it is to be the *Servant*. A mirror is nothing in itself. It can reflect light only when there is light to fall upon it. The word *splendor, pa'ar,* occurs as a verb in the Hithpael, and so we have: "I shall show myself in splendor —*in* thee." The noun is very close in meaning to "glory," *kabhodh;* and God has promised to give his glory to no nation but Israel (42:8; 43:7; 46:13; 48:11). So God now promises to reveal his splendor in the servant (cf. John 17:1).

4 For my part, I had thought: "I have toiled to no purpose,
My strength I have used up for negation and vanity.
Yet surely the meaning of my existence lies with Yahweh,
And my raison d'etre is [secure] with my God!"
5 So now, declares Yahweh, who formed me from the womb to be his Servant,
That I might bring Jacob back to him, and that Israel might be gathered to him;
That I might be honored in Yahweh's eyes,
Once my God had become my strength:
6 (He said:) "It is too easy for thee to be my Servant
[Merely] to reestablish the tribes of Jacob,
[Merely] to restore those Israelites who are held [in exile].
I shall make thee into a light for the nations,
So as to be my salvation to the ends of the earth."

4.

I had thought is merely "I said" in Hebrew; Israel is represented as ruminating within herself. In the previous verse, however, God has just *said* an important word. It is therefore ridiculous of Israel to say anything at all in reply about what she has been thinking in herself. The Servant has just received an extraordinary call, even while she is still a pariah amongst the nations. How could the splendor of God be revealed in her? Fifty years of struggling to be faithful—more or less—in distant Babylon had made her feel that *my strength I have used up for negation and vanity*. Her life in Babylon clearly exhibited the opposite of what she had been called to become. Obviously her life was now meaningless, *hebhel, vanity*, the word which was so central to the thought of Ecclesiastes in later years. And *yet surely*, life has a meaning for her, even in exile. Israel does not claim here to have any righteous saving deeds of her own. All she claims is that she believes that her *mishpaṭ* is still with God.

This word unfortunately can mean many things. Initially it signified judgment. Then it came to cover the idea of justice in general, and so could be used for our word ordinance or even for a man's legal right. Then it spread into the meaning of the fitness of things that are just and right, and so became what we mean when we speak of custom or of an accepted manner of doing things. Then of course it was used to describe God's justice as it has been revealed to man. Since God's revelation is concerned with the whole man and with the whole of his life as it must be lived out here on earth, the word *mishpaṭ* may even be translated by the German term *Weltanschauung*. Here we can take it to mean that whole, true, wholesome, and creative way of life which it is God's will that Israel should understand and live; in other words it is *the meaning of my existence*, as Israel says in this poem. And if the latter is to be understood in terms of God's reward to her—the usual translation of *pe'ullah,* here rendered *raison d'être*—then it must surely be rooted and grounded in *my God* alone.

5.

So Yahweh is still for Israel *my God*. "I believe," Israel is virtually saying, "help thou mine unbelief." God now seizes gladly on this little vestige of faith in his Servant, and at once makes a basic statement about his purpose in Israel for the world. This comes at vs. 6. Vs. 5 is a long parenthesis leading up to the central affirmation which follows. *So now* (*'attah*), *declares Yahweh*—that is, here and now *in* this exile situation—Yahweh's plan will find its way. *Who formed me* is the same word as potter at 45:9, 11. There potter is paralleled by creator and is linked with those great words of redemption which are to apply even if Israel has to go through fire and water. Here DI is reminding Israel that the creative activity of the living God, ever since he *formed me from the womb to be his Servant,* obviously cannot end in *tohu.* His purpose must still be to win Jacob back to co-operation with himself in his plan. *And that Israel might be gathered to him* is the Hebraic way of saying, in poetic parallelism, "that is to say, Israel has still to be brought back, gathered home from exile."

Note that it is Israel herself who is speaking here and actually quoting what Yahweh has said. Thus Israel now confesses what God's purpose *in* her is beginning to mean to her. It begins with the reality that the glory of God is becoming apparent on earth. "The heavens declare the glory of God," Hebrew poets had already declared (Ps. 19:1). But the heavens show only the hem of his garment, DI adds. The heavens are dead matter, whereas Yahweh is the living God. DI therefore has to employ anthropomorphic language to express what it means to conceive of Yahweh in personal terms. To do so, he brings forward a great variety of active participles to describe the living God in action. He calls God creator, fashioner, potter, giver, spreader-out, refiner, redeemer, carrier, sitter, judge, bringer-forth, speaker, planner, opener, shutter, shouter, wiper-away. Such transitive, creative, purposive verbs describe the action, not primarily of One who made the heavens with all their beauty and majestic spread, but rather of One whose true glory can become visible only in human relationships. Moreover, those relationships are to be with Israel alone, not with any other. *That I might be honored in Yahweh's eyes* therefore means something like "that I might bear the glory of Yahweh as he reveals himself in action." [1] Such an interpretation of the first half of the line is upheld when it is seen in the light of the second and parallel half: *once my God had become my strength.* For God alone, not Israel, possesses strength, and his alone is the glory that is to be revealed on earth.

6.

He said. Note that "to me" is not required and is not stated. For what follows is a divine fiat for all the world to hear. Yet at the same time it is a repetition of the *declares Yahweh* of the previous parenthetic verse, in order to give sequence to the theme. Now follows mention of the two functions

[1] Many editors would place vs. 5*c* after vs. 3. But in this way they empty vs. 5 of its content. This is too facile a change and shows an unwillingness to wrestle with the text against its context.

assigned to the Servant Israel. (1) The Servant is to *reestablish the tribes of Jacob, . . . to restore those Israelites* who are at present *held* [*in exile*] in Babylon. But that is too easy a thing for the Servant to do, if he is the Servant of a plan that is intended to embrace the whole of humanity. (2) Therefore the Servant is to become *a light for the nations, so as to be my salvation* to the extremity of the earth.

DI would know the contents of Ezek. 37. There we find two distinct themes. First, says Ezekiel, God is about to resurrect the dead body of Israel, and to bring them out of their graves in the great Mesopotamian valley. He is about to breathe into their corpses his own life, as he did when he first created man (Gen. 2:7), and so this resurrection will become a new creation. Second, God's purpose in this resurrection is to work itself through all the twelve tribes of Israel and not just through Judah, that tribe which had retained the leadership of the Davidic line; it was to embrace even those tribes who had seemingly lost their identity almost two hundred years before. Thus Ezekiel looked for the promises of God, spoken as they were so long before to the patriarchs, to become flesh, so to speak, in a reconstituted Israel that was representatively the whole people of God. Here DI is speaking of the same great hope for all twelve tribes that Ezekiel had enunciated some years before in the ears of the exiles in Babylon.

Yet we are faced with a difficulty in interpretation. If Israel is the Servant, then how can Israel raise up Israel? Must not the Servant be identified with someone else who has a mission *to* Israel, but who is not Israel himself? It is clearly only a modern, individualistic reader of DI who would think in such terms and ask such questions. Till now we have been aware that the Servant in DI's sequential narrative has in every instance been a title given to Israel and to none other, except when in another respect it is used of the person of Cyrus. Again, vs. 6 follows in direct sequence from vs. 3, and there is the explicit sentence, *Thou art my Servant, Israel.* So the Servant here must still be Israel, difficult as that is to understand. The Servant must be the whole people of God as it is represented by the remnant (46:3).

However, when we recall that the NT conception of the Church is in continuity with the OT conception of the corporate personality of Israel, we find a clue to the puzzle of this verse. A local congregation may decide to hold a mission to its own people, for it has newly discovered a sense of responsibility for all those who dwell within its parish area. But the whole membership does not at once become the instrument of evangelism. It is the faithful few, the inner core, who are the first to become the vehicle of the Word to others. On the other hand, those others to whom the parish mission is being addressed will certainly regard themselves as Christians, for they have been baptized and confirmed and are to be found on the roll of church membership. Who then is to say that they are not as truly "Israel" as are the more self-consciously confessing group who are quite clearly Israel in the sense that DI is using here? What we have is the servant-group Israel seeking to reestablish and restore the whole servant-people Israel to their rightful place in the plan and purpose of God.

Then again, whenever a congregation regains its understanding of what it means to be the servant-people of God, it also regains its understanding of the world mission of the Church. It is too easy for any local congregation just to restore its lapsed and lost members; its greater task is *to be my salvation to the ends of the earth*. For without his Servant God cannot act. And so it is, even as the Servant witnesses by word and deed to God's salvation, the glory of God is revealed—not in the inanimate heavens, but in the active, fashioning, giving, spreading-out, carrying, refining, speaking manner in which living man can reflect the living actions of the living God.

A light for the nations is repeated from 42:6, and now its significance is made crystal clear. For since ch. 42, we have learned that it is God who forms the light, not man (45:7; cf. 60:3). Moreover, since *light* and *salvation* are set down in parallel, the one word illumines the meaning of the other. The God who forms light is light himself; and so he is salvation itself; or rather he is light in action; he is saving love in action. And yet, paradoxically, the salvation that DI speaks of can be conveyed to man only in the body of the Servant Israel (cf. Luke 2:32; Acts 13:47).[2]

Here we have Israel preserved in the dungeon and darkness of Babylon, "waiting for the consolation of Israel," to use the words of Luke 2:25 at this point. DI tells her three things about her present situation: (1) Her time of consolation or comfort has come (40:1-2). (2) God is now about to use her despite her state of rebellion, because he has forgiven all her sins. (3) God is now preparing to make use of her even while she suffers rejection in Babylon, and will do so in such a manner that her suffering

[2] Note that the Qumran community undoubtedly regarded themselves as this true, inner core of Israel in their day (circa 100 B.C.; Black, *op. cit.*, p. 129). Thus it is quite natural for some of the NT writers to adopt a similar exegesis of DI's lines with reference to the young Christian Church of which they were a part.

will become his instrument for the world's redemption. But as the reader is aware, DI leaves the development of this tremendous theme until a later chapter.

7 Thus says Yahweh, the Redeemer and Holy One of Israel,
To one heartily despised and abhorred by people,
to the servant of tyrants—
"Kings shall yet see, and stand up, princes too, and shall
then bow down,
For Yahweh's sake, the trustworthy One, the Holy One of Israel;
It is he who chose thee."

7.

DI left us at vs. 6 with a one-verse cameo of the Servant, now clearly portrayed as one who suffers. The words *to one heartily despised* are only one possible translation of the phrase, and much depends upon the interpretation of the words. The more study that has been given to the DSI text, the less willing are scholars, generally speaking, to believe that it can add much to our knowledge, yet here its reading seems to make better sense than the received Hebrew text. The word *heartily* is the Hebrew *nephesh,* person, soul, life, and many other things in English. So it could be translated, "despised of soul," by himself or by others. The LXX translators later on must have read "he who despises his own soul" (cf. 53:3). Yet a previously noted truth emerges again even from this difficult text. Once more we see that the Servant in himself is nothing. God is still all in all. On the other hand, the Servant is needed by God. What God needs is his obedience, and that alone. However, the servant Cyrus could give more than his obedience, unwitting as that was, for he offered God his strength and his many abilities both as a warrior and as a king. But Israel, we have learned, has neither strength nor native abilities to offer to her God. In consequence all that God wants and needs of her is an emptiness of self, for it is only then that God can reveal himself in her body (cf. Heb. 10:5). Nothing else can be its medium, for nothing else leaves room for it.

Yet, as the parallel passage at 52:15 *ff.* declares (cf. also 49:23; Ps. 72:10-11), the *tyrants* who now despise the Servant will eventually make obeisance to him in the abject manner customary at the period. But note that they will bow not to Israel but to the *Holy One of Israel,* who is now made manifest in and through the self-emptying of Israel. That is why

God, as the *trustworthy* or faithful *One,* can be relied upon to uphold his Servant at that moment when the Servant is no longer himself; for in despising his *nephesh,* the Servant is no longer clinging to his own ego. *It is he who chose thee* obviously points to the end in view, to which God's Servant is called.

8 Thus says Yahweh:
"It was at the moment I willed it that I answered thee:
At the day of salvation I aided thee.
I kept thee so as to make thee a covenant to people;
So as to reestablish the [scorched] earth and let desolate heritages be reinhabited;
9 Saying to the prisoners: 'Come out,' and to those in darkness: 'Show yourselves.'
Along [all] roads shall they feed, and even on all bare hilltops shall be their pasture.
10 They shall neither hunger nor thirst, neither shall the sirocco nor any heat wave smite them;
For he who pities them shall lead them,
And shall guide them to springs of water.
11 All my hills I shall make into roads, and my highways shall be built up.
12 Behold, these ones are returning from afar!
Behold, these others are coming from the north, and from the west, while still others are coming from the land of Sinim."

8.

Just as the NT can use the word *kairos* with reference to Christ and speak of his time as having "arrived" (cf. Matt. 26:18), so too DI can use the word *'eth.* Here it occurs as the emphatic first word of this new section. *Thus says Yahweh, "It was at the moment I willed it that I answered thee,"* almost "answered thy prayer." This line is a development of the news headline, as we have called it, with which DI opened his announcement of God's good news: *Speak to Jerusalem's heart . . . that her forced labor is ended, that the punishment due her for her iniquity has been accepted* (40:2). Now he goes on: *At the day of salvation I aided thee* (see 42-6). In fact, D day in God's plan has now arrived (cf. 54:8; 57:17; 61:2; Luke 22:53*b;* and Paul's quotation at II Cor. 6:2). Cyrus is pounding at the gate of Babylon—or proleptically he is just about to do so. "Now is the day of salvation; I have come to thine aid." God then has come to do two things in one. He has come (1) to save Israel; (2) to save her that she might become that covenant to people which he has proclaimed above (vs. 6), in order that the whole world might be saved.

But now DI takes a step farther. He knows with Hosea (cf. 2:1 *ff.*), Jeremiah (cf. 4:20-31), and the author of Gen. 3:16-19 and others, that natural disasters are bound up in some way with the fall of man. Evil is in fact no more static a thing than is goodness. We have seen that DI regarded goodness as the in-breaking of creative love within Israel's life. Israel's goodness thereby becomes the counterpart of God's goodness to her and is visible as acts of compassionate love. Goodness is thus inconceivable without either God or man as the instruments of good in action. So too in the case of evil, which cannot exist per se (cf. 45:7). For evil is the expression of the evil purposes of living beings. The prophets before DI's day, in looking forward to the day of redemption, saw the latter as the day when the evil in nature would be done away with as completely as the evil in the human heart—for God's universe is one *uni*-verse. Thus Amos can speak of the coming redemption of the cycle of nature (9:13), as Hosea also does a few years later (2:21-23), and as Isaiah does even more particularly when he promises the redemption of nature red in tooth and claw (11:6-9).

So as to reestablish the [*scorched*] *earth and let desolate heritages be reinhabited* thus points beyond the rebuilding of Jerusalem and the cities of Judah. There are those who limit the function of the Servant to the latter task, and who would read *earth* as "land" of Judah. But they are not seeing the passage in the light of DI's great heritage of thought. So he can say of the world: God *did not create it to be negation; he fashioned it for civilized life* (45:18), i.e., to be inhabited, not to lie in ruins. DI believes that this is a fallen world, and that it must therefore be raised up. That is, the earth must be *reestablished* according to God's initial purpose for it when he saw that it was good (Gen. 1). This will eventuate once the *tohu* with which it is riddled is reclaimed for order and *shalom* (45:7). Before proceeding further, note that Trito-Isaiah advances DI's argument still another step; for he sees the renewed people of God themselves bound up not just with a renewed nature, but with a new heaven and a new earth as well (65:17 *ff.*).

9.

The redemption *of* Israel is bound up with the redemption of others *through* Israel. But Israel though a corporate body is composed of individuals. Of course it is only individuals who can respond to God's call or can risk their lives rescuing prisoners from dungeons. We know that many Israelites did not respond to this challenge and never gave up the flesh pots of Babylon for the rigors of life in a ruined Jerusalem. They imagined perhaps that one can be saved apart from sharing in God's great saving purpose for his whole creation (cf. Matt. 16:25; 27:42). For the saving activity of God is visible only as we see men breaking down prison bars, or venturing into the dungeons beneath the public buildings of Babylon or Birmingham, there to meet with a stench and a filth that appalls. Yet without this human action God's purpose could not advance (cf. Matt. 25:35-36). On the other hand, God takes the initiative in love. The Good Shepherd, spoken of at 40:11, 29-31 promises that *along* [*all*] *roads shall they feed*, as they return to their Promised Land.

10, 11, 12.

So DI develops this theme once again as in ch. 40, and in a manner closely parallel to the passage we call Isa. 35, whose authorship it is hard to determine, and which some editors actually ascribe to DI. But now he sees the exiles returning not just from Babylon, but from every point of the compass. We need not dwell on determining where *Sinim* was. For no agreement has been reached whether DI meant Syene, which is Aswan in Upper Egypt (cf. Ezek. 29:10; 30:6), or the Sudan, or even an area of Eritrea. Probably DI did not know himself, nor was he concerned to know.[3] What mattered was that these people lived at the ends of the earth, and the redemption of Israel was to reach to the ends of the earth. That is a reality which has interested the author of the book of Revelation also much more than the geography of God's activities, as we can see when we read his beautiful development of DI's words at Rev. 7:16-17.

These last lines, let us note, speak of an action of God with which Cyrus and Babylon have nothing to do. DI has thus departed from an exposition of the immediate historical situation and has entered upon a broader theological discussion of what God's redemption of Israel means as a thing in itself. In doing so, however, he remains true to the biblical method of the presentation of truth. The prophets never discuss the meaning of concepts or of propositions. What they do is to expound the actions of God in and from historical situations. It is thus imperative for us to make sure we know all that we can know about Israel's history. On the one hand, DI

[3] *Sino*-Japanese War includes an English word built from *Sinim* in misunderstanding.

gives us no discussion of the concept of redemption. On the other, however, he expounds the historical situation in which he and his contemporary Israelites found themselves, even as Cyrus the Persian marched upon the city that held them captive.[4]

The significance of Cyrus' advance thus became existentially true for him as in turn his hopes rose and fell with the daily news; and anxiety, depression, hope, and certitude followed each other in the depths of his sensitive soul. But once the events had happened and become past history, and the interpretation he had made upon them had become definitive for him in his own mind, then that interpretation became normative for an interpretation of all similar acts on Yahweh's part. Salvation had now been expounded to his mind through an historical situation. Thus salvation had now become a theological concept about which it was possible to philosophize. But it was not a concept that had arisen through a dream put by God in the mind of a man, nor one arrived at after much cogitation or even by reading the works of one's predecessors; it was one arrived at existentially from knowing a historical moment from the inside. History never repeats itself. But incidents can become types, and these may aid the human mind to see the working of God in typical instances similar to the historical situation through which the prophet has lived. Moses had already interpreted the Exodus-Sinai series of events in this way, as DI knew, and had left his interpretation to posterity to study. DI accepts Moses' view, for he makes use of it as the basis of his own interpretation of what he perceived was to be a new exodus from the dungeons of Babylon.

With this in mind, we are able to recognize that DI was both a prophetic voice—and, as such, an interpreter of events to his contemporary exilic hearers—and also a theologian whose works will stand for all time. We might even call him a systematic theologian, for the interpretation which he gives to one single event, that of the redemption of the exiles by Cyrus, he generalizes upon and uses as a theological proposition that can apply to the exiled Hebrews even if they live in the land of the *Sinim*.

13 Shout for joy, you skies, exult, O earth!
Burst into singing, you hills!

[4] To suppose that Isaiah of Jerusalem wrote these chapters therefore is to reduce the biblical method of exposition to absurdity, for Isaiah was dead 150 years before Cyrus rose to power. If God gave Isaiah of Jerusalem the thoughts we read in chs. 40–55, then he gave them to him in the form of propositions apart from historical fact. But DI lived through these stirring events himself.

For Yahweh has comforted his people,
He shows compassion on his afflicted!

13.

This little, single-verse poem becomes a generalization from the actual incident of the fall of Babylon. Moreover, the significance of the incident has now become greater even than the redemption of all the Hebrews scattered amongst the nations. God's people, God's afflicted, are to be found, in point of time, both before and after this particular moment that is bound up with Cyrus the Persian; whereas in point of space, the reality of the redemption is now to obtain with respect to the whole cosmos. We dare not dismiss the call to the *earth* and the *skies* to shout for joy as just poetry. For the Hebrews employed poetry along with the parable as a vehicle to convey truth at those moments when no prose language could do so.

The words *his afflicted* force us to pause, however, and examine an important theological issue, one that is possibly the chief stumbling block at the heart of DI's exposition. How can God use, to serve his ends, a people who are *his afflicted* when it has been he who has afflicted them as punishment for their apostasy? How, in other words, can a sinful nation *be* the instrument of the Holy God's salvation of the rest of the world?

Israel had received from God special revelation in the form of Torah. This light had then had an effect upon her which she did not realize. In a negative sense, she had rejected and failed to use the light. Positively speaking, the light had blinded her eyes, stopped her ears, hardened her heart, so that her failure surpassed the sinfulness of any other nation on the earth (cf. Isa. 6:9-12). Yet God must have foreknown that this would happen. Was it fair of God to choose Israel at all, knowing as he would (1) that Israel would necessarily fail him, and (2) that his own light would blind her eyes and render her even more rebellious than she would have been without it?

The full judgment of the living God had now fallen upon Israel, and she had met with *just* retribution for her disloyalty. For she had failed not merely to be good, the position that all nations found themselves in; she had actually let God down as he sought to use her to save the world. Accordingly she bore the unspoken execration of all mankind as the nations of the earth dumbly sought for a salvation whose source they knew not. DI has spoken of the ugliness of sin. Now he has declared the judgment of the all-holy God upon it. For the Holy-One-of-Israel cannot tolerate union with a corrupt Israel. God must therefore reject her even when he never lets her go. So finally he did act, and Israel became what she is called here—*his afflicted*.

DI thus comes to the extraordinary conclusion that Israel had been chosen to become—that. She had been chosen to become the scapegoat required to carry the judgment of God upon the sins of the world. God had rendered her so by blinding her eyes still further. Instead of being accursed, for allowing her heart to grow hard, Israel was in fact the most highly privileged nation of all. Actually her hardness of heart was necessary for her election.

Yet we are to remember that Israel had not offered herself to be the scapegoat as if that had been her own good idea and the expression of her loyalty to the covenant. Israel was in fact quite unconscious of the uniqueness of her calling. For was she not just an ordinary, despondent prisoner-of-war, just a pariah people that had been conquered in war?

Here is where DI makes a contribution to our knowledge of the ways of God with men that is without precedent. What he does is to combine two realities which, humanly speaking, seem to be total opposites. In the first place, DI acknowledges Israel's rebellion, acknowledges that she is a worm, acknowledges that she has suffered justly for her sins. But he has kept asserting that even while she has been suffering justly, Yahweh has never let her go. In fact, he has been beside her in her sorrow and pain all the time. DI even dares to use the simile, following Hosea, of a loving husband sharing, even bearing, the pain that results from the folly of his wife's disloyal ways.

But in the second place, he asserts that the suffering undergone by Israel, which she has so richly deserved, God has accepted as if it were suffering voluntarily undergone on Israel's part. That is to say, God imputes to Israel the good intention she never had. God imputes to her the complete self-emptying, which she had to undergo when her *nephesh* was despised and abhorred by her conquerors. Thus in reality it is no longer she, the stiff-necked, proud, self-confident Israel of old with whom her God is dealing; all that man can now see is the mere broken body of Israel as it suffers the strokes of the lash of a terrible judgment. For Israel is no longer there, so to speak. Rather, the place where she had once been is now taken by the Word that dwells within her. For as a *nephesh* in her own right she is dead (42:6, 8; 43:2; 48:11; 49:3, 8). So her body is now merely the form through which the Word becomes flesh. Therefore it is the Word—a masculine noun in Hebrew—who has now borne the consequences of Israel's guilt, *in her place.* No wonder therefore the cry goes forth: *Shout for joy, you skies, exult, O earth! Burst into singing, you hills! For Yahweh has comforted his people, he shows compassion on his afflicted.*

14 Whereupon Zion replied, "Yahweh has abandoned me, my Husband has forgotten me."
15 Can a woman forget her breast-fed babe, and feel no compassion for the child of her womb?
Yes, women may forget this way—
But I shall never forget thee!
16 Behold, I have incised thee on [my own] two hands!
Thy walls are constantly before my eyes!
17 Those who shall rebuild thee will outstrip those who have been tearing thee down;
While those who have been laying thee waste shall depart from thee altogether.
18 Lift up thine eyes, and look around, and see!
They are all there, gathering together and coming to thee!
By my life (is Yahweh's utterance) [I declare] that thou shalt put them all on like ornaments, and wear them like a bridal crown.
19 [It is true] that *I* devastated thee and laid thee waste, and razed thee to the ground;
But now thou shalt be too confined for all thy inhabitants,
Once those who swallowed thee up shall have gone away.
20 Those children who were born in thy period of grasswidowhood will once again say in thine ears:
"The place is too small for me; move aside to make room for me to dwell."
21 Then shalt thou ask thyself: "Who fathered me all these?
For I was a grass widow and barren;
An exile and pushed aside. So these—who brought them up?
Behold, I was left alone all by myself—so where did these come from?"

14.

The humanity of Israel is clearly underlined in this verse. Here she is quite unable to appreciate and understand the wonder of the gospel that

DI is proclaiming to her about her God. In fact, all down the ages men have found the good news of God's love too good to be accepted as true (cf. 40:27). DI here calls Yahweh Israel's *Husband*. While the word normally means "Lord," *Yhwh,* yet both the OT words for Lord, viz., *'adhon* and *ba'al,* may be used for husband too.

15.

The remarkable metaphor that follows is DI's way of showing still another facet of Yahweh's special relationship to Israel. For here we learn of the mother love of God. The figure occurs a number of times in the OT and serves to balance the usual masculine image of the Almighty that men have held. However, if only the early Church had fed the ordinary believer faithfully with the truths of revelation as they are given us in the OT, as well as with those that come to us from the NT, the felt need for a mother image in the heavens would never have developed, and the Virgin Mary would not have been exalted to the position she now holds in the imagination and respect of many. In fact, the Virgin Mary is really the representative of the feminine figure of Zion, the people of God, of the OT. For it was Zion, the people of God, even as she humbly "waited for the consolation of Israel," whose body Yahweh used to be the temple of the Holy Spirit. At vs. 14 Zion has just spoken in the feminine singular of her heavenly Spouse. The pity and compassion in God's reply can be heard in the choice of the word *breast-fed babe*—for that is what poor, abandoned, helpless, ridiculous Israel obviously appeared in his sight. But now, how can the omniscient One forget (cf. Pss. 13:1; 77:9; Hos. 4:6)? *But I shall never forget thee* comes the emphatic reply—*thee* being in the feminine gender. Thus "thee" is no longer the Servant in the masculine; "thee" is now the beloved wife.

16.

Now we have a moving picture of divine grace. For it is not possible to conceive of grace in the abstract. The picture has been adapted from a practice with which Israel would meet in Babylon. Some of Israel's neighbors, including the Babylonians, were in the habit of tattooing the name of the god they worshiped upon their hand, in order to remind them to whom they belonged, and who was the controlling power in their lives. Similarly, Israel was called to witness to God's act in bringing her out of Egypt by wearing on her hand a reminder of that great event (Exod. 13:9). On that occasion God had been the sole actor. He had done everything for Israel, and all that Israel needed to do was just to accept in gratitude what he had done. But in this picture the tables are turned, so to speak, and we are given a picture of *God* showing Israel that he has her name inscribed not just on one but actually on both of his hands. Moreover, although the walls of Jerusalem are now lying flat on the ground, God declares that he sees them reerected, protecting the city that he has promised to keep forever as his own. This can only mean that the walls shall be built; what God sees cannot be a mirage, for God sees both the beginning and the outcome of every situation in every age.

17, 18.

God in fact now sees feverish activity in progress as Zion's sons work faster at rebuilding the city than her enemies are able to destroy it (cf. Neh. 6), and all marauding desert nomads vanish in the mist. Back to their predestined home come all the sons of Mother Zion from every corner of the earth—and so not only from Babylon, as we saw before. And then comes a heartening declaration from the lips of Zion's God. Beautiful as her walls and buildings may be, Zion's real wealth and beauty reside rather in her—and God's—sons and daughters. Unlike Queen Babylon who will soon be mourning the loss of her sons, Queen Zion, when the marriage is later renewed, as the bride of God, will possess all the children she desires (cf. Gen. 22:17). And while Queen Babylon will be putting on widow's weeds, Queen Zion will be attiring herself with the glory of her sons.[5]

DI may however be saying the same as 60:4. We should examine his words in the light of what he has said before (cf. 44:5), though he is not wholly explicit on the matter. For Mother Zion here seems to be surprised at seeing some of her new children, and evidently does not recognize how she came by so many. Moreover, it is unlikely that Jews were at that time living in the very far-off land of Sinim (vs. 12). The DSI actually reads "the people of Sinim," from whom also "sons" will return to Zion, as if it were expecting not just Jews but gentiles to come home to God. This scroll seems to be interpreting DI aright, and agrees with what Paul had in mind when he insisted that there is only one Israel of God, one original stock, into which the believing gentile is grafted by baptism (Rom. 11:17-32; I Cor. 10:18).

[5] Note that Trito-Isaiah quotes this verse (60:4), but he adds to the returning sons and daughters of Israel representatives of all nations of the earth, for they too will be among God's sons returning home to Zion.

19, 20.

The same God who had *laid thee waste* was now, beyond the death of Zion, bringing new life abundant to the city he had chosen. It is true that for a time God had had to put away his bride, Mother Zion (cf. Hos. 1–3; Ezek. 16), because she was unclean; she had consorted with other lovers and had given her loyalty elsewhere. But God had long since sworn to give his glory to no other than his faithless bride.

21.

Now that she had been forgiven therefore, one of the joys of setting up house again which Yahweh granted her was wondering where all her children had come from. So long as she remained an exile in Babylon she had not been in physical contact with Yahweh her Husband—for the temple, where Yahweh had put his name to dwell, was then in ruins. Without a Husband, who could have sired her with all these children? The only answer is that they must have been born of grace (vs. 15), the grace of a Husband's love that had remained unchanged throughout the whole long period that she believed herself to be barren and a grass widow in exile.

How daring this figure appears to us, with our Western conceptions of delicacy in matters of sex. Yet no figure conceived in an Eastern mind could express more movingly the reality of grace, the grace that becomes worded explicitly in the annunciation narratives of Luke's Gospel. Moreover the figure unashamedly includes both *agape* and *eros* in the love of God for Israel; and so if DI believes that both concepts are needed to expound the love of God, then there is no reason for us to be ashamed to make the identification too.

22 Thus says the Lord God:
Behold, I have only to beckon to the nations,
Or raise my signal to the peoples,
And they would fetch thy sons in their bosom,
And carry thy daughters on their shoulders.
23 Then kings would become thy guardians, and their queens thy foster mothers;
They would prostrate themselves before thee with their faces to the ground,
And lick the dust of thy feet.
Then wouldst thou know that I am Yahweh.
Those who wait for him shall never be ashamed.

22.

Nothing now can stop the outworking of God's *ʿetsah,* or plan. DI here refers to a daring saying of Moses as the latter expostulates to God: "Have I conceived all this people? Have I begotten them, that thou shouldst say unto me, 'Carry them in thy bosom, as a nursing father beareth the sucking child?' " (Num. 11:12.)

23.

In fact DI's language could easily be and has often been misconstrued. His expression: *They would prostrate themselves before thee with their faces to the ground, and lick the dust of thy feet* has led expositors to exclaim with disgust that what is portrayed here is a highly undesirable trait in the nature of the chosen people. But this is to misunderstand the *ʿetsah* of God. In Israel's total obedience and self-emptying, the nations would not see Israel, for Israel's *nephesh* would have been emptied out; they would see Yahweh *in* Israel, for there is no other possible way of seeing God or even the glory of God. Thus were the nations to *lick the dust of thy feet*—"thy" is still feminine. We are given a vision of the nations of men, in typically Eastern language, bowing down and prostrating themselves before not Israel but God-in-Israel. *Then wouldst thou* (Israel, feminine) *know that I am Yahweh.* He is the God, as the whole world will one day discover, who will never let any *who wait for him be ashamed.*

24 Can a warrior's booty be taken away from him?
Or can a tyrant's captives ever be rescued?
25 Surely, says Yahweh:
Yes, a warrior's captives can be rescued,
And a tyrant's booty recovered.
But when I contend with thine adversaries,
Surely I can save thy sons.
26 In fact, I could make those who oppress thee eat their own flesh,
And they could be drunk with their own blood as if it were sweet wine.
Then would all flesh realize that I, Yahweh, am thy Savior and Redeemer, Jacob's Mighty One.

24, 25, 26.

DI now allays a final doubt that Yahweh may not be strong enough to effect his purpose amongst men. Yahweh, he says, is surely stronger than any human dictator, for he has made them all (45:9). In fact, he *could* effect the terrible picture drawn in vs. 26; and yet even if he were to do these things, they would represent even less than justice for the evil in the thoughts and plans of the nations. For God, being the living, active God, must do something, no matter how shocking that something may be. *Then would all flesh realize that I, Yahweh, am . . . Jacob's Mighty One* (*'abhir*). This last word is the old poetic name for Yahweh that Isaiah of Jerusalem had used (1:24), and which was employed by the narrator of Jacob's story in Genesis (Gen. 49:24; cf. Ps. 132:2, 5). It was discussed at 46:12. By using this word *'abhir,* DI is declaring that God's purpose and plan, now about to be revealed to the nations, are rooted in the far distant past of the patriarchal period, even before *Heilsgeschichte* began. But *'abhir* seems to be but a variant of *'abbir.* This word means "bull" or "violent" when applied to men. Now the king of Assyria had been such (Isa. 10:12-13), and Israel knew what had happened to this Nebuchadrezzar, who once had been known as king of kings and lord of lords. The tradition of his fate is preserved in Dan. 4:28 *ff*. For if left to its own devices evil finally will *eat its own flesh* and fall down in the stupor of death as it drinks its *own blood.* Even Yahweh could of course behave as Nebuchadrezzar had behaved, for Yahweh is the *'abhir* par excellence, the *Mighty One* of Jacob. But Almighty Yahweh has chosen a wholly different way to effect his purpose on the earth.

CHAPTER 50

1 **Thus says Yahweh:**
"Where is your mother's divorce certificate with which
I dismissed her?
Or which one of my creditors did I sell you to?
Behold, it was for your own iniquities you were sold;
it was for your own transgressions that your mother
was sent away.
2 **Why was it that when I came in to her, no one was there;**
when I called, no one answered?
[Do you really think] my hand is too short to redeem,
or that I have not the strength to rescue?
Look! If I were to rebuke the sea I could dry it up!
I could turn rivers into a wilderness!
So that the fish in them would stink for lack of water,
or simply die of thirst.
3 **I could clothe the heavens with blackness,**
and make them wear sackcloth for a covering!"

1.

These chapter divisions are of course artificial. DI is here proceeding with the question of the estrangement between Mother Zion and her Husband which occupied his attention in the previous chapter. What God is saying here to Zion's children—in the plural—is this: "I didn't *divorce* your mother (when I sent 'Zion' into exile), and the proof of that is that she can show no certificate to that effect." Such a certificate was necessary by the Law of Moses (Deut. 24:1-4; cf. Jer. 3:8, where the Northern Kingdom is given such a certificate, but not Zion). Within Israel it was only the husband who could divorce his wife. All that the woman could do was to be unfaithful. No divorce therefore became legal unless the husband presented his wife with such a certificate. "I had to deal with you in some way for your unfaithfulness," God explains. "It was not that I was bankrupt of love. Yet I had to make a plan. My plan was to allow you to leave home, and so to let you suffer a just punishment (40:2) for your unfaithfulness; but I vowed to have you back thereafter." "Selling to creditors" is a figure of speech for giving into the power of a conqueror (cf. Judg. 2:14; Deut. 32:30).

2.

What Zion did not realize when she went whoring after other lovers (cf. Hos. 1–3) was how much she hurt her Lord by doing so. In love he *came in to her,* but she had gone; when he *called, no one answered.* In this one line we are shown the pathos of the empty home, the loneliness of God's heart, the pain at the center of the universe. Yet at the moment we get only a glimpse of that pain, for here is only a foretaste of a later theme. Instead, God asks at this point whether Israel does not realize that, being the Almighty, he could compel his wife to return home to him if he so decided. The Almighty could do anything. He *could dry up the sea,* and thus reverse the order of creation (Gen. 1:9). He *could turn rivers into a wilderness,* leaving death and devastation behind him.

3.

He could even produce the *blackness* of chaos and thus reverse his gracious purpose of creative redemption. But that way of redeeming the world is unthinkable. For God is not like that. His method is to use a Servant who is wholly dedicated to his mission.

4 The Lord God has given me a tongue such as
disciples have,
That I may know how to prophesy to the weary a word
that will waken them up.
Day after day he wakes my ear,
So as to hear as disciples (hear).
5 The Lord God has opened my ear.
For my part, I was never refractory, nor did I ever
turn round and run away.
6 My back I even offered to bullies,
And my cheeks I even turned to those who pluck
out beards.
I have never hidden my face from shame or spitting.

4.

This ideal, wholly dedicated Servant now speaks. And his first word is Yahweh, not self, and his second is *has given*. The Servant thus witnesses to Yahweh alone and to his acts of grace. *A tongue such as disciples have* reveals that the speaker is aware of his need to learn, and has the humility to confess that need. This word for *disciples* occurs substantivally only in the book of Isaiah. Its first occurrence is at 8:16-17. There the prophet Isaiah of Jerusalem declares: "Bind up the testimony, seal the teaching among my disciples. I will wait for the Lord, who is hiding his face from the house of Jacob, and I will hope in him." (RSV.) Then the word does not occur again until here, except for two occurrences in Jeremiah, where it is virtually an adjective, and where it must be translated by "trained" or "accustomed." Buber suggests that Isaiah of Jerusalem really coined a new and special term in this word, and sought to demonstrate by means of it that it was his own *disciples* who were eventually to be "the remnant that shall return" (Isa. 10:21). Napier follows Buber in proposing that Isaiah evidently did not think that the time was then opportune for the full-scale prophetic Word of redemption to enter into the life of Israel. That was why he had to seal it among his disciples until God's good time. Both scholars suggest that DI believed himself to be the second Isaiah, and as such authorized by God to declare that the time had come at last when the seal could be broken. If this is so, then DI believed that the seed of Isaiah's disciples was now to be identified with the whole (remnant) Servant people of God; for, as he declares later at 54:13, "All thy sons shall be Yahweh's disciples." This time again, and for the last time, he uses this strange word *limmudhim.*

However, the Servant does not learn merely for the sake of learning, but in order to *know how to prophesy to*—or possibly "help"—*the weary a word that will waken them up,* that is, arouse them from the sleep of death. For the Servant has learned from Yahweh, learning it in fact day after day, to be compassionate towards his *weary* fellow men to the point of searching out those who are sleeping the sleep of death.

5.

Once again the Servant emphasizes that *the Lord God* is doing this, not he. His task could possibly have rendered him *refractory,* or frightened him enough to make him *run away;* but he had withstood the temptation.

6.

Far from taking this ignominious course, the Servant had actually tried a new thing in the face of the world's violence—obviously again as taught by Yahweh. The vast majority of peoples at all ages of the world have known only one answer to the problem of commanding obedience—strike your servant and compel him to obey. However, this Servant had learned from Yahweh neither to run away nor to rebel, nor even to hit back, but instead to offer his back to the *bullies,* the average men. The most telling insult that the East could perpetrate on one whom the average man sought to insult and so to render inferior, or to put him in his place, was to pluck the hairs from his *beard* (cf. Neh. 13:25). But the Servant had now learned to turn the other cheek. He had never even tried to escape from the shame and spitting (cf. Num. 12:14; Deut. 25:9; Matt. 26:67) of a world that could only show its inverted inferiority complex by mean and ugly acts—instead he quietly accepted them. Why did he do all this? We are not told as yet. DI's brilliant psychological understanding of his reader's mind prompts him to withhold that secret till the great denouement that he plans for later on.

Now how did DI conceive of this extraordinary new approach to the problem of man's inhumanity to man? Of course it is utterly new. He did not find it in the Tammuz ideology that some expositors have adduced. One of a vast concourse, he may well have stood and watched as the Babylonian high priest ceremonially struck his monarch on the face. The latter then symbolically fell dead. For the king of course had to die and be raised to life again, for such an act of sympathetic magic would make the world of nature come alive again with the advent of the autumn rains. Though such a ceremony was undoubtedly a very ancient one among the Canaanite peoples, we are not as certain today as scholars were a generation ago that the king in Babylon ever underwent such an indignity.[1] But if he did, he accepted it as a staged ceremonial act, knowing that the eyes of all men were upon him—DI's eyes included perhaps. This act may indeed have set our prophet thinking and reasoning. But DI's portrait here of the servant as he humbly accepts the obloquy of a vicious-minded humanity belongs in the sphere of divine revelation—for no human being had ever yet consistently acted in this way since the world began.

How then are we to understand this portrait of the perfectly obedient

[1] See ANET, p. 334, col. 1.

Servant—who, let us note, is *not* named Israel here—if we compare it with that of the diffident and sinful Servant that DI has already portrayed Israel to be? The key to this question must lie in the method DI uses to unlock the secret of his message only step by step. At 49:16 he proffered one of his hints on the important theme he will develop later. At 49:14 we heard the empirical Israel speaking: *Yahweh has abandoned me, my Husband has forgotten me.* But at 49:16 God replied to Israel's whining complaint. That reply assured doubting Israel that he retains before his mind's eye the vision of his beloved Zion not as she is now but as she shall be in his sight in the days to come. This is DI's manner of affirming confidently that the Servant can yet become God's perfectly humble and self-emptying Servant that Israel was called in the beginning to be, and that the basis of this realization is no less than the intention of God himself. God knows the end from the beginning. God sees Israel in the future become the perfect Servant, because he has said that she shall be. Therefore she shall be what God sees she shall be. Reality, we recognize, is to be adjudged and interpreted on the basis of the Word of God alone.

7 The Lord God helps me, that is how I
have never been confounded;
That is how I could set my face like flint, and
know that I shall never be shamed.
8 My Advocate is beside me; who would dare enter a
suit against me? Let us take our stance together!
Who is my adversary? Let him approach me!
9 Behold the Lord God is helping me—who is he
that would convict me?
Behold, they will all wear out like a garment; moths
will eat them up.

7.

We are not told *why* the Servant acts this way—except that Yahweh had taught him so—but we are now told *how* he can face the pain and obloquy spoken of in vs. 6. He can do so because *the Lord God helps me, that is how I have never been confounded; that is how I could set my face like flint, and know that I shall never be shamed. Shamed* or "let down" by Yahweh! The speaker knows that he is the Servant of a God who will be wholly loyal to him and to this method of meeting evil. How silly it is even to suggest that Yahweh could ever let the fish stink in the sea as a means of redeeming the world, or turn the light into darkness and so reduce the world to chaos (vss. 2-3).

8, 9.

Yahweh is in fact *with* his Servant in a very potent manner. He stands beside him as his *Advocate* in court. What *adversary* dares come forward to take legal action now? As Paul says in another context with regard to the Christian man: "If God be for us, who can be against us? . . . Who shall lay anything to the charge of God's elect? It is God that justifieth. Who is he that condemneth?" (Rom. 8:31, 33-34). It would take the accusers so long to stand and make their case that they would *wear out like a garment*. Moreover, this vivid analogy is introduced by "behold," in the typical biblical manner. It is the genius of the Bible to pictorialize theological issues, for ordinary men can grasp these only when they can see them in a mental picture.

Now a new picture of the Servant is building up. At vs. 5 we saw that he could be God's completely willing Servant. But as such his obedience is not to be construed as merely passive. His response to evil is that of God himself, viz., positive and recreative. Vs. 7 confirmed this view, for here we read that with God's help he is able actively to turn the other cheek toward wicked men. Finally at vs. 9 we discover that the Servant's secret is an inner spring of joy and assurance, for he possesses an unshakeable faith. He can trust God about the unknown future on the ground that he has discovered that Yahweh is wholly reliable in the here and now.

10 Which of you fears Yahweh? If so, let him obey his Servant's voice.
He who has walked in darkness, and possesses no shining light,
Let him trust in Yahweh's name, and so [learn to] lean upon his God.

10.

Because of his total obedience, the servant actually empties out his own self. In this way he leaves room for God to act through him without any block or hindrance. He who *fears Yahweh*—the most representative OT expression for our modern phrase "being religious"—now has the chance to know Yahweh's will. This is because Yahweh's will has materialized, so to speak, in *his Servant's voice*. In obeying the Servant, the God-fearer will now find himself leaning *upon his God,* directly! In obeying the *Servant's voice,* he will *trust* not in the Servant but *in Yahweh's name.*

Both Yahweh and the Servant are here spoken of in the third person. This verse is therefore DI's own note appended to the direct speech of the Servant that precedes it. In this note, moreover, he makes an extraordinary equation: The voice (i.e., words) of the Servant *is* the Word of God; he who obeys the voice of the Servant finds himself leaning upon—*God.* The Servant thus enables those who walk in darkness and have no light of their own (cf. vs. 11) to find their way to God who is the light himself (cf. Isa. 9:2), there to *lean* on him in utter dependence. This word of DI's is therefore much more than a historical note about the Israelites in the darkness of Babylonian prisons (cf. 49:25). It is a theological utterance, based indeed upon the contemporary historical situation, but one which thereafter has repercussions throughout the whole of the biblical revelation.

11 Behold, all you who kindle fires, you who equip
yourselves with brands of your own,
Depart into the furnace of your own fire, and to the
brands you have kindled!
From my hand this then will happen to you:
You will lie down in torment!

11.

Finally DI turns and addresses the pagan world, Babylonians and all others. Probably he includes even the Persians because of their interest in fire worship. How stupid it is to worship a fire which you yourselves have kindled, he says (cf. 44:16). For Yahweh is the true light, and so Yahweh is the source of all fire, not Ahura Mazda nor any other. DI thus connects the concept of the true light available to those who trust in Yahweh (vs. 10) with a terrible reality also connected with light and fire. That reality is that fire destroys as well as gives light. DI is therefore saying to the heathen world the kind of thing that we today might put in proverbs, such as, "He who plays with fire will get burned"; "Be sure your sin will find you out." There is a law of life that ensures that in the end evil devours those who worship it. And if it is in fact a law of life, then it comes from God. This truth DI now expresses pictorially. For along with Isaiah his predecessor, DI knows that it is *God* who is the real furnace, so that to enter the fire is to meet with God (Isa. 30:33; 31:9; 42:25; 47:14; 66:24).

If men *depart into the furnace* which they themselves have lit, they are walking into what is no less than the judgment of the living God. But if a man walks in the light of the true God, he learns something very different; for as the psalmist says, "In thy light do we see light" (Ps. 36:9 RSV; Isa. 10:17). On the other hand, the guiding light of God and the fire of the wrath of God naturally cannot be dissociated one from the other, for they are one and the same reality. This is because there is one God, and it is he who creates both light and darkness, both peace and evil (45:7). Suddenly DI passionately utters the words of the living God himself: *From my hand this then will happen to you: You will lie down in torment!*

The doctrine of hell is just as integral to the Old Testament revelation as it is to the new. For the God of whom Paul can say, "Do not be deceived; God is not mocked: for whatever a man soweth, that he will also reap" (Gal. 6:7 RSV), is the same God whom DI came to know and trust in the days of the Babylonian exile, and whom he found to be both light and fire at once.

CHAPTER 51

1 **Listen to me, you who pursue [God's] saving righteousness,**
who seek after Yahweh,
Turn your gaze upon the rock whence you were hewn,
and upon the quarry from which you were digged.
2 **Turn your gaze upon Abraham your father, and upon**
Sarah who bore you.
For when he was only one I called him, and I blessed
him and made him many.
3 **[Realize that] Yahweh has comforted Zion, that he has**
comforted all her ruins.
He has made her wilderness like Eden, and her desert
like Yahweh's garden.
Joy and rejoicing shall be found in her, thanksgiving
and the sound of music.

1.

Before this point DI has made two opposing statements. First, he has shown that Israel, called to be Yahweh's Servant, has signally failed in her calling. But second, he has outlined what the calling of the Servant could be; and so he has pictured for us the perfect Servant, that is, one who is wholly obedient to the will of God. Here he reconciles these two disparate statements in a remarkable manner. For he now calls upon the actual, empirical, historical, wholly sinful Israel, composed of the exiles in Babylon, to trust and believe in God as Abraham did of old. Obviously Yahweh intends to accept sinful Israel's act of faith, and through her faith to impute to her the power really to be the Servant, even though she is far from being like the ideal picture that DI has drawn.

Abraham was an individual. It is only individuals who can believe. So

God here doesn't address Israel as he has been doing till now in the singular feminine, regarding her as a corporate personality; now he addresses her in the plural. For Israel is also an aggregation of individuals. He accepts these individuals as purposeful personalities, as *you who pursue* [God's] *saving righteousness, who seek after Yahweh.* Did they really believe thus in God? However, such a divine utterance gives us the real secret of faith. Israel in exile has faith in Yahweh only because Yahweh first has faith in Israel. It is Yahweh's faithfulness, not man's faith, which is the basis of the hope of Israel. DI makes this clear by quoting what must have been a well-known metaphor, since it also occurs in the song of Moses (Deut. 32:4). He does so of course by way of illustration, not to make etymologists of his readers. There, as elsewhere throughout the Bible, God alone is the rock. The Rock is not the faith of DI, nor even that of Peter (cf. Matt. 16:18), nor of anyone else. The verb "to believe," *he'emin,* basically means to find oneself standing on something secure or, to pictorialize it, to find that one's feet are upon the Rock. Some of the Jewish exegetes of the early Christian centuries did not realize the truth of this metaphor as it is portrayed in Deut. 32:4, 30 and Ps. 18:2, nor did they notice that DI is here quoting Deut. 32:18 directly. For they discuss whether Abraham was the rock that DI mentions. In the same way, in the case of the seminal NT passage, Matt. 16:18, some exegetes have supposed that Peter and not God was the rock. But Abraham's faith in God was derived only from God's faith in Abraham. Having taken his stand upon God, Abraham shows his faith as simple obedience; he knows that a servant must obey (cf. Gen. 26:5). For the words of Gen. 15:6, quoted by Paul at Rom. 4:3, "And he believed in Yahweh, and he counted it to him for righteousness," mean literally, "And he found himself firm upon Yahweh, and he counted it to him as saving activity." We discussed the meaning of this last word at 45:8. That is to say, when Abraham found himself standing upon the Rock, God imputed to him the power to become a rock to others (cf. Isa. 32:2). He had pursued *tsedheq,* [God's] *saving righteousness,* and had been rewarded with the power to display *tsedhaqah,* compassionate concern for his fellow men. This at least is how DI understood the words of Gen. 15:6.

2.

Israel then is summoned to turn her gaze upon God, who is the sole ground of her faith and her very existence. But she must also look back upon the derived faith of Abraham, who was one and alone when God initially *called* him to faith. The potency of the ancient blessing is here accepted as a natural experience. A blessing was a word uttered with intent; it was quite unrelated to mere idle chatter that was of no consequence. How much more effective must be the blessing of Almighty God. The DSI misses this point, for it alters the word "bless" to "make fruitful." It concerns itself only with the fact that Abraham's descendants had indeed multiplied in number (cf. Exod. 1:7, 19; Ezek. 33:24). But this took place only as the outcome of the blessing that followed upon Abraham's taking his stand upon the Rock (Gen. 12:2-3).

DI mentions Sarah, the only time her name occurs outside of Genesis. Gen. 12 has nothing to say about Sarah's faith, only about Abraham's. Yet as we read the Genesis sagas we find that Sarah, who had no visionary experience such as Abraham had, sets off from Haran with her husband to go to the land of promise. DI did not need to mention Sarah at all even to provide himself with a poetic parallel; another patriarch would have done for that. Then why did he draw attention to her at all? Evidently for two reasons:

1. Despite the fact that Abraham was *one* when he received his call, he was not one in the mathematical sense of the word. "One, and all alone," "only," "unique" are all the word *yaḥidh* in Hebrew, as we saw at 44:6. That is the word which is used later in Genesis for Abraham's one and only son (22:2). But the word that is here used for "one" is that employed for the oneness of husband and wife together, also found in Genesis at 2:24. The Bible does not seem to reckon with the idea of mere individuality in the modern sense. A man in OT times is always one with his tribe, his family, his wife, his children, and even his slaves and possessions. These all reflect his personality as he does theirs. Abraham would not have been the Abraham that we—and God—knew if he had not had Sarah for his wife. Without her he would have developed a different personality. His faith, DI implies, was dependent on the kind of wife he had, for he was one flesh with her in trust and love. Sarah as an individual does not need to make the decision to travel, for she makes it *in* Abraham's decision. Her part in their joint act of faith is the expression of "loyalty-in-love." This hyphenated concept represents the word *ḥesedh*, which Hosea before DI's day had stressed in his own existential decision to continue in loyal love with his apostate wife.

2. The second reason for mentioning Sarah is this: Sarah, the *quarry from which you were digged*, was a barren womb. It was a miracle of God that

she bore a son at all. DI wants us to recognize that what God has done once he can naturally do again. He can raise Israel up out of the womb of death, for new life can spring forth for Israel now in Babylon as truly as new life once came from Sarah's womb.

3.

Yahweh is doing for Zion now what he did originally for Abraham, Zion's progenitor. He kept his promise to Abraham despite all appearances to the contrary. DI here returns to the feminine singular and ceases to address Israel in the plural as "you." He must therefore be emphasizing once again how all Israel is truly one, in the same sense as Abraham was one with Sarah, and even with Lot, and with "all the souls that they had gotten in Haran" (Gen. 12:5). At that time Yahweh had accepted Abraham as his servant and friend (41:8). Now he was accepting Zion in the same way. He was comforting and forgiving her—as DI began by saying at 40:1-2—and was imputing to her his own quality of being rock to others (cf. 49:6), a quality which was certainly not inherent in Israel herself. So the contrast between the one and the many in the person of Abraham, showing him to be an individual and a corporate personality at one and the same time, is DI's approach to the problem of the personality of the Servant also. Therefore his allusion to Abraham here is important for our understanding of the Servant concept later when the issue is more fully developed.

Before he develops this theme, however, DI opens a door to the cosmic hope that his great predecessor Isaiah also held (cf. 11:6-9). This hope is that the end of Yahweh's plan through his Servant is much more than just the redemption of individual men. DI looks for the redemption of this whole fallen universe, and in saying so in lyrical vein he again uses the language of that great passage, Isa. 35, which may or may not be attributable to him. That is to say, he uses the mythology connected with the concept of the return of the Garden of Eden or paradise regained. It was a very widely held theme in the ancient Fertile Crescent. The prophets took it over, but they used it to serve a theological not a cosmogonic end.

This end DI refers to several times (cf. 41:17-20; 42:14-17; 43:16-21; 55:12-13). It is like what the NT calls the *anakephalaiosis ton panton*, the recapitulation of all things; for DI sees it as the return of the Garden of Eden, or the reestablishment of the garden of the Lord (Gen. 13:10) with which the world began. But Gen. 2, in contrast to Gen. 13:10, speaks of the garden not as that of the Lord but as God's home for man. Now it was Zion in particular that was this special abode, for Zion was God's home for his chosen Servant. We found at 47:8 that Babylon in contrast to Zion is given the adjective *'adhinah,* "voluptuous," which is a feminine form of this same word *eden.* DI may have thought of Babylon as Eden after the fall of Eve. But DI is soon to describe Zion in terms of the Garden of Eden restored (54:11-14), in the manner that Ezekiel speaks of his Eden (28:12 *ff.*), even though the latter is understood differently in the tradition that Ezekiel uses. DI may well have known all these various meanings of Eden. His recapitulation that is to come at the end of God's plan, however, is expressed in terms of the reversal of the concept of *wilderness,* which is one of Israel's pictorial terms for chaos, so he portrays the end in terms of *shalom* or peace. Here the words *her wilderness* mean virtually "she who has become a wilderness," or "she who is living in a spiritual state describable in terms of wilderness," and likewise in the case of the word *her desert.*

4 Hearken, my people, and give ear to me, my nation:
[I declare] that Torah shall go forth from me, and my revealed way of life shall become the peoples' light.
5 I shall cause my saving activity suddenly to flash near;
My salvation is about to go forth [like light],
when my arms shall rule the peoples.
The isles are looking to me in hope! They are eagerly awaiting my arm!
6 Lift up your eyes to the heavens, and turn your gaze on the earth beneath.
The heavens have actually dissipated like smoke.
The earth is disintegrating like a garment.
Its inhabitants are dying like gnats.
But my salvation shall continue forever, and my saving activity shall never be dismayed.
7 Listen to me, you who have experienced [my] saving activity,
The people in whose heart is my Torah:
Do not be afraid at human reproaches, nor dismayed when they revile you.
8 For moths shall devour them like a garment, and grubs eat them up like wool.
But my saving activity will continue [in you] forever,
and my salvation [working in you] to all generations.

4.

This explicit universalism (cf. 54:5), this ultimate redemption of the whole cosmos, was dependent upon something about to happen at that moment in history. DI pinned down the moment to the events of 539 B.C. This whole cosmic movement was dependent on Israel's giving *ear* to Yahweh. Such a little act of obedience, at such an obscure moment in the obscure history of an obscure *people!* And yet in the providence of God that little act of obedience meant that God could act for the salvation of the world. Without it, God could not act, as he could not act without the faith of Abraham. Torah is the revelation that was given in the days of Moses, and that subsequently evolved into what we today wrongly call the law of Moses. For the noun *torah* comes from the word "to teach." DI, with all the prophets, used the word as a technical term for the revealed knowledge of God delivered to Israel in the form of instructions on how to live together as the people of God in obedience to his will. Through Israel's obedience, Torah will go forth "from within God" (as the Hebrew says), not from Israel; for Israel is the mere pied-à-terre where the glory of God will be revealed (49:3). The double Hebrew preposition "from with," in connection with Torah, is reminiscent of the language used to describe the relationship between wisdom and God in Prov. 8, and between the creative Word of God and God himself in Genesis and John (Gen. 1:3; John 1:1-3).

Parallel with God's Torah, his *mishpaṭ*, his "way of life," *shall become the peoples' light*. This is the language of 49:6 once again. *Mishpaṭ* has already been defined as "true religion" or, better still, as "total way of life" (see commentary at 42:1). For since *mishpaṭ* is paralleled in this line by Torah, DI must intend these two nouns to complement each other. It is interesting that God's *mishpaṭ* can be expressed only in and through Israel's life and obedience. DI sees therefore that Israel is more than the pied-à-terre God will use on earth. Israel has actually become the body which the Torah and *mishpaṭ* of God occupy while the process develops as the Word becomes incarnate before the eyes of the gentiles.

5.

God is about to act at any moment (cf. 46:13), as DI knew. For DI was convinced that Cyrus' capture of Babylon, obviously now only a matter of days away, was the historical moment that God would use for his own mighty ends. Not that God would confine himself to that relatively unimportant historical incident. DI thought of God's use of the fall of

Babylon in terms that we today can best understand as a chain reaction. The capture of Babylon by Cyrus was not *all* that Yahweh planned to do. The first effect of the fall of the city would be the rescue of the exiles. But then the rescue of the exiles would initiate a new understanding by Israel of the ways of God with man. That new understanding would thereupon interpret the suffering which Israel had newly undergone. Israel would then give herself in *saving activity* for her neighbors till the redemption of all *the peoples,* and, till the redemption even of the cosmos would finally be reached. Yet it was all to begin like a *flash* of lightning or, to use our idiom, like an atomic reactor's first explosion. *Rule* is the verb connected with the noun *mishpaṭ* and thus means something like "rule with the application of that justice which will regulate the whole of life." It is most interesting to recognize that DI evidently believed in their heart of hearts all men, even in the chaos and turmoil of their short and brutish lives, desire above all else the revelation—*arm*—of the living God.

6.

It is a mistake to imagine that apocalyptic imagery is only a late phenomenon in Israel's story. The preexilic prophets used it; DI does here too. The sentence *the heavens have actually dissipated like smoke* uses the perfect of the verb to show completed action; for to the mind of the poet the event is actually happening before his eyes.[1] This verbal form is known as the prophetic perfect, for it is used when the prophet is utterly sure that what he is declaring will come to pass.

The emphasis of this apocalyptic picture, however, is not on what we today would call the end of the world. It is upon the contrast between the transiency of this world, with man upon it, and the everlastingness of God's continual saving activities. Neither the Exodus in the past nor the return of the exiles in Cyrus' day is to be the climax of God's saving purpose. That purpose is to *continue* forever,[2] just as God's Word endures forever (40:8). God's saving love does not reach an end when we come to that moment which we call the end of the world. God's saving love must continue with him to all eternity.

7.

After such a tremendous utterance, how ridiculous it is for Israel, with God's Torah in her heart and actually knowing what God's saving activity

[1] In the OT God does not, of course, dwell in heaven. He sits above the heavens. Heaven is as much part of creation as is earth, and will pass away at the end just as the earth will pass away.

[2] The verb *hayah* normally means not "to be" but rather "to become," "to endure."

is—for Israel has already *experienced* salvation—to be afraid of short-lived man. The Hebrew word for man—*human* in the translation—is that which emphasizes his weakness and dependence. So DI says of this human obloquy: *Do not be . . . dismayed when they revile you.* This verb, rendered "dismayed," is the same one that in vs. 6 was translated *my saving activity shall never be dismayed,* even though in English "dismayed" needs a personal subject.

8.

As DI has said before, evil finally devours itself, even though it may be as slow a process as the disintegration of a *garment*. A garment cannot last forever, and we ought to recognize that fact as clearly as we realize that *my salvation* will continue [*working in you*] *to all generations.*[3] This must be so, simply on the ground that God is God (cf. Ps. 102:26-27). DI in concert with his predecessors is not concerned to show that Yahweh's transcendence is to be understood in terms of space, so that he dwells outside his universe. Both the ancient Greeks and modern man regard the spatiality of the divine Being as a problem for the mind. What DI is concerned to express is that God's transcendence is to be understood in terms of time. Yahweh is both first and last; therefore because of that he must be the same forever (41:4; 43:10; 44:6).

9 Awake, awake, put on strength, thou arm of Yahweh;
Awake, as in the days of old, as in the generations of
long ago.
Art thou not she who hewed Rahab in pieces? who didst
pierce the dragon through?
10 Art thou not she who dried up the sea, the waters
of the great abyss?
She who made a way in the depths of the sea,
for the redeemed to cross?
11 So shall Yahweh's ransomed return and enter Zion
with shouts of joy.
Eternal rejoicing shall be on their heads,
joy and gladness shall they attain;
While sorrow and sighing shall flee away.

[3] In this verse both "saving activity" and "salvation" are in the feminine.

9.

"Arm of the Lord, awake, awake!" runs the favorite missionary hymn. Yahweh's arm is here apostrophized as if she—for "arm" in Hebrew is feminine—were an independent entity apart from God. But no arm can act without motivation by the will of the person to whom it belongs. A man's arm in fact bears the same kind of relationship to his person as does his word or his spirit—spirit and breath or "word" are one word, as we saw at 42:5-6. That is why DI can call upon not Yahweh but Yahweh's arm. We can see how the Church father Irenaeus could speak of Christ and the Holy Spirit as "the two arms of God." For DI however, the arm signified action. He may have learned this concept from the Deuteronomist (cf. Deut. 4:34; 5:15), who speaks of God's arm as that which delivered Israel from Egypt. DI consequently daringly summons God's arm to *put on strength* again as one puts on clothing. If Yahweh's arm has done so before, says his faith, then she can do so again.

The mythological language that follows was the common property of the ancient Near East.[4] *Rahab* was the West Semitic name for the monster of the "waters under the earth" (cf. Exod. 20:4) who in herself represented the powers of chaos in which she swam. *The dragon* is a poetic synonym for Rahab. DI knew of several names for this symbolic evil force; he could have used Isaiah's and Job's word, viz. Leviathan (Job 41:1; Isa. 27:1). In Isa. 27:1 Leviathan is paralleled with serpent as well as dragon. This is because the mythical monster of the deep was conceived of in more than one guise. DI however takes the important step of demythologizing the monster; and instead of recounting myth, he theologizes upon the religious significance of the whole concept.

10.

He now doesn't allude to the primal battle between the god of the sky and the goddess of chaos that the Babylonians believed in, that battle which underlies the theological picture presented to us in Gen. 1:1-3; he alludes to the crossing of the Red Sea. To show that he is theologizing and not repeating a myth, DI now equates *the waters of the great abyss* (the *tehom* of Gen. 1:2) with the waters of the "Reed" Sea through which Yahweh *made a way . . . for the redeemed to cross*. DI thus speaks in terms of soteriology and rejects the myth, although myth was the only science

[4] See T. H. Gaster, *Thespis* (Anchor Book ed.; New York: Doubleday & Company, 1961), pp. 135-200.

that was available to the ancient world. We ought therefore to interpret the Exodus not by asking scientific questions as to what actually happened, but by seeing in it the arm of the Lord in action, ready to save. Job 26:12; Isa. 30:7, and Ezek. 29:3, all equate Egypt with Rahab in this same theological vein. Since DI's hearers were certain, or ought to have been, that Yahweh had won the victory over Rahab at the crossing of the sea, he now declares that it will be an easy matter for Yahweh to do so again at any time he wills (cf. Job 9:13). In fact he can and will do so *now,* for the fall of Babylon by the arm of Cyrus is certainly contemporary evidence of the power of Yahweh's arm over the dragon at all times (cf. Ezek. 20:33 *ff*.).

11.

This vivid section now ends on an eschatological note. *Eternal rejoicing* is rejoicing that will only begin not cease with Cyrus' act. In a sense it is parallel with the NT term "hilarity" (II Cor. 9:7), which is an outrageous kind of joy that is shocking to the faithless (cf. Acts 2:13, 15). The word *rinnah, shouts of joy,* is a joy which comes from God and belongs to God. So DI in a few lines passes from mythology to theology and finally to eschatology. This fullness of meaning in DI's language is implicitly recognized at Rev. 7:16-17.

12 I, I am He who is comforting you.
Who art thou then to fear mortal man, the sons
of Adam who are thrust [like] grass [into a stove]?
13 Hast thou forgotten Yahweh thy maker, who stretches out
the sky, and who keeps the earth firm?
Wilt thou continually, daily, be scared
At the oppressor's wrath, whenever he prepares to act
destructively—yet where is the oppressor's wrath?
14 Those who are now bowed down will be quickly released;
They shall not descend to the Pit in death, nor shall
they even want for bread.
15 For I, Yahweh, am thy God, who can stir up the sea so
that its waves roar. Yahweh of hosts is his name.
16 Moreover I have put my words in thy mouth, and have
covered thee with the shadow of my hand;
Even while planting the heavens and founding the earth
I was saying to Zion: "Thou art my people."

12.

With such a future in prospect, *who art thou* (feminine) *to fear* frail, *mortal man,* or "what kind of person art thou to," "in what condition art thou to" (cf. Ruth 3:16), as if the question is asked with astonishment. Yet *you* is plural in *I am He who is comforting you.* This interesting swing from the plural to the collective singular, as noted earlier in this chapter, has a basic significance for understanding the person of the servant. Meanwhile God comforts the hearts of the exiles one at a time, then expects them to respond in his service as a body. We can see here how the NT doctrine of the Church is firmly rooted in the words of DI. The word *ecclesia* in the NT is both feminine and singular, just as Israel, Yahweh's bride, is both feminine and singular.

13.

Israel's response must take the form of opposition to the wrath of man, for man is evil. The question is of course what form that opposition should take, in face of the fact that in the end the *oppressor's wrath* is only transitory. *Whenever he prepares to act destructively* uses a verb that offers a picture of a man determinedly preparing his bow and fixing an arrow to it with intent to kill.

14.

But those who are at present the object of the oppressor's wrath (the Servant people of God in exile) must ultimately know the saving power of God, simply because the oppressor's wrath is indeed transient, while Yahweh's Word endures forever. *The Pit* is the lowest level of Sheol, the abode of the dead. We are reminded of another promise in a parallel situation: "Verily I say unto you, There be some standing here, which shall not taste of death, till they see the Son of man coming in his kingdom" (Matt. 16:28). DI uses a typically Hebrew pregnant verb here. His verb means: "They shall not die and go down into the pit." On the contrary, they shall live, and living never lack for their daily bread, for God knows his Servant cannot live without it.

15.

The reference here is to Israel as the Servant, for the *thy* of *thy God* is expressed in the masculine gender once again. Finally Yahweh concludes this promise by appending his signature, as we might say, to the promise he has uttered.

16.

What a contrast DI now draws between the God who can raise a storm at sea and the God who acts with the gentleness of the uttered Word. Yet astonishment at the contrast, which after all Elijah had already experienced (I Kings 19:11-12), is as nothing compared with the profundity of the subsequent declaration.[5] It is that Israel's election to be the Servant was made contemporaneously with creation itself. This does not mean that empirical, sinful Israel was in any sense preexistent. It means that God's purpose of love was prepared from the beginning for all eventualities. It means that the eternal Word has needed this body in which it could become flesh since *planting the heavens*. It means that at the beginning of God's purpose he said of Israel: *Thou art my people*. Since God had said this *dabhar* (word), and it had come forth from his heart and mouth, it necessarily had to become event (*dabhar* again). For the two are one, and need but one word in the Hebrew language.

17 Rouse thyself, rouse thyself, get up, Jerusalem,
Who hast drunk from Yahweh's hand his cup of wrath,
Who hast drunk to the dregs the chalice of reeling.
18 "She has no one to comfort her of any of the sons she bore,
nor anyone to take her by the hand of any of the
sons she has reared."
19 The following two [ills] have befallen thee—
who will condole with thee?
"Destruction and devastation," "Famine and sword."
Who even am I to comfort thee?
20 Thy sons have collapsed; they have fallen down at
the top of every street like netted antelopes.
They are (drunk) full with the wrath of Yahweh,
with the rebuke of thy God.

17.

DI is not averse to presenting us with shattering contrasts. He first proclaims God's premundane purpose in Israel. Then immediately he reveals what Israel is really like, figured as she is once again by the feminine personality of *Jerusalem*. Even as he summons her to *rouse thyself, get up, Jerusalem,* he knows that she cannot do so in her own strength. Herein rests the paradox of the way God works in the heart of his Servant.

[5] The infinitive absolutes of the Hebrew may be understood in more ways than one.

DI is at one with his predecessor Isaiah, who believed that his preaching would serve only to harden Israel's heart, not enlighten it (cf. Isa. 6). This conception of the hardening of the heart the Hebrew mind pictorialized under the figure of drinking the *chalice of reeling.* The concept of reeling obviously originates from the experience of the drunkard whose legs cannot hold him up. But the prophets use it with a theological aim. As such it becomes the picture of the effect of drinking a cup which the Lord has handed a man to drink. Throughout history the idea of sharing the cup has been universally employed as the symbol of fellowship and so by derivation, of covenant. We read in Nathan's parable how the lamb shared his master's cup rather than his plate (II Sam. 12:3). To the psalmist his cup could be "the portion of his heritage" offered him by a loving God (Ps. 16:5), a cup running over with grace (Ps. 23:5).

But *corruptio optimi pessima.* That which was symbolic of the reality of fellowship and covenant love, if misused could become the veritable cup of damnation itself. On the one hand, the psalmist who received the cup in faith could exclaim: "I will take the cup of salvation" (Ps. 116:13). But on the other hand, if that cup should be taken "unworthily" (as Paul says at I Cor. 11:29), the drinker thereby drinks damnation to himself. "For in the hand of the Lord there is a cup, and the wine is red . . . ; but the dregs thereof, all the wicked of the earth shall wring them out, and drink them" (Ps. 75:8). No more terrible use is made of the figure than by Jeremiah (25:15-33). In that parabolic experience which he undergoes, God hands him the cup of reeling to give to all the kings of the earth, with the words: "Drink ye, and be drunken, and spew, and fall, and rise no more." DI would regard it as inconceivable to except Israel from drinking the cup, for he had no illusions about her being part of all the wicked of the earth. Election, he knew, was not to salvation but to service. That was why Israel had now suffered the ultimate outcome of her apostasy, the total damnation which God must in fact offer to those who prefer blindness rather than sight (cf. also Lam. 4:21; Ezek. 23:31 *ff.*). She has *drunk to the dregs* not just the cup but the huge Babylonian *chalice* of reeling.[6]

[6] The word *cup* in the English versions toward the end of vs. 17 is the translation of a Hebrew interpolation meant to interpret the Babylonian word for *chalice.* The latter was probably a large bowl that was used in the service of Marduk.

18.

Now if there is anything more degraded than a drunk man it is a drunk woman. So Zion—feminine—is drunk, too drunk to find her way home. Comes a sorrowful voice, pointing out that Zion has no sons left capable of performing the filial duty of guiding their mother home in her drunken state. For they themselves are all too drunk to help her.

19.

Thus *two* pairs of evil have befallen the exiles, two pairs because DI names those evils in doublets. His words moreover illustrate the inner and outer aspects of the situation. For his words portray the moral collapse that accompanies the material distress that Israel had found herself in. Is this another reason why DI began his gospel by declaring that Zion had now suffered *double* for all her sins (40:2)?

20.

All Israel has drunk from the cup of *the wrath of Yahweh*. Israel has now reached the lowest ebb of her whole existence. Her whole *nephesh* has been emptied out, and there is nothing left of her former self. *Who even am I to comfort thee?* (vs. 19, literally "shake the head with thee") asks even the Almighty as he looks at the pitiful husk of her who was once his bride. Was there any point of contact left at all in Israel's bemused and befuddled mind which even God Almighty's words of comfort (40:1) could reach home to, and obtain a response? No, there was none at all, DI declares. Israel could not now even hear the words of comfort, far less make any movement to respond to them. For poor, stupid, egotistical Israel was now dead, and was even buried in the grave (cf. Ezek. 37:11 *ff.*). In fact, her descent into Babylon had become her descent into hell.

21 In face of all that, listen to this, thou poor soul,
drunk, but not with wine—
22 Thus says thy Lord Yahweh, thy God who pleads the
cause of his people:
"Look, I have taken the cup of reeling out of thy hand,
the chalice of my wrath; thou shalt never drink it
again.
23 Moreover I have placed it in the hand of those who
made thee suffer,
Who said to thee: 'Lie flat, so that we may walk over thee!'
So thou hadst to make thy back like the ground,
or like a street for them to walk over thee."

21.

But it is just at that point when Zion needs God most that the God of all grace acts (cf. Hos. 2:14-15). Even though she is in a drunken stupor far more terrible than anything occasioned by wine, God remains her lover and her faithful husband. God says: *Listen to this, thou poor soul.*

22.

And then he acts, in the manner that a doctor may have to act to save an unconscious patient. What we now observe is the Word becoming act. God is now doing for Israel what she cannot do for herself—he takes *the cup of reeling out of thy hand*. It is as her Advocate too that he does this, as one who stands beside her and *who pleads the cause of his people* (cf. John 14:16; Rev. 14:8-10; 16:19).

23.

For in his infinite pity and compassion he has had to watch his beloved treated with all the brutality with which ancient peoples handled their prisoners of war. DI's choice of words at vs. 23 possibly rests upon the last line of the so-called blessing of Moses (Deut. 33:29), "And you shall tread upon their backs." For we know today from our study of the Ugaritic language that the word *bamoth* ("high places") should probably be translated in this way. The Ugaritic sagas were already a thousand years old in DI's day. Such cruelty had evidently been the accepted thing ever since those far-off days.

DI has now brought us face to face with an amazing conception. It is that this virtual suicide, for an alcoholic is a suicide, this emaciated body of Israel now brought down to the point of death by her own deliberate decision and freely executed choice of loyalties, in God's eyes is still not merely his own beloved elected Servant but actually his suffering Servant. DI will soon expound this paradox in detail.

On the other hand, Israel was not the only sinful nation on God's earth. We have seen before (ch. 47) what Yahweh thought of Babylon, for example. The justice of God demands that all the sinful nations of the earth should in their turn drink from the cup of reeling too. How this cup is finally snatched from their hands before it becomes too late only the NT can tell us, for only it can tell us who drank the cup in their stead (Matt. 26:39-42).

CHAPTER 52

1 **Rouse thyself, rouse thyself, put on thy strength, O Zion;**
Put on thy splendid garments, O Jerusalem, the holy city;
For the uncircumcised and unclean will never again
enter within thee.
2 **Shake thyself from the dust, get up, O captive Jerusalem,**
Free thyself from the fetters round thy neck, thou
captive daughter of Zion.
3 **For thus says Yahweh: "You were sold for nothing, so when**
4 **you are redeemed it will not be for money. For thus says**
Lord Yahweh: At the first my people went down to stay in Egypt, then
Assyria oppressed them for nothing.
5 **But now, what am I to say about this situation? For has my people**
been taken away for nothing after all? Their rulers mock [at them],
says Yahweh, and all
6 **day long my name is continually despised. Therefore my people shall**
know my name; therefore [shall they know it] on that day; for I am
He who speaks [the effective Word], Here I am."

1.

The poem continues. God has to call upon Israel a second time (cf. 51:17) and tell her to wake up from the sleep of death, from the intoxication resulting from drinking the cup. DI's words are now clearly a theological interpretation of contemporary events. They are couched in language that becomes valid for all ages. Vss. 1-6 do not contain a prescription to the exiles of what they are to do when Babylon falls.

The poem is written in plain contrast with that to be found at 47:1 *ff*. There the queen of Babylon is doomed to destruction, for she is the personification of sinful pride. But here it is Zion that is addressed. She is Yahweh's bride, and because of that she is to put on her wedding gown. This gown is not of course her own, for the gown is part of the dowry that the husband supplied to his bride. Zion's is a clean and beautiful gown; as such it is symbolic of purity and of sins forgiven (cf. Zech. 3:4). But what actually is this gown? It is nothing less than Yahweh's own strength. *Put on thy strength, O Zion,* does not refer to anything Zion herself possesses. Her strength is God himself (cf. Ps. 21:1; 27:1; 28:7; 46:1); *ʿoz* means both strength and glory at once. So her *strength* is defined by God's gift to her of her *splendid garments.*

At Judg. 6:34 we read: "The Spirit of Yahweh clothed itself with Gideon." Here is similar theological picture language, but in reverse. DI has already summoned Yahweh's arm to put on strength (51:9); here Israel in her turn is to put this newly revealed divine strength on herself. When she does so, two things will result: (1) She will move from the prison dungeon of Babylon into freedom, and so find herself moving from the death of the exile into the life of God. (2) She will become *holy,* even as God himself is holy, for all those who associate with him partake of his holiness (cf. Exod. 19:6; Isa. 48:2). That is why *the uncircumcised and unclean will never again enter within thee* (cf. Rev. 21:27).

2.

"*Qumi, get up,* daughter of Zion," says Yahweh to this poor girl bride who is now sitting in the dust into which Queen Babylon is about to descend (cf. Mark 5:41). For dust represents all that is unclean, and one must *shake* it off before the clean new garment is put on. Yet Israel cannot raise herself any more than can Jairus' daughter. Only if she uses her divine Husband's strength will she be able to strike off from her neck *the fetters of* servitude. In this verse there is a curious juxtaposition of genders. *Captive* in line *a* looks like a masculine form of the word; in line *b* it occurs as feminine. Probably DI is referring to the idea of the captivity of an Israel that is both Servant (masculine) and bride (feminine) at the same time.

3, 4, 5.

Till now Israel has been a useless Servant and a fruitless bride. That is the essence of the rather obscure verses that follow. What DI is saying, as he looks back into the past, is that God's handling of his people till this time has been of no effect. Israel had learned nothing from her *stay in*

Egypt; and the Northern Kingdom had learned *nothing* from being overwhelmed by *Assyria* in 721 B.C. Israel had profited nothing at all from her training or her discipline, nor had she learned what it means to be called to be Yahweh's Servant. So God himself now explains why the exile that began in 587 B.C. has been necessary. The pain and suffering following upon the fall of Jerusalem have not been a pointless experience. Even when their Babylonian masters *mock* at the exiles in their bullying manner, and God's *name* is *despised,* God can weave it into his plan. Even though Israel had been sold into Babylon's power *for nothing* (vs. 3), that is, without effect, yet God of his own free sovereign grace will now redeem her *for nothing* too; but now the phrase means "freely," "without payment," "from grace alone."

6.

Till now Israel has been only an empty shell of a Servant, has not even had the form of a Servant. But *on that day* the form will take on new content, for the name of God, God's very self, will dwell within that form. Remember that to *know* God's name meant for DI's hearers to know his essential being. Thus to know God meant vastly more for DI than merely to know about him. It signified virtually that oneness of almost physical union that can produce new life (cf. Gen. 4:1—new life, *'eth Yahweh,* from or by means of Yahweh). That is what Yahweh now promises, his actual presence, *Here I am!* Yet the ultimate union of God and Israel was not to coincide with the return to Jerusalem by the exiles rescued from the prisons of Babylon. It was to happen only *on that day.* This is the phrase used by the prophets to refer to the final outcome of the chain reaction that had been set in motion by God at the historical moment of which they are witnesses. Thus the perfect union of God and Israel which will create the perfect Servant must eventually come about, for the chain reaction had now been initiated through "my servant Cyrus." However, this perfect union was not to happen in 538 B.C. with the return of Israel to the ruins of Jerusalem, for Israel had not yet become the perfect Servant. That event still lay far in the future. It would happen only *on that day.* But *that day* when it dawned would not, surprisingly enough, reveal a wholly new and unprecedented movement on the part of God. What it would reveal would be the inevitable and final perfect outcome of what God had now begun to do in calling Cyrus from the east to set his people free.

7 How beautiful upon the mountains are the feet of him
who brings good news,
Who tells of peace, who announces good things, who
proclaims salvation,
Who says to Zion: "Thy God is reigning!"
8 Hark! Thy watchmen have lifted up [their voices]; hark!
they are shouting for joy together,
Standing shoulder to shoulder they watch for Yahweh's
return to Zion.
9 Burst into song and shout for joy together, you
ruins of Jerusalem.
For Yahweh has comforted his people and has
redeemed Jerusalem!
10 Yahweh has bared his holy arm before the eyes of
all nations,
Thus all the ends of the earth shall see the
salvation of our God.

7.

How thrilling it is to discover that, unimportant as a man is in himself, he is a link in the great divine chain reaction. *On that day* an extraordinary thing is going to happen (vs. 6). Yet that eventuality is dependent on DI's contemporary hearers as at this juncture they take their place in the evolution of the cosmic plan. Till now the exiles in Babylon had been utterly depressed, because the mainspring of their existence had gone. No man possesses any élan vital within him if he has lost purpose in life; in consequence he sees no reason to continue living. But he who learns that he is needed, that he has a necessary place in a mighty campaign whose outcome if he is faithful is assured—for God has spoken it—that man gains an exhilaration of spirit that the world can never understand. So DI pictures this exhilaration in much the same form as a NT parable. He sees an exile who has been raised from the death of meaninglessness, of *tohu,* of negation, in the dungeons of Babylon, now bursting with the joy of one who has found that life has meaning and purpose, for he has discovered that God is alive and he cares. Naturally this exile cannot keep the news of this new birth to himself. Like the new manna, unless it is used the news is lost in *tohu.* So he speeds over the intervening mountains to poor, ruined Jerusalem with this new song in his heart: "God is not dead after all: he is reigning still, despite all appearances to the contrary" (cf. Rom. 10:15).

8.

The excitement spreads. The watchmen on the ruined walls are the first to see this herald and catch the infection of his spirit themselves. The whole city as one man is moved to accept the news that is announced as the opposite of *tohu,* viz. *shalom,* fullness of being, salvation, the victory of the living God over *tohu* in all its forms, whether the latter is experienced as black despair in the human heart, the darkness of the prison cell that is symbolic of the Babylonian exile, or the horror of dwelling in a ruined city at the mercy of nomad marauders. The offer of this good news, being the Word of Yahweh himself, implies that Yahweh is present in his word; so the people of God who are still living within the ruins now stand up eye to eye, or better, *shoulder to shoulder,* and watch for the very presence of God himself.[1]

9.

DI's parable continues. Since the uttered Word of God bears within itself the power to fulfill itself, DI sees that it can inspire even the inanimate stones of the city to burst into song; for this is an otherworldly joy that has entered their midst by means of the human lips of a human messenger. And so he points to the mystery of the total redemption of God, who when he *comforted* and *redeemed Jerusalem,* comforts and redeems her very stones. Similarly with the mystery of the divine choice of vehicle for the Word. For the word "messenger" means either a human being or an angelic agency. Here again DI obviously draws no line between them.

10.

However, if *Yahweh has bared his holy arm,* and the strength of that arm has in fact become visible *before the eyes of all nations,* then this can have reality only if the invisible God reveals himself through the very visible and tangible agency known to us as the empirical people of God.

11 Depart, depart, get out of there! Don't touch anything unclean;
Get out from within her; cleanse yourselves, you who are to carry Yahweh's utensils.
12 There will be no need for you to depart in a hurry, nor will you need to flee;

[1] The Church has presented this truth since those days by employing the pregnant words, *Deus in verbo suo praesens.*

In fact Yahweh is going ahead of you, and the
God of Israel will be your rear guard.

11.

This empirical people is faced with an existential decision: whether or not to get out of Babylon when the city falls; whether to decide for freedom from servitude to a pagan empire and so to enter that service to Yahweh which alone is perfect freedom, or whether to remain in Babylon and thus to reveal more concern about mammon than about obedience. Yet here again the situation goes far beyond the moment of Israel's decision. For *Yahweh's utensils* are primarily the implements used in the temple worship at Jerusalem, but which Nebuchadrezzar had stolen and which were still preserved in Babylon. As a matter of history, it was only many months after DI had told the exiles to *depart, depart, get out of there*—his use of "there," not "here," shows he is not in the city itself but in some village nearby—that Cyrus finally gave orders to have the temple vessels restored (Ezra 1:7-8). DI could not be sure at the time of speaking whether Cyrus would do this or not. *Yahweh's utensils*—the word is simply "things"—could therefore refer also to any of the Israelites' possessions that were to be restored to Yahweh's holy city. All Israel had originally been called to be a "kingdom of priests" to Yahweh (Exod. 19:6), even though there were in Israel men specially set apart to fulfill the office of priest. Thus it is all the exiles who are addressed here, and who are summoned to recognize their original calling to be "a holy nation, a kingdom of priests."

12.

However, unlike the exodus from Egypt, when things had to be done in a hurry, this second exodus is to be completed at leisure, for no one will prevent their leaving. Moreover God is both before it and behind it. Just as he went before his people at the Exodus (Exod. 13:21) yet also came behind them in the form of the angel of the covenant (Exod. 14:19), so will he do again. Going both before and behind he will lose no stragglers on the way, but like the Good Shepherd, will finally bring home all his ewes and lambs to the fold of the holy city (40:10-11).

13 **Behold, my Servant will succeed. He will be exalted;**
he will be lifted up, and he will be exceedingly high.

14 In proportion as the masses were appalled at thee (so inhumanly
marred was his mien, and his appearance so unlike the
sons of Adam),
15 So many will be the nations he startles.
Kings will shut their mouths because of him;
For they will have seen for themselves something
beyond all telling,
And will ruminate on what is quite unheard of.

13, 14.

When *that day* (vs. 6) finally arrives, as the ultimate outcome of the redemption of the exiles from Babylon, what will the Servant look like that Israel was chosen to embody? And how will his task appear to the world?

It is not always possible to differentiate between God's messengers in heaven and those on earth. DI draws no line between the task of the Servant on earth and the nature of the divine plan for the whole of creation. Or, to use another mixture of concepts, one can speak of the Spirit's clothing itself with a man and, at the same time, of a people putting on divine strength like clothing. In conformity with this type of thinking, therefore we are not surprised to find that the Servant is here described in terms both of God and of man, with no line of demarcation between the two.

Behold, says DI. That is to say, use your mental powers to delineate the substance of the extraordinary theological picture I am about to draw: *My Servant will succeed*. Man, we know, is never effective to the point of complete success in anything he undertakes. This verb implies having the intelligence, insight, and capability to bring to a successful conclusion what one plans to do. As DI declares, it is only the word of God and never the ephemeral word of man which really endures, and which can therefore reach its goal. Yet, some centuries later than DI the book of Daniel actually employs the active participle of the verb which is here translated as *succeed*. It is used in the form of a name ("they that be wise," Dan. 12:3) that describes what Israel's function is as Servant of God. In this way the word becomes finally linked with the resurrection of Israel that is spoken of in that chapter of Daniel, and which is regarded as the ultimate outcome of Israel's unique relationship with God. This word *maskilim* in the book of Daniel, is synonymous with *matsdiqei ha-rabbim*, "they that turn many to righteousness," or, as the verb has been translated in earlier chapters of DI, "they who make many compassionately concerned for others."

The Servant here is actually described in terms of divinity. The phrases *he will be exalted* and *lifted up* are representative expressions from earlier literature, such as Isaiah and the Psalms, used normally of God. But DI immediately couples these terms with others that can only be used of a man. For once again (cf. 50:5-6) he describes the Servant as a man whose face is *marred* by suffering.

It is an interesting fact that the DSI scroll vowels this word in such a manner that it means in English "I have anointed," or even, "I have made Messiah." But most scholars agree that the insertion of a *yod* here to give this rendering has been done for dogmatic reasons, so it is to be rejected. The word which is rendered *the masses* or *many* occurs twice in this pericope, and it will appear again in the next chapter at a significant point. Both times it seems to mean, not "the majority" of mankind, but "virtually all" men. Thus while *ha-rabbim* is translated by the *many,* its anarthrous form *rabbim* is rendered "*the masses.*"[2] Our verse declares that once the masses of humanity see this *one* Servant, they will be appalled at his marred mien, even though God does not seem to be appalled at it.

15.

In fact, this *startles* them out of the normal attitude toward the weak and helpless that unredeemed man naturally assumes.[3] For the average man reveals himself as a bully at heart; he seems to take a sadistic delight in hurting the one who meekly accepts his cruelty (50:6). When Easterners *shut their mouths* under the influence of a powerful emotion, they show by their compressed lips and by drawing back the corners of the mouth that they are reacting with astonishment to a situation that has taken them unawares. Now a nation in those days took its cue in its whole national life from its leader and his royal decrees. Thus, for example, if the king declared war, then all his subjects naturally fought for his cause. In like manner, if the king should be startled into new ways of thinking, the commoners of his realm would eventually follow suit. DI is obviously aware that the best strategy one can employ in the propagation of an idea is to begin with the man at the top.

The Servant's task is to give *the masses* a wholly new view of life, one

[2] If this translation is correct, then it has important consequences for our understanding of the words of Christ, as at Mark 10:45.

[3] Some scholars understand this last verb to mean "sprinkled." But this meaning does not fit the context well. Sprinkle is a word that belongs to the cult and so is inappropriate here.

that, as DI has already told us, is to be in accord with the Torah which God has already given (42:1). But the startling *new* element in its propagation is that it will be enunciated by one whose *mien is inhumanly marred*. Such a thing is so utterly new that it is *beyond all telling* and *quite unheard of*.

CHAPTER 53

1 Who could have believed what we have heard? Whoever
had Yahweh's arm revealed to him before?
2 For he grew up before him like a sucker [from a dead
tree stump], like a root out of dry ground.
He had neither form nor charm, that we should look at him,
nor appearance to attract us to him.
3 He was despised and avoided by people; a man who
suffered pain and who was familiar with sickness.
He was like one from whom people hide their faces;
he was so despicable that we took no account of him.

1.

The thing is so utterly new that it is *beyond all telling* and *is quite unheard of* (52:15). The last words of comment in the previous chapter are repeated here to emphasize the unity of ch. 52 with ch. 53. For of course the chapter divisions in our English Bible are no part of the original text. And so the speaker continues: *Who could have believed what we have heard? Whoever had Yahweh's arm revealed to him before?* (Cf. 63:5; John 12:38; Rom. 10:16.) One would have thought Yahweh's arm would rend the heathen or tear asunder the hills, for "arm" denotes power put forth in action. But when it was revealed, no one, neither heathen nor Israelite, could ever have imagined that this is what it would do. We are reminded of the words: "Blessed art thou, Simon Bar-jona, for flesh and blood hath not revealed it unto thee, but my Father which is in heaven." (Matt. 16:17.) Similarly no human onlooker, be he Israelite or heathen, could ever have uttered the succeeding lines had not the Holy Spirit been interpreting to his mind the scandal of the scene.

2.

A pest in all our gardens is the *sucker* which grows from the root of our rosebush, for it does not present us with a flower. Such a sucker develops when the ground is uncultivated and hard and dry; it grows straight with thorns on its whole length; it has no *form nor charm*, no *appearance to attract us to it*. The good gardener cuts it out and throws it away. The word *sucker* has two meanings in Hebrew. It can mean what its parallel implies, a sapling growing straight up out of the ground. But it can also mean one who sucks at his mother's breast, a little child.[1] It is interesting that by means of the parallel with *root*, DI reveals that he is making direct reference to the words of Isa. 11:1, spoken so long before his day: "There shall come forth a shoot from the stump of Jesse, and a sucker shall grow out of his roots." There the word for "sucker" is *netser*, which means the same as *yoneq* here. Job 14:7 says, "For there is hope for a tree, if it is cut down, that it will sprout again, and that a sucker (*yoneq*) from it will not cease." A tree stump can appear to be dead. Not a leaf or a branch seems to have survived the felling. Yet months later, after the long reign of a winter's death, a *sucker* may appear through the ground several feet from the dead stump, but obviously from a root that is still alive. From that small beginning a tree will grow once again. In this way Isaiah of old had foreseen how his kingly Figure would arise, not necessarily as a physical son of David, whose tree would eventually be cut down, but from David's roots in Jesse (Isa. 11:1). He would thus be the outcome not of flesh and blood but of the divine promise lying behind all that David was called upon to do and to be.

Similarly the Israel to whom DI is now speaking is a vine that has been cut down to the ground (cf. Ps. 80:8-16) and is now lying dead on the dry soil of Mesopotamia. But the power of the Word of God is stronger than the destruction of Jerusalem and the felling of the vine Israel, for the Word of God endures forever (40:8; cf. Ezek. 37).[2] The Hebrew here speaks of this Figure as growing up *before him*, which can mean only something like "in the presence of Yahweh," "under the eye of God," "in conformity with the will and purpose of God."

[1] See my *Christian Theology of the OT*, p. 313.

[2] It is interesting to note that the LXX version translates *yoneq* by its other meaning of "small child." Yet it makes no explicit suggestion that the child here is equated with the messianic child of Isa. 9:6. See also Wisd. Sol. 2:13; 9:7-20; 19:6; Acts 4:27.

3.

The portrait before us, however, is that of one whose rejection goes beyond even the humiliation and pain which the Servant people of God have had to suffer in Babylonia. It is the portrait of one who is wholly abject, who has encountered evil in its ultimate form. He is not shunned because he has met evil arising from natural causes; rather he is shunned because he has been disfigured by human malignity.

Remember that for OT man, even more than for us, communal life was a sine qua non. No man at any period can develop to be truly human unless he lives in society; in fact a man goes mad if he is completely shunned by his kind. DI therefore puts his finger on the point of the greatest sacrifice of all which the perfect Servant has to make. He is to be utterly lonely. *We took no account of him:* we thought him an idiot in the Greek sense of the word—we regarded him as an isolated fanatic. In other words, his calling is to lead him to tread a completely lonely path, even as God himself must pursue the path of redemption alone (63:3).

4 Actually it was our sickness that he was bearing, and our
pains that he was carrying;
Yet we thought he was affected by a stroke from God,
and that that was why he was degraded.
5 He, however, was pierced by our rebelliousness,
crushed by our iniquities.
The punishment by which fullness of life [is effected] for us
was upon him,
And through the blows that he accepted, healing
came to us.
6 All of us have wandered away like sheep, each of us
has turned along his own way;
So Yahweh made to alight on him the guilt of us all.

4.

The content of this line comes as a great shock. Normally man supposes that the only reason for punishment is penal. But DI has long since warned that a new thing is about to be revealed (cf. 48:6*b*, 16). He has declared that God has long been preparing his Servant people, first to understand this new thing, and once they have accepted it, to live it out in the world (49:2; 51:16). It is neither wise nor possible, as we are now in the position to recognize, to isolate the so-called "Servant passages" in the pages of DI from the rest of the text; for they contain the flowering of the slowly developing argument that runs through all of DI's sixteen chapters.

We, that is to say, humanity at large, had imagined that this Figure was suffering from a natural illness, so that his suffering was something that God had sent him as a punishment for his sins (cf. Jer. 10:19). However, we might have gone so far as to suppose that God was making him suffer for the sins of his forefathers (cf. Lam. 5:7).[3] Yet we must recall that this chapter paints a portrait or offers a theological picture of the historical situation in which empirical Israel once found herself. The Servant Israel was then meeting suffering which, while in part penal, was also just that ordinary suffering that all men must necessarily meet in this fallen world.

5.

But DI now makes the remarkable statement that it is *we,* humanity at large, free as we are to choose the evil as well as the good, who have chosen to pierce the Servant by *our rebelliousness,* and crush him *by our iniquities.* It is understandable why DI should mention *rebelliousness* as the first of all human sins. The man who, through pride, chooses to follow the dictates of his own ego and to disregard the Word of God has thereby rebelled against God's loving offer to him of fellowship and peace. Quite possibly DI had in mind here, as the type of all human rebellion, the disloyalty of the bride Israel to the Lord and Husband who has never ceased to exhibit his *ḥesedh* or "loyal love" toward her, so the pain that she has caused him in her folly has pierced him to the heart (43:24; 50:1-2). For of course as DI has already said of God, *Thou hast turned me into the Servant* [*who has had to deal*] *with thy sins, and it is I whom thou hast made weary at the cost of thine iniquities* (43:24).

If it is indeed true, as many suggest, that DI borrowed some of his ideas and certain specific terms from Akkadian liturgical texts to which he would have access in Babylon, then it is all the more remarkable how much he has transformed them. For ideas belonging to very human documents, reflecting as they do a pagan cult, have now become vehicles of the deepest revelation of God that the Old Testament can offer. DI now emphatically declares that the suffering experienced by this Figure was not

[3] In passing, there is no need to discuss, as some expositors do, whether it was leprosy from which this Figure was suffering here, for of course this chapter is not to be regarded as a photograph of any historical personage. Yet if leprosy is indeed the intention of DI, then the Servant was expelled from the people of God, was removed from the circle of the elect, was accursed from the covenant of God. This forms an antinomy to which we must return in a later chapter (55) when DI brings his whole impressive argument to its conclusion.

caused by a stroke, nor by the living death of leprosy, nor by his being reduced to poverty and shame from ruin or misfortune as was Job. Rather he was voluntarily accepting the sufferings that had come upon him. At first glance it had looked indeed as if he were passively accepting his suffering in abject misery. In reality, however, his suffering was vicarious. His suffering was actually intended to effect the will of God. God's will, as DI has already told us, is no less than that all men should possess the full life in a covenant of peace (cf. Num. 25:12; Ezek. 37:26; see 54:10), and so be healed of all their diseases (cf. Exod. 15:26; Ps. 103:3).

6.

DI now connects the task of Israel with the historical picture of her that has been employed by the prophets before him, in fact, ever since the days of the shepherd king David. Ezekiel had newly painted the portrait of Israel as a forlorn flock of sheep, and had applied it to the exiles in their lost state in Babylon (Ezek. 34). Yet *all of us* of this verse must not be limited to the lost sheep of the house of Israel, but should embrace within its sweep *the masses* (see 52:14), that is to say, the whole world of men (cf. 52:15 and 53:1, 6); for this verse surely describes the manner in which humanity as such behaves.

For humanity is one and is bound together as one by a common guilt and a common fate (cf. Gen. 6:5; Isa. 6:5). To make this clear the picture changes to punishment; we see a wild beast before which isolated and lost sheep are in danger. But the beast turns from them and attacks the shepherd instead, and the sheep escape. Yet paradoxically, man's common guilt is revealed as the innate desire in the individual human heart for each to turn *along his own way,* and thus to be wholly selfish and live a self-contained life (cf. Gen. 11:7-9). Moreover, it is this common guilt that unites all men, not renders each man unique. It is this common guilt which *Yahweh made to alight on him,* and this means again that the guilt of the *all-of-us* communally has fallen upon him individually. If two people, such as husband and wife, are so closely associated that they regard themselves as one (cf. Gen. 2:24), then each shares in the suffering of the other. DI has explicitly stated in an earlier stage of his argument that God reveals himself as Israel's husband. Therefore, when Israel suffered, God suffered too. Thus the extraordinary inference can be made that it was God who became the Suffering Servant that Israel was elected to be, for Israel could not fulfill her calling alone (43:22 *ff.*). The Servant is a masculine and not a feminine figure. On the other hand, Israel continued to suffer. But in his grace the divine Husband accepted her deserved sufferings as if they were one with the vicarious sufferings he was undergoing on her behalf. In his capacity as the Suffering Servant himself and by means of his union with his wife Israel, God subsumed her justified and penal suffering into his own vicarious bearing of the *rebelliousness* and *iniquities* (vs. 5) of *the masses* (52:14).

7 He was mishandled and he was humiliated, yet he never opened his mouth.
Like a sheep led to the slaughter, or like a ewe that remains dumb in the presence of her shearers,
He never opened his mouth.
8 He was taken from restraint unjustly; and as for his fate, who gave it a thought?
In fact he was wrenched from the land of the living; because of our sins the stroke lighted on him.
9 So men made his grave with the wicked, and with the rich when he was dead,
Although he had never done any wrong, nor was deceit ever in his mouth.

7.

DI would have before him as he wrote the words of Jeremiah, "But I was like a gentle lamb led to the slaughter" (11:19 RSV), a sentence which would only deepen his admiration for this ordinary sinful man who had had to bear so much suffering in his life. Yet Jeremiah complained bitterly at the suffering that came his way and never suggested that his suffering could bear away *the guilt of us all* (vs. 6). So the theme of this important verse presents at long last the content of the new thing which DI has kept reiterating God has been about to reveal (cf. 42:9; 48:6). For the new thing is not just the return from Exile, as some suggest, although it is rooted in that historical situation. This is because the return is but part of the total action of God which, once he has initiated it in Babylon, comes to a head only as the outcome of this extraordinary revelation. The completely surprising thing here is the twice-repeated phrase *he never opened his mouth* (cf. Acts 8:32). Yet why should this phrase give the surprise that it does? Surely suffering is part and parcel of this natural order and world in which we have to live. Yes, but to suffer vicariously, to bear unmerited suffering for another man, that is not normally considered an ethical action at all, unless of course the action is accepted voluntarily and spontaneously. Even then, the other man for whom one suffers also suffers, suffers as a consequence of his sin, and rightly so; for that is the penalty he must carry, the penalty of the burden of guilt.

However, the new situation revealed to us here is that it is the one who is rightly suffering for his own sins who becomes aware of a new and transforming reality in his experience. The other person is sharing the suffering with him which he ought to be carrying alone. This vicarious suffering on the part of the volunteer is therefore participative; it is neither substitutionary, nor yet is it penal. It reveals the act of enduring the pain that the other also suffers, so that it is endured, not *instead of* the other party, but *on his account*. In this way vicarious suffering actually becomes a remedial and redemptive force. How strange that it was Israel who was called to be this redemptive force by becoming a sheep or a lamb led to the slaughter, for of course she did not appreciate her calling. In fact DI believed that redemptive suffering had been God's plan for Israel from the very foundation of the world (51:16). Historically speaking, of course, there was no doubt that Israel had been led to the *slaughter* at the hands of evil men. Consequently, it had now become evident that Israel, through her union with him whose Word endures forever, had been called to be the lamb slain from the foundation of the world (51:16; cf. Rev. 13:8).

8.

At this point scholars for centuries have felt it necessary to make countless emendations in the Hebrew text. Vss. 8-12 are indeed in places quite obscure. This state of things has arisen in all likelihood from the fact that the Church has always felt that this chapter is highly important, and that the subject matter is itself mysterious, and so is couched in suitably mysterious language. In consequence the cryptic and concise original language has always been regarded as a challenge by scholars as they have sought to interpret it, with the result that ever since the NT was penned, it has been easier to proffer some kind of an exegesis than to give a literal translation. The LXX varies from the Hebrew in a number of places. The Targum, containing the Jewish exposition of the chapter emanating from the time of the fathers, yet set down in writing only about the seventh century A.D., deliberately takes the essential scandal out of these verses and renders them quite innocuous. It does so in evident reaction against the contemporary Christian interpretation. It is easy to make additional emendations, but then it becomes all too tempting to read the poor thought of man into what is the surprising new revelation of God. The Targum should remain for the modern scholar the awful warning of this possibility. Even at those points where the Hebrew is obviously not as it was left to us by DI, we should make every endeavor to translate the text as it stands.

The Hebrew text behind *he was taken from restraint* (or prison) *unjustly* could mean several possible things in English; yet one essential emphasis comes home from the line, no matter how we translate it. That is the fact that the Servant is pictured as suffering unjustly. Some understand the oppression to be restraint *in* prison; others that he was taken *from* prison, unjustly—that is to say, without a proper trial—and so to death. Others translate that he was "led to death" or even "smitten to death." However we read these words, we see that the Servant pays the ultimate penalty. *As for his fate* is the translation of most modern commentators; yet if the traditional meaning of the word, usually "generation," is retained, we are given still another cause for suffering. For then we see a man dying before our eyes, knowing that no one is caring either for him or for his children (cf. John 19:26).

The only arbitrary emendation made here—with the scholar Budde [4]—occurs next: The last line of vs. 8 is read *because of our sins,* instead of "because of the sins of my people." A case can be made for either reading. It is the sins of the world that cause the Servant's death, not just those of Israel. We, the heathen world, express astonishment at the sight of the Suffering Servant at the beginning of 53:1. The heathen are the speakers at vss. 4, *5a,* and *6b.* Moreover, at vs. 5 there occurs in the text the very word suggesting the true reading for vs. 8, viz. *mip-pishaʿenu,* so it is no stranger to this passage. Dogmatic ends may lie behind what is faulty in the present Masoretic text reading. In later centuries when the return from Exile had become a matter of history, yet before NT times, it was not easy for an expositor to substantiate DI's interpretation of God's action. For Israel, unknown to herself, was then living in the period between promise and fulfillment. Once again the case of the Targum is adduced as a warning against preconceived dogmatic interpretations of the biblical text.

On the other hand, the present Masoretic text reading also belongs in the general sense of DI's thesis. The worm Israel, the stubborn and stiff-necked Servant whom the prophets never ceased to castigate, cannot be excepted

[4] Karl Budde, "Das Buch Jesaia, Kap. 40-66," in Kautzsch-Bertholet, ed., *Die Heilige Schrift des Alten Testaments* (4th ed., Tübingen, 1922) I, *ad loc.*

from the sinful sons of Adam. Therefore it may be sufficient to speak only of the sins of "my people" rather than the sins of humanity. The sin of Israel must in fact fall on this Figure even more heavily than the sin of the gentiles. As Amos had long since insisted, Israel was peculiarly liable to the sin of rebelliousness, for she alone was in the position to rebel against the bonds of the covenant which bound her to Yahweh, and so to commit the basic sin with which no gentile nation was in the position to be tempted (Amos 3:2).

9.

So *men made his grave with the wicked* is again only a hypothetical translation. The words could also mean "He made the wicked his grave," that is, he met them head on, and they killed him for his opposition to them. *And with the rich when he was dead;* curiously enough, *dead* here is in the plural. This plural form of the word possibly emphasizes the horrible nature of his end—but this again is only hypothetical. On the other hand, if we continue to recognize that the basis of the thought of this chapter is the existential experience of Israel, then the plural word "deaths" might be understood to refer to the individuals who comprise the corporate body of the people of God. This is a likelier interpretation, since DI's mentor, the song of Moses, also makes use of this oscillation between the singular and the plural with reference to Israel (cf. Deut. 32:6, 21); and as we have already seen, this is a feature of DI's own thought (ch. 51:1-3). In this way Israel is both a corporate entity and a collection of separate persons at one and the same time.

Does *rich* refer to the wealth of the Babylonian empire (cf. the discussion at 43:28) and the nations generally who are to serve Israel's God when they eventually behold his glory when it is revealed *in* Israel? (Cf. 49:23.) Or could it simply have been axiomatic in ancient times that no man can gain riches without learning to be wicked in the process? Again, slight changes in the text—those that many editors support—could create a poetic parallel with *wicked,* viz., "evildoers." Then some interpret *his grave* as "his burial mound," though this meaning is highly doubtful, or again as "his house of death." In the Akkadian language of DI's day, the phrase "to ascend one's mountain" had become a euphemism for the verb "to die," the thing that all men wish to avoid; the same idiom appears as well in the Ras Shamra texts of the western coast of Syria. Such a conception may thus possibly be in the prophet's mind. The Masoretic text may even contain two meanings in one word, a poetic device mentioned in the Introduction.

Whatever the individual words mean, however, the main idea of the phrase is apparent. The Figure now accepts violence—and this word pictures rude excess and vicious spleen—so that he is brought down both to death and then to burial thereafter. In a passage which may be Jeremiah's, but could come from the exilic period, the action of Nebuchadrezzar in destroying Israel is likened to Israel's death; for in the vigorous words of the passage Israel is described as being swallowed by the monster of chaos, just as Jonah was swallowed by the monster of the deep (Jer. 51:34). Such a picture is in full conformity with that which Ezekiel envisaged, for he too regarded the destruction of Jerusalem and the deportation of Israel into exile as the death and burial of the people of God (Ezek. 37:11-12).[5]

10 But it was Yahweh who had planned to crush him;
It was he who made him sick; indeed it was thou who madest his person the atonement.
He will find satisfaction in [his] seed; he will prolong [his] days:
And Yahweh's plan will reach its fruition in his hand.
11*a* Out of the torment of his soul (person) he will shed forth [light] and in knowing it will be satisfied.

10.

But it was Yahweh who (cf. Mic. 6:13)—this sentence holds in perfect balance the twin problems of divine predestination and human free will, the interrelationship of which was as evident a reality to DI as it was to Peter centuries later (cf. Acts 2:23). It also contains the inference that the Servant is innocent, so that his sufferings are undeserved.

The poet's swing from the third person to the second person in this line need not disturb us, for this is a characteristic device of prophetic oracles generally: *Indeed it was thou who madest his person the atonement.*

DI has inherited various theological ideas which we must bear in mind in seeking to understand this surprising statement. A man's *person, nephesh,* was his whole personality. To use for a moment the Greek trichotomy of the personality, his *nephesh* included all three parts of him, his body, soul, and spirit, though of course the Hebrews did not think in this way. It was not his soul that God made the atonement, nor was it even his body, or

[5] Ezekiel interprets the loss of Yahweh's bride by death (24:25-27; 33:21-22) by the loss of his own wife (24:15-18).

his breath of life. It was the whole man that he was by the accident of birth —not just man but Israelite man, a man with a history and a place in the scheme of things, a man with parents and friends and possessions and hopes and fears.

Moreover, he was a man with blood in his veins, blood which would pour forth when he met this violent death. In this connection, one theological idea which DI would inherit from those who had gone before him was that the blood was not merely nor chiefly the vital stream in the veins of the body; it was actually regarded as the life itself (cf. Lev. 17:14). Death therefore meant for DI "life" that had been poured out in death. And since this concept arose from within the cult and was applied to matters pertaining to it, the pouring out of blood must have meant for DI the symbol of sacrificial death. Again in Leviticus, most of whose sacrificial ideas precede the period of DI, the word for *atonement, 'asham,* also has a cultic significance. At Lev. 5:14-19 we read how the "trespass offering" which a sinner is to bring to Yahweh is accepted as an atonement only for the individual who is presenting it. Even though at the presentation of such an *'asham,* the altar receives all the blood, we do not read of its having any effect upon God himself. Such is the case once again at Lev. 7:1-7 and at I Sam. 6:3. But here at vs. 10 a new element appears. Here the offering of the *'asham* is not for the good of the offerer; what we find instead is that God is making this innocent Figure *into* the *'asham,* so that the latter now pours out his own blood—or life—even unto death. This too is a surprising new thing that the law of Moses knows nothing of.

Yet the purpose of God cannot be checkmated by death, especially when God foreordains that death. For when a seed falls into the ground and dies, that is not its end. The question arises, however, whether the succeeding words of this verse actually mean that this Figure is to rise again from the dead. First we read: *He will find satisfaction in* [*his*] *seed,* or "he will see seed." So we ask, whose seed is this? Is it his own? The answer is that the words can mean nothing else. But whether the word "seed" requires us to understand that our Figure has children of his own, or children in the sense of disciples or followers (cf. 8:16) is another matter. Again, it is not easy to determine whether they are to be understood in the sense of a continuing but now believing Israel, or even whether it is *he* who prolongs his days *in* his seed, or whether it is the seed who prolong their own days. Yet without doubt DI means that the *'asham* carries within it its own inevitable outcome (cf. discussion at 46:10), and that therefore the self-offering of the Figure cannot be considered to have been made in vain. Indeed, *Yahweh's plan*—corresponding to *Yahweh . . . planned* at vs. 10*a*—must necessarily be effective (see ch. 55). It will be made so by *his hand*. This could be Yahweh's hand, for hand and arm are synonyms, and we already know that here we behold the revelation of his arm (53:1). But it could also be the Servant's hand. In light of DI's theology, need we now differentiate between them?

11*a*.

DI expresses this new and astonishing truth in another fine poetic line, one that issues from the mouth of Yahweh himself. *Light* has always seemed to commentators to be the necessary word after *will shed* in order to complete the sense of the line. It is interesting to discover that the DSI now confirms the LXX reading in preserving the word that the Hebrew had evidently lost at some point in the transmission of the text (cf. 49:6). *He will shed forth* [*light*] *and in knowing it will be satisfied*. That is to say, he will continue in the knowledge that his death will be effective for salvation. DI may even mean that beyond death the Servant remains creative and actively continues to save. Yet of course if his death is effective, that can be the work of God alone, for it is only the uttered Word of the living God that ever reaches its promised goal.

11*b* Victorious, my Servant will win salvation for the many,
and their iniquities he himself will carry.
12 Therefore, I shall divide the many for him as his
portion, the majority he shall have as his
share of the spoil,
Because he emptied out his life (self)
unto death, and was numbered with the rebellious;
And because he bore the sin of the masses, and
interposed himself for the rebellious.

11*b*.

If his death is really effective, this Figure will naturally be *victorious*. For that word conveys the idea of completing an action. To know that fact must constitute a joy and a satisfaction beyond anything that this world can give. For him to know that he is able to *win salvation for the many* means that he knows that he is doing what God alone can do and even has the right to do; for God alone is Savior—there is none other (cf. 43:11). Yet even while he acts as the arm of God revealed (51:9 along with 53:1; 63:5), he remains the Servant that Israel is called to be; for it is the human Servant who *will carry away* the *iniquities* of *the many* by accepting the office of one led like a sheep to be slaughtered. The verb to *win salvation for*—from the same root as the noun "saving action" which DI has used so often—does not mean to declare another to be in the right in a forensic sense; rather it operates in the ethical realm, and so means to bring another to righteousness, or help another to attain a new quality of life. Yet the tense of the verb as it is used here implies that this action has now been performed once and for all and so is final and complete.

12.

So the Figure finally receives his reward. This reward is not to be understood in terms of selfish grasping at payment or of a boy receiving a prize at school. Rather, as in the case of the man who used his talents to good purpose (Matt. 25:29), the reward is shown to comprise sharing one's innate satisfaction with *the many. Therefore, I shall divide the many for him,* says God himself. *Therefore* God will do this! The Figure here is actually ready to share with the *majority* that joy about which Isaiah of Jerusalem has already spoken, and which enters also into DI's thoughts so frequently (cf. Isa. 9:3; 41:16; 49:13; and cf. 65:18-19). For at 9:3 in one short picture we see the joy of ordinary men, of poverty stricken peasants rejoicing over harvest home or treasure trove that has unexpectedly come their way; or as in the NT, the joy of sitting down at a supper table together after having persevered to the end through the toils and tribulations of the life of obedience that marks the true Servant (cf. Rev. 19:9). *Because he emptied out his life* (*self*) *unto death* (cf. use of this Hebrew verb at Ps. 141:8): the words *taḥath 'asher,* that signify consequence, mean "in reward for" and are thus a strong *because. And because he bore the sin of the masses, . . . the rebellious:* at 52:14 the anarthrous *rabbim* was translated by *the masses* of humanity. In vss. 11*b* and 12 it carried the article "the." Here however it is clearly in parallel with *the rebellious,* who are of course all mankind. We should note too that the word *bore* is identical with that used for *bearing* at vs. 4. The inference is that the sins of humanity are to be understood in terms of sickness (cf. Ps. 103:3). So to bear these away he *interposed himself,* even as Moses long before had offered to do (Exod. 32:32). But Moses, as a sinful man, was not acceptable to God. At last God has found one worthy to be the *'asham* for the sin of the world.

CHAPTER 54

1 **Cry aloud with joy, thou barren one who hast not been bearing;**
Burst forth into song and neigh, thou who hast not been travailing!
For her children from the period when she was desolate shall be the masses,
More than her children when she was married, says Yahweh.
2 **Make more room for thy tent; stretch out the curtains of thy dwellings—don't stop!**
Lengthen thy cords, and strengthen thy tent pegs!
3 **For thou shalt burst forth to right and left;**
Thy seed is to inherit the nations, and to inhabit the ruined cities.

1.

By setting the figure of the perfect Servant alongside the reality before his eyes, viz., the sinful, empirical Servant, Israel, bemoaning her fate as she is in Babylon, DI reveals with clarity the grace of Israel's God. For Israel now knows exactly what she has been called to do and be and must recognize at once that she is in fact totally unlike what she is meant to be. Even as the consciousness of this unlikeness enters her soul, God stoops, not to point the finger of scorn, but to show pity and to comfort his chosen one in her vexation of soul. So DI is here reiterating—but now with deepened content—the call to believe and proclaim the good news with which he began his narrative (40:1 *ff.*). At 40:6 he himself had asked, *What am I to call?* He has his answer at last. The new, deeper content of his message arises from the fact that Yahweh still loves Zion, not only when her failure has been shown up in relief, but also now that the perfect Servant has been delineated. What Yahweh has to say to Zion now is therefore spoken in a setting very different from that of ch. 40. And yet Yahweh himself has not changed—he is the same Yahweh; for *the Word of our God remains forever* (40:8).

No wonder Zion is to jump for joy, and even *neigh.* This is an extraordinary word for DI to use. The NT uses the word "hilarity" to seek to express the eschatological joy which can be known now that the Church has received the gift of the Holy Spirit. Yet in classical Greek "hilarity" was used of one who was unbalanced in mind. Here too the joy of Yahweh that sinful Israel can share is so strange an experience that only strange words can seek to describe it. We are to remember that Yahweh has now revealed his love for Israel. He has shown her how he himself, in the form of Israel, will be the Servant that she is called to be herself. He has shown her how he can bear away the sin of the world, provided he can be united with the body which he had planned to use from the foundation of the world (51:16). When this happens, God will have revealed his glory as he had promised he would (40:5)—in Israel (42:8; 44:23).

The occasion of Israel's joy is the revelation of the coming successful outcome of God's action in the Servant. We read of it in 53:10: *He will find satisfaction in* [*his*] *seed,* or *he will* see his seed *prolong* [*his*] *days. The masses* whom the Servant is to receive as his portion, we remember, are to be his own *children.* These are to be born from the reunion of Yahweh and Israel; for Yahweh has now brought home his bride in triumphant love.

2.

So Zion is to make more and more room for her children yet unborn. She is to *stretch out the curtains of thy dwelling* on earth—now that she has the strength of Yahweh in her (50:7; 51:9)—even as Yahweh stretches out the curtains of his dwelling in heaven (40:22). For she is going to have countless children (cf. 49:19-26). *Don't stop* making room, says God, but do with faith what Elisha commanded the widow to do when pouring out her oil (I Kings 17:14).

3.

The returning exiles are to receive from *the nations* the countryside of Judah which they have overrun and whose *cities* are now *ruined.* But since DI is now speaking in eschatological terms, this very factual recovery of Israel's ancient territory is only the historical basis for a far wider hope. The hope for the future that the Bible offers never appears to be hanging in the air, so to speak. It is always based on, though not limited to, the factual experience of Israel in this life that is set within space and time. But the very fact of Israel's finiteness is also part of the good news which DI is now proclaiming, for the ultimate end of the promise of God to his people will not be something alien or strange. It will be new indeed, but new only in the sense of the Greek word *kainos,* in the sense of something developing out of what is already known. It will not be new in the sense of that other Greek word *neos;* that is to say, it will not be utterly different from man's knowledge of God in this life. Yet its newness will contain within it a miraculous content too. For the barren wife, like Sarah of old (51:2), is to bear children in her old age. Eschatologically speaking, *thy seed is to inherit the nations* includes within it the miracle of the masses of the world sharing in the benefits of the Servant's self-offering (44:3-5; cf. Gal. 4:27). No wonder Jerusalem is not just to grow quietly and naturally; she is to *burst forth to right and left* as her population explosion forces her children to find their homes far afield. The promise made to the patriarchs then continues to be valid.

4 Do not be afraid, for thou shalt never be shamed; and do not
feel humiliated, for thou shalt have no cause to blush.
[I declare] that thou shalt forget all about thy youthful
indiscretions,
And shalt no longer be able to recall the sneers at thy
(grass) widowhood.
5 For thy Maker is—thy husband! His name is—Yahweh of hosts!
The Holy One of Israel is—thy Redeemer! He is called
The God of all the earth!
6 [Realize] that Yahweh has called thee back like a wife
abandoned and broken in spirit;
"The wife one married when she was young—could she be
cast aside?" asks thy God.
7 I let thee go, indeed—but only for a brief moment; but now
I am hugging thee close with great compassion.
8 In a rush of wrath I had to hide my face from thee for a moment,
But because of (my) everlasting covenant love I have had
compassion upon thee, says Yahweh, thy Redeemer.

4.

Once again, as at every eschatological moment throughout the whole Bible, there sounds the command: *Do not be afraid!* What might Israel be afraid of? Primarily of the consequences of her sin. When Hosea took home his licentious wife, she had just cause to be afraid of what he might do to her (Hos. 3). A century after Hosea had expounded through his own personal tragedy the disloyalty of Israel to her covenant God, Jeremiah made use of the same figure (2:2) for the same purpose. Israel had been fornicating with other lords by giving her loyalty to anything except Yahweh. She had originally promised to be faithful to him at that time when Yahweh, her true Lord, took her to himself at the foot of Sinai (Exod. 19:1-6). But those *youthful indiscretions,* her experiments in extramarital relations, were now a thing of the past. Israel would now no longer remember them with a sense of guilt. This is because she has just been given a vision into the very heart of God. There she has seen how, as the true Servant himself, God has now borne her guilt away. Therefore her recollection of her sins can affect her not with a sense of guilt but only with a deep knowledge of the grace and love of her faithful God. Then again, her period of being put away (50:1) in exile, when she could bear no children, because she was not in contact with her divine Husband, will also turn from evil into good.

5, 6.

This is because her whole existence depends upon who her Husband is. Yahweh is no god such as the heathen worship, one who exhibits all the vices and failings of mortal man. Who is he then? In awed wonder and adoration DI now applies to Yahweh four transcendental names that no heathen god could ever bear. *Husband* and *Maker* are both written in the plural to show that they refer to *'elohim,* the Hebrew plural word for God. This all-holy One had actually claimed Israel as his bride when she was an attractive young woman in the days of the wilderness wanderings (Hos. 2:14; Jer. 2:2). What honorable husband could ever forget the girl he had loved when they were young together? Then how much more will Yahweh love her if she is *abandoned* and *broken in spirit* or "sick at heart" —a pun in the Hebrew—and thus all the more in need of the love and loyalty of her husband. Yet imagine being married to Almighty God, the creator of the stars—and having children of the union. The language of the biblical revelation is scandalous indeed (cf. 62:4).

7.

How God must then have hated to *let thee go.* Note that, as in 50:1, he did not divorce her; yet he had to find some way of making her discover the blessedness of the married state. For centuries she had played fast and loose with her divine Husband. But now at last she knew his love for her as never before. In his wisdom God had made her taste the death of separation from him, *for a brief moment*. This was essential if Israel was ever to learn that God Almighty was in earnest about her election.

8.

In a rush of wrath—the words are highly onomatopoeic in the original Hebrew—could we say that God allowed the dam to burst that held back the wrath he eternally feels toward the evil in his world? Was his beloved bride then suddenly overwhelmed in the great waters over which he rules (cf. Ps. 46:1-3)? Yet his wrath is but a necessary expression of the *covenant love* which he had laid upon Israel at the marriage that he contracted with her at Sinai (see commentary at 49:20). Even within the covenant, Israel had had to experience alienation from God before reconciliation could be possible. Satan must first lead Job to the dunghill, where he curses his day, before Job can understand the joy of life in God.

But God's love never changes even when his wrath flows as a flood. When the time of the flood is past therefore, the divine Husband is found still *hugging thee close with great compassion*. We notice that it is not only DI's transcendent themes which are expressed in scandalous language, so is his imagery of love. Yet others before him had employed this very verb "to hug" to delineate God's passion for Israel (e.g., Deut. 30:3-4; Mic. 2:12; Jer. 29:14; Ezek. 11:17). DI knows that no line can be drawn between the two types of love that the Greeks call *agape* and *eros*. The physical passion that is the basis of true love between man and woman DI actually regards as the basis of the transcendent love of him who is the Holy One of Israel, and whose nature is utterly other than that of mortal man.[1]

9 I see the present situation like the days of Noah.
For just as I swore then that the waters of Noah should
never again overwhelm the earth,
So I am swearing now never to be angry with thee again,
nor rebuke thee.
10 [I swear] that the mountains shall remove and the hills
depart,
But my covenant love shall never remove from thee,

[1] It is interesting to note that the Károli version of the Bible in Hungarian uses the word for physical love to represent the love of God even in the NT.

nor my covenant of peace depart from thee,
Says he who has compassion upon thee—Yahweh.

9.

The picture of the dam bursting reminds DI of the flood in the days of Noah, and so he puts this simile in Yahweh's mouth. He wants it to be clear to Israel that if she had never known a period of separation from her Husband, she would never have believed in the reality of a time of wrath. It is terrible indeed for any man to be overwhelmed by the flood when it comes. The man who is walking in thick fog can have no idea how near he is to the edge of it—or to the edge of destruction. But when he does eventually come out of the strangling, choking fog and realizes his nearness to the precipice, it is then that he values the warmth of the sun as never before; for previously he had just taken it for granted. Yet the heat of the sun is a permanent entity; it is God's wrath which is but *for a moment* (vs. 8), not his love (cf. Ps. 30:5; Isa. 26:20; II Cor. 4:17). In the same way the Word of God also is permanent, that Word which Yahweh now swears just as he swore in the days of Noah (Gen. 8:21; 9:11-17; cf. Matt. 24:37; Luke 17:26). For God swore that never again would his wrath overwhelm his creation. Thus DI shows, after the present experience of exile—the time of wrath—the reality of this unique event will become apparent. For it is then that the significance and the timelessness of the Word of God will become evident, and the era of salvation will dawn.

10.

Mountains and *hills* were naturally the most permanent things that Israel knew. But someday, DI declares for Yahweh, these are going to *remove* and *depart*. On the other hand, Yahweh's *covenant love* will remain, for it is the expression of his *compassion* for his bride—Israel is still addressed as "she." So the corollary of this statement must be that the object of God's covenant love also will remain forever before him; or, to put this truth in other language, that experience which Israel thinks of as physical death will never be able to end the covenant relationship or disrupt the marriage which Yahweh has sworn to uphold to all eternity. This is now the second time (cf. 40:8) that DI has made use of this particular argument to claim the reality of the life beyond. It is the same argument that Jesus used in discussion with the Sadducees (Mark 12:18-27).

Yahweh is a God who likes covenants. He made one with Noah and then with the patriarchs. Through the lips of Moses he made a covenant with all Israel. Within the context of this new relationship he then made a covenant with David and his line. Shortly before DI's day, he had even been proposing through the lips of Jeremiah another and still more wonderful covenant to come (Jer. 31:31). The concept of covenant is therefore central to God's way of working, because through the bonds of covenant he is enabled to do everything for his partner in the covenant even when the latter fails to keep his side of the bond. Thus God's continued offer of covenant in the OT is the practical expression of his grace. Being aware of the reality of God's covenant relationship with Israel therefore, DI describes how Israel is rescued from the far country of the soul and brought back home where she properly belongs. We see all this through the lens of three vitally important and central words: (1) wrath, (2) covenant love, and (3) compassion.

11 O thou poor, storm-tossed, uncomforted soul!
Behold, I am going to inlay thy stones in antimony,
and lay thy foundations in sapphires.
12 I am going to make thy minarets like rubies, and thy gates of
sparkling jewels.
Thy whole city wall will be of precious stones.
13 All thy sons will be Yahweh's disciples, and great will be
thy sons' peace.
14*a* In redemptive love shalt thou be established.

11.

Our eyes have newly been directed to the ultimate outcome—beyond the age of the hills—of God's covenantal love (vs. 10). So the Jerusalem that DI paints for us here is no longer the poor, ruined capital city of Judah on her forlorn hilltop. Yet this picture is based upon the empirical city to which the exiles were soon to return (see vs. 3). We need not pause to identify the precious stones, for it is their significance that invites our attention, not their chemical composition. The motif that is in this picture of the new Jerusalem is what scholars of Near Eastern thought have called *Urzeit=Endzeit*. The belief of many ancient peoples was that in the beginning the ultimate purpose of "God" had been expressed in a perfect creation. Israel too believed this and described that perfection in terms of the precious stones of the earth (cf. Gen. 2:11-12). Ezekiel had newly drawn just such a picture of Eden (28:13 *ff.*), and his Eden too had been studded with sparkling gems. But DI has now asked us to lift our eyes, not to the beginning this time, but rather to the end of the city of Jerusalem. This end must of course necessarily emerge from events that have already taken place in the empirical city of Jerusalem; for Jerusalem is the "holy city" (52:1), "the city of our God," the "navel of the earth," as Ezekiel had said (38:12), that spot in fact where "God has put his name to dwell" (Deut. 12, passim); so it is that place where ultimate events must surely come to pass (cf. Luke 9:51-53; 13:33-35; 18:31; 24:47, 49). Yet they will come to pass only after the completion of the self-offering of the perfect Servant. Otherwise, of course, DI would have placed his present picture of the lady Zion alongside that which he had painted of the lady Babylon (47:1 *ff.*), the wicked city that epitomized the reverse of the self-emptying of the Servant.

Once again the sex motif unashamedly obtrudes. Antimony is the *kohl* which an Arab girl employs today to make her eyes attractive to the opposite sex. God is obviously not ashamed of the significance of sex. Zion of course needs to be adorned, for she has lost her attractive power in her dejection of spirit. So God himself will give her back the attractiveness she needs in order to make him love her. She is an *uncomforted soul.* This is the negative of the word that DI used in the beginning of his message—"Comfort my people" (40:1)—and we are also reminded of the name of one of Hosea's children, *Lo-ruḥamah,* "unpitied" (Hos. 1:6), which rhymes with our word *lo-nuḥamah.*

12.

The precious stones therefore are just the ordinary limestone blocks in Jerusalem's walls, yet now glorified to be the precious stones of the new Jerusalem glinting in the sunshine of the love of God (cf. Rev. 21:2, 18-21). The coming of the new Jerusalem is of course a miracle; but that miracle is only consequent upon the still greater miracle of the resurrection of the Servant, which in the sequence of DI's argument is now a future certainty.

13.

Then he declares that Israel's *sons will* one day all *be Yahweh's disciples* (see comments at 50:4). That also will be a miracle, a miracle of grace, since a hundred percent change of heart is something that man can never expect to see. The intent of the law of Moses was that Israel should dwell together in *shalom,* peace, in the complete well-being and fullness of life which DI has said before can come from God alone (45:7).

14*a*.

Yet, as DI knew, God purposed that Israel should offer to all the peoples of the earth God's *redemptive love* (49:6). Here DI gives us insight into one of the great truths of the Bible. For it is in offering the new life to others that Israel herself will find fullness of life. It is as if DI knew the words: "For whosoever will save his life shall lose it: and whosoever will lose his life[2] for my sake, shall find it" (Matt. 16:25).

14*b* Keep away from oppression, then thou needst never fear;
and from terrorizing, then it will never come nigh thee.
15 Behold, if any man picks a quarrel, it is definitely not
from me.
Whoever quarrels with thee, shall fall upon thee
[to his ruin].
16 Behold, it is I who have created the blacksmith who blows
on a fire of coals,
And who then produces a weapon to suit his need.
Thus it is I who have created the power to destroy.
17 No weapon that is formed against thee shall succeed;
And thou shalt refute any tongue that brings a case
against thee.
That will be Yahweh's servants' heritage, for their power
to save rests with me;
Is the oracle of Yahweh.

14*b*.

This last section of the chapter reads like an afterthought, almost as if DI did what all writers do, that is, decide on second reading to fill up a gap in the argument. Similarly, at the second half of Rom. 12, Paul gives his readers some practical advice following upon his sustained theological argument. Here DI warns the people of God not to play with fire, so to speak; for if they do not oppress or terrorize others, then they will not need to fear reprisals.

15.

On the other hand, as we have clearly seen in ch. 53, oppression can come unprovoked, for man is quarrelsome by nature. So DI asks Israel

[2] *Emptied out his life,* as did the perfect Servant at 53:12.

not to put the blame on God for the iniquities of man. In fact, since God is *in* Israel, he who falls upon Israel falls upon the wrath of God.[3]

16.

We are reminded of DI's clear declaration of faith about the nature of God at 45:7: *I fashion the light, and I create the darkness; I make order and I create evil.* His illustration of the *blacksmith* is interesting. By it he shows that God is ultimately responsible for evil, that is, for weapons of destruction, be these earthquakes, *fire,* sword, or the atomic bomb.

17.

But that does not mean that God is responsible for the sin in the heart of man that leads him to oppress his brother with the sword he has made. Actually, in fact, it is the way of the *Servant* that wins in the end, not the sword. If Israel, the people of God, were to be the form of the Servant, as DI declares they are called to be, then it will be their *heritage,* even their divine calling, to accept the oppression of violent men. These they need never fear, for *their power to save* others *rests* with Yahweh—the noun *tsedhaqah* once again. The passage ends with a very emphatic phrase. It is not the usual "says Yahweh," but *is the oracle of Yahweh.* That is to say, declares DI, the eternal Word has now been spoken in the above words with intent.

[3] The LXX paraphrases this verse and infers that proselytes will take refuge in Israel as they flee from the wrath of God.

CHAPTER 55

1 **Hi! Come for water, all you who are thirsty! Come along,**
even you who have no money!
Buy wheat and eat! Come along, buy wine and milk without
money or cost!
2 **Why do you spend money on what is not bread? And your**
energy on what does not satisfy?
Pay close attention to me, and you will eat what is good,
and will regale yourselves on the choicest of food.
3 **Incline your ear! Come unto me! Listen, that your whole**
being may live,
Let me make an eternal covenant with you
With the unshakable covenant love [I gave to] David.
4 **Behold, I appointed him to be a witness to the nations,**
An expositor and commander to the peoples;
5 **Behold, thou shalt call nations unknown to thee, and**
nations to whom thou art unknown will run to thee
Because of Yahweh thy God, the Holy One of Israel,
for he will have glorified thee.

1.

We now reach the climax of DI's great thesis. Ch. 53 seemed at the time to form the peak of his message to the world with its description of the Servant. There he was God's arm revealed, God's instrument for the redemption of the world. Yet ch. 54, standing on the shoulders of ch. 53 as it does, rose to an even loftier peak of revelation. For it demonstrated what the love of God actually is. It showed how, through the *perfect* Servant, God reveals his love for the *sinful* Servant. It showed how by grace God has identified the empirical, sinful Israel with the Figure who is here revealed as his own almighty "arm." But in this chapter the outcome of God's purpose in the Servant is finally revealed. That purpose is the redemption not only of Israel herself but of all mankind, including even the earth on which mankind takes his stand. That surely is good news and the climax of all that DI has to say.

Whose voice do we hear at this point? Is it DI's or is it God's? Obviously the answer is meant to remain open. The prophet has now become so completely the mouthpiece of God himself that the word he speaks is not his own but the Word of God.

This message takes the form of a gracious invitation.[1] As such the speaker does not compel his hearers to come. He respects their personality and leaves them room to refuse. This of course is wholly unlike the manner in which man is accustomed to address his fellow man (cf. 53:7).

Notice the eschatological provenance of the whole chapter. We can take it for granted that normally the exiles in Babylon would not lack for food or water. But once in the desert on the way home to Zion they would become completely dependent upon God for their daily needs. Moreover God had promised to open pools of water for them alongside the highway home (41:18). Such a figure of speech therefore removes DI's words from the historical moment in which he is speaking and turns them into an eternal invitation. However, in conformity with the holy materialism of the biblical manner of revelation in general, this eternal Word that DI is uttering is not to be understood as a mere philosophical or metaphysical idea. For it arises from an existential situation.

We recall that the summons to Israel to enter the promised land of Canaan in the days of Moses had been bound up with the very material action of eating and drinking. For example, the covenant between God and Israel had been sealed with such a mundane thing as a feast (Exod. 24:11); again, the wilderness journey had offered Israel the opportunity to discover God's ever-watchful concern for her daily bread (Exod. 16:11-15; 17:1-7; Deut. 8:3). As Deut. 8:3 asserts, God's intention in feeding Israel had a sacramental import: "That he might make thee know that man doth not live by bread alone, but by every word that proceedeth out of the mouth of the Lord doth man live." Thus when Canaan's delights are eventually visible to the itinerant Israelites, and the new land is described as "a land flowing with milk and honey," the eschatological overtones of

[1] Is it the basis of Christ's parable at Luke 14:16-24? The latter describes the banquet that follows the eschatological marriage.

the phrase become abundantly clear. For milk and honey were the traditional food of the gods throughout the whole Fertile Crescent in Moses' day. Israel was thus being invited by means of these words to sup with the Lord of the land of Canaan, viz. Yahweh, in a sense that went beyond the eating of material food.

And so we come to DI's day when Israel was facing a new exodus that was to begin at any moment. Surely with a knowledge of her whole past history in mind, Israel would readily discover that it was the bread of "life," in the eschatological sense of the word, that she is here invited to come and get and eat and live (cf. Pss. 42:2; 63:1; Prov. 9:5). The verbs occur in the plural, so that the invitation is to the individuals who comprise the people of God. In the same manner it is the *water* of life (cf. Isa. 12:3) that Israel is summoned to come and drink, that water of which Ezekiel too in days of exile had spoken and which he had described as the river of life (Ezek. 47:1-12; cf. John 4:10; 7:37-38). As for *wine*, it was the symbol of joy, for it was in wine that a wedding toast was drunk and it was wine which made a dinner a merry occasion. The imagery which DI uses here then is that of a banquet spread by Yahweh himself to which he invites his bride, the sinful Israel. For we have learned that Yahweh loves her still, and that she has now been brought back, proleptically speaking, to where she belongs in her divine Husband's home. It is from this and similar verses that so much of the later imagery of the Bible is taken, where Israel's hope for the future is pictured (cf. 25:6—a passage later than DI—Matt. 22:2 *ff.*; Rev. 19:9). The Qumran community, even before the advent of Christ, evidently understood their own sacred meal partly in the light of this passage. For as Black[2] points out, their banquet and their song were concerned with the celebration of the mighty acts of God's deliverance of Israel in the future as well as in the past.

2.

Unless he eats this spiritual bread, man's life is vain. Getting and spending we lay waste our powers, that is to say our *energy on what does not satisfy*. Normally man seeks to live on what the Hebrew calls here "non-food," that is, the gratification of his own selfish desires. The result is that in the end he is left hungry and unsatisfied. Why should man be such a fool? *Why* indeed, asks DI with emphasis. (1) This food is free. (2) It is for all—the verbs are plural. (3) Yet it is offered to each individual person

[2] *Op. cit.*, p. 112.

one at a time. (4) This food is the whole answer to human need, viz., it satisfies. *The choicest of food* means in the Hebrew the fatty parts of the fatted calf or sheep, or else any food that has been cooked in olive oil. For these were both considered the greatest delicacies of which a humble farm worker or artisan could partake (cf. 25:6; Pss. 36:8; 63:5; and see Jeremiah's introduction to his "new covenant" passage, 31:12-14).

3.

If a man then will but *come unto me* and eat this bread and drink this cup, he will *live* in the sense that only divine food can enable a man to live. Also, God's will is not that men should just eat and drink once only and then return to their old and stupid ways. His will is that this new experience of fullness of life should remain as man's eternal heritage. Consequently, God now offers to pledge this eternal life to Israel within the bonds of the covenant, but to an Israel that has now tasted the bitterness of death and the descent into hell.

This new and exciting fullness of life is understood, first, to be rooted in the historical moment of the resurrection of Israel from the grave of the exile (Ezek. 37:12-14); and, second, to be one with the eschatological outcome of this historical experience of Israel's resurrection. That is to say, it is to be understood in terms of the final moment in the chain reaction set off by the events of 538 B.C. when Cyrus issued his famous decree. For while the chain reaction is going off, the Word is in the process of becoming flesh. Third, since sinful Israel shares by grace in the action of the Servant, this new fullness of life is the reward that the Servant is offered; for the Servant is to share with *the masses* the spoils he has seized when he rescues them from the bonds of evil and from death (53:12).

This *eternal covenant* is now given a surprising new content and direction. This is because it is defined in terms of *the unshakable covenant love* [*I gave to*] *David*. We must first look to see what such an idea meant for DI himself. DI was well aware that Yahweh had chosen David in an earlier century even as he had chosen Israel as a whole (II Sam. 7:8). Moreover, David himself had recognized his election to be set within the larger covenant. So it had been ordered in all things and made "sure" (II Sam. 23:5), or "established" (II Sam. 7:16, where we find the same word as is translated here as *unshakable;* cf. Ps. 89:28-29). The election of David was meant to last forever, even as Israel as a whole was to be God's Servant people to all eternity.

4.

Yahweh had *appointed* David, says DI here, and with David was included of course his house or dynasty. Together they were appointed to be *a witness to the nations*. They witnessed to the reliability of God, who had made a covenant with his line, and who never changed. One psalmist notes that David was called to be "the head of the gentiles" (Ps. 18:43). That is what DI must mean when he names David as *commander to the peoples*—i.e., one who gives them orders, evidently the divine commands in the Mosaic law. But he is also called to be God's *expositor*. The word *nagidh* is usually translated by some such word as "ruler." But here it means one who "tells forth," *higgidh,* and expounds the mind of God; that is to say, here is an idealization of David that is not historical.[3] Later OT writers certainly idealized him in this way, or else they would not have attributed to him the authorship of so many psalms. Probably they based their belief on I Sam. 16:13 among other passages: "Then Samuel took the horn of oil, and anointed him in the midst of his brethren: and the Spirit of the Lord came mightily upon David from that day forward."

Yahweh's covenant with David would never have been made, if the prior covenant with all Israel at Mount Sinai had not been entered into first. David himself was an Israelite and was thus king over the covenant people; he could not have been the man he was, had he not been born within the covenant, and had his whole life and thoughts not been shaped by its content and force. Thus the Davidic covenant is the lesser of the two covenants, and is dependent upon the greater for its validity. On the other hand, David was the head of Israel. The king in Jerusalem was both the representative of his people in the sight of God and the mouthpiece of God to all the people. The Davidic line, in other words, was encouraged by the prophets to see itself as the apex of a triangle. That triangle was Israel. The king, placed at the top of the triangle, represented in himself all those who were contained within the three sides. The people for their part were all summed up in him, took their direction from him, and lived their whole life in him. Thus what happened to "David" happened to them; and what Israel as a whole suffered, "David" too felt in his soul. For David was the epitome, the essence, the representation, of all Israel; he was "the breath of our nostrils, of whom we said, 'Under his shadow we shall live among the heathen,'" in the Babylonian exile (Lam. 4:20).

[3] For this translation of *nagidh* see Alt, *Staatenbildung*, p. 29; and Vischer, *Les Premiers Prophètes*, 1951, p. 196. Note that Dan. 9:25 equates *nagidh* with *mashiah*, "anointed."

The king was thus both singular and plural at the same time, depending on whether one regarded him as the apex of the triangle, or as the whole of the triangle at once; he included within himself all the people of God who were sheltering under his wing. In fact, he was the head of a living body. As such he guided and directed its life; but at the same time he suffered pain too when the members of this his own body felt the pains of life upon their individual hearts. The Gospel writers are aware of this representative function of King David (cf. Matt. 2:2; 21:5; Mark 15:2, 9, 12, 18, 26, 32; John 1:49; 18:37.

Now in the larger covenant with Israel, God had laid upon her shoulders the very tasks which "David" was later called upon to accept. DI had emphasized repeatedly that it was Israel who was to be God's *witness to the nations* (42:6; 43:10), his *expositor*, one on whom the Spirit rested (42:1; 44:3; 48:16; cf. Num. 11:29), and *commander* to the peoples, that is, one who gives God's *mishpaṭ* or commandments to the world (42:4; cf. Matt. 16:19). This point of view is expressed elsewhere also. It is found, for example, in Ps. 89:38 *ff.*, which was written during the exile probably just before DI's day. The sentiments of the psalm would almost certainly be familiar to DI. Here the line of David is called by the same two names as are given Israel at 42:1 *ff.*, where "David" is hailed as God's *chosen one*, and he is called God's *servant:*

> I have made a covenant with my chosen one,
> I have sworn to David my servant:
> "I will establish your descendants for ever,
> And build your throne for all generations." (Ps. 89:3-4 RSV.)

No line therefore can be drawn between David's task in covenant and Israel's. Israel's task could be summed up in David's, and David's could be exercised by each and every member of the covenant people, insofar as the latter acted as a representative of the whole body of which he was a member. Again, just as Yahweh's *covenant* with Israel was *unshakable* (vs. 3) so was it with "David." Yet the equation could be expressed equally well in reverse.

Finally we should note an interesting grammatical question. The word for *covenant love* here is written in the plural in the Hebrew. This is an unusual form. Most expositors regard it as an intensive plural. It may very well be such. Yet it may also be what grammarians call a distributive plural. If so, by means of it DI declares the oneness of God's covenant love, first, between himself and David and, second, between himself and each and every member of Israel as the people of God. Moreover, this covenant love God will give to Israel as a gift—*lachem,* "to you," and not the usual *'immachem,* "with you"—since it is something she cannot possibly earn. Then again, since it is no past covenant that is referred to here, we must be hearing of a future event. This means that Israel is to enter into the new covenant through that action of the Servant (53:11) which DI has shown to be the vital hinge in the whole scheme of God's cosmic plan of redemption.

5.

Now comes a swing from the plural back to the masculine singular. This change is not visible in the RSV. But the original Hebrew suddenly abandons the plural of the verbs that have been used since vs. 1 and startles us by declaring, "*thou shalt.*" Evidently "David" is now Israel epitomized. But this is not difficult to understand, for we have seen that he is the whole body even while he is its head, that is to say, and to use the language of Ps. 80, he is both the vine and the branches at once. At 43:10, DI could say: *You* (plural) *are my witnesses, . . . and my Servant* (singular) *whom I have chosen.* Yet now, addressing Israel in the singular, he declares, *thou shalt call nations unknown to thee,* virtually employing words that occur in Ps. 18:43 in connection with the individual King David. What DI wishes us to understand is that the call of the perfect Servant, who has now subsumed sinful Israel within himself, could well be fulfilled in a single "David" yet to come. The identification of "David" with the perfect Servant, and so with Israel, is expressed still more clearly in the next two lines. *Nations to whom thou art unknown will run to thee* is an echo of what was said of the imperfect Servant Israel at 42:4; yet it was not said at that point for Israel's own sake, for of herself Israel is nothing. There it was pointed out that Yahweh's glory is to appear *in* Israel (40:5; 42:8; 43:7; 45:25; 46:13; 48:11). We have now been shown what the new thing is that DI expected, and how the glory of God is revealed when the arm of the Lord offers himself as an *'asham* that the masses may be saved. So DI is now in the position to sum up his whole argument with the words: *Because of Yahweh thy God, the Holy One of Israel, for he will have glorified thee.* In other words, the *glory* of *Yahweh,* revealed as it is by the perfect Servant, is now to be made manifest in empirical Israel by that David who sums up in himself the calling of Israel.

To make this final point clear, DI does two simple things with language. First, he recapitulates the idea of running to (*'el*) *thee* by employing the preposition *l^e^* to mean the same thing before *the Holy One of Israel.* There he declares that if the nations run to Israel, then they are in fact running to the Lord of Israel. He will be known to them only as they see him *in* Israel. Second, DI suddenly and unexpectedly employs the feminine form of the word *thee.* In this context, *thee* can naturally be no other than Zion, the people whom God has chosen to be his Servant and his bride at once. How the paradox "God was in Israel, reconciling the world unto himself" is to be understood is the theme only of the next section of his argument. Yet first, if this paraphrasing seems to be a rather far-fetched reference to II Cor. 5:19 and a forcing of DI's words beyond their limit, remember that the language he uses in the Hebrew can never be adequately translated into English. Consequently it is the duty of a commentator to seek to make what was clear to the reader of the original Hebrew equally clear in his own language and in the very different forms of expression used in his own day and generation.

Let us note the following issue also. It is obvious that DI had a wide and penetrating knowledge of the earlier literature of his people. He obviously knew that the Servant concept had already been employed to describe not necessarily the nation as such but a group within Israel as a whole (see comments at 42:1). For example, in I Kings 8:32 and Ps. 34:22, the concept applies only to the true believers in Yahweh. And in II Kings 9:7; Amos 3:7; Jer. 7:25; Ezek. 38:17, it appears as a generic title for the prophets of Yahweh as a group *within* the people of God. In the Psalter the Servant is sometimes an individual, yet one who speaks as a representative Israelite and in the consciousness that the whole nation of which he is the mouthpiece is the Servant (e.g., Ps. 19:11, 13; 27:9; 37:16; 69:17). Again, the Servant may be an individual prophet. As such, however, the prophet is fully aware that he would not be the called one that he is, were he not one with the whole people whom God had already called to be his Servant (e.g., I Kings 14:18; Isa. 20:3). This is true of Moses as well (Deut. 34:5; Josh. 1:1), for he, par excellence, is the apex of the triangle that represents the chosen people as a whole. Thus it follows naturally that "David" becomes the representative, the mouthpiece, the idea, the father image, the essence of his people. That is why he is called the Servant of Yahweh even when it is the whole nation that has been called (e.g., I Sam. 2:10; II Sam. 3:18; I Kings 3:6; Isa. 37:35).

6 Seek Yahweh while he is to be found: call upon him when
he is near.
7 Let the evil man give up his course, and the wicked man
his plans,
And let him come back to Yahweh, and he will have
compassion upon him; to our God, for he will
abundantly pardon.

6.

The motivation in the Servant's self-emptying DI sees as in the very heart of God himself, viz. compassion and eagerness to forgive and restore. DI returns now to the plural, for here God is addressing individual men and women: *Seek Yahweh, while he is to be found: call upon him when he is near.* For Yahweh himself is the water of life and the bread that wholly satisfies. And he has now come near in the glory of the Servant. Yet included in the invitation is a note of urgency. For God is not always available, says DI. If he were, he would show disrespect for the integrity of our human personalities. Yet to miss him when it is possible to find him would not be mere folly; it would be sin.

7.

We notice that DI does not identify the crass nonsense of idol worship with sin. In an earlier chapter he laughed it and the idol makers out of court. Sin is something far more terrible than idolatry, now that we have been shown what man will do to the Servant if left to his own devices. For sin is quite simply planning one's own plans and going ahead with one's own course in self-centered disregard for the plan of Yahweh that has now been revealed. This line of verse reads strangely when we recall all the heinous sins that man can commit. Yet DI makes no mention of what we call the flagrant sins, which all derive ultimately from the one fundamental concept that the human mind is so prone to entertain: a man believes that he knows better than God his maker what he is meant to do with his life (cf. Gen. 3:5). In the Garden of Eden story, however, we read that God takes fallen man even as he is in all his pitiable emptiness, and with compassionate love gives him clothes to cover his nakedness. DI's gospel is that God offers forgiveness to man at the very moment when man is committing the fundamental sin from which all others issue. God will *abundantly pardon* such, DI declares, or "multiply to forgive" as the Hebrew has it, because such full and total forgiveness is the expression of a love which is willing to empty out its *nephesh* even unto death. The "arm" of God that has now been revealed is his forgiving and renewing love become flesh.

DI has already declared that Yahweh forgives sinners even *before* they are able to repent. Nowhere therefore does he affirm that repentance is a condition of forgiveness. Forgiveness is in fact offered free to all men even before they are aware that they are sinners (43:25). The awareness of that forgiving love, however, and man's tremendous need for it must on the other hand be brought home to sinful man. Of his own free will he must be led to *shubh*, that is, turn round and *come back* to Yahweh. The Israelites had an initial advantage in this regard, for Yahweh chose and redeemed his Servant people even before they were able to make a conscious choice of him. In fact, every little Israelite boy on the eighth day was circumcised in order to reveal sacramentally that the grace of God precedes any statement of faith he may later wish to make, for this circumcision was the sign that he belonged to the already redeemed community. Thus in coming back to Yahweh, who will *abundantly pardon,* the Israelite was but coming back to the home where he originally belonged.

Forgiveness then lies at the very heart of the self-emptying act of the perfect Servant of Yahweh. No wonder DI announces the loving, forgiving call of God in the beautiful language he does as the climax of his thesis.

8 [Realize] that my plans are not your plans, and that your ways
are not my ways, is the oracular utterance of Yahweh.
9 [Realize] that even as the skies are higher than the earth,
So my ways are higher than your ways, and my plans
than your plans.
10 [Realize] that just as rain and snow come down from the sky,
But never go back up there; watering the earth instead,
And letting it give birth to living creatures and producing
vegetation,
Furnishing seed for sowing and food for eating,
11 Such happens too with my Word which issues from my mouth—
It never comes back to me fruitless,
Without having accomplished what I will,
Or succeeded in what I sent it to do.
12 [Realize] that you are going forth with joy, and will be
led in peace.
The mountains and hills are to burst into shouts of
joy before you,

And all the trees of the field will clap their hands.
13 Instead of thornbushes, cypresses will come up,
Instead of briers, myrtles will come up.
Then will be the revelation of Yahweh himself,
An eternal sign that shall never be cut down.

8.

These well-known lines are each introduced by the particle *ki.* This particle can mean "for" or "because," but it can also introduce direct speech[4] or even represent the two together. This means that a verb of strong asseveration is to be understood before the clause of direct speech, such as "I swear" or "realize." This usage is common in DI's forceful language and has been taken into account in the translation. Next, note that the usual translation of "thoughts" is not quite adequate here, for the reference is to what immediately precedes. We have seen that the wicked man's thoughts issue in wicked plans. God's loving thoughts must therefore issue in loving, creative *plans* and then actions. The word *plans* consequently is to be understood in a theological sense. It does not mean that God as creator has many scientifically discernible marvels still up his sleeve for men to wonder at thousands of years from now. Rather, as we see from Jer. 29:11, the emphasis is that God's purposes, which transcend what any human being could ever have thought out—*my plans are not your plans*—have now been revealed. In fact they are now in process of becoming flesh through the ideal self-offering of the Servant.

9.

To DI such a plan is a far more astonishing reality than the mysteries still hidden in the wonders of God's natural world. In fact, man cannot even begin to comprehend the depths and heights of the love of God and of his plans of salvation that embrace the whole of creation. How sordid were the ways of the proletariat of Babylon—bowed down with superstition as they were, riddled with jealousies and fears, their homes cramped and mean, their morals bestial and repulsive—compared with the self-emptying of the Holy One of Israel in his Servant for the redemption of the world.

10.

Yet a vital element in the good news is that God's way of salvation will win in the end over the sordid ways of men. In fact this is inevitable. This

[4] See p. 17.

verse contains the longest sustained simile that DI employs. In it we are reminded that God is in full control of the processes of nature. Moreover, these processes are orderly, and they work together according to natural law. Interestingly enough, they are creative and are not merely mechanically conditioned. As such they form the sacramental woof and web of man's life under God. For man lives on bread (55:1) and cannot hope to find fullness of life unless he first sustains his body on meat and drink. Thus the food that grows out of the ground is the inevitable outcome of the movement of God's loving purpose for man in the processes of nature. Moreover, this movement cannot reverse itself. It must go forward according to the pattern that God has first created, a good pattern, for it is a pattern that reveals a purpose of love. In other words, it is an effective pattern, for it results in the fulfillment of the divine plan.

11.

This is DI's analogy by which he declares the effectiveness of the divine plan of redemption. His choice of language rests upon the generally held ancient concepts of the potency of the word and its substantive existence once it has been uttered. As we have seen in the commentary at 44:24, this view is basic to DI's argument. When God speaks, he naturally speaks with intent. For he is the faithful God. *My Word which issues from my mouth—it never comes back to me fruitless,* that is to say, without hitting the target at which God has aimed, *without having accomplished what I will, or succeeded in what I sent it to do.* Thank God, we may say, that DI's God is really what we know him to be—not Marduk or Nebo, the messenger god who conveys the will of Marduk—but that he is in fact the Holy One of Israel. For only he has a purpose of love; only he is Savior (43:10-13). Once his Word is uttered, therefore, it necessarily becomes effective to save, even though it may be deflected from its course for a time by the resistance of the free will of man (cf. Jer. 30:23). In the end, however, God's Word must inevitably reach its target: *By myself have I sworn; from my mouth a Word has gone forth with saving purpose; it will not come back—that unto me every knee shall bend, every tongue shall swear* (45:23).[5]

This great Word of promise bears within it a corollary, however. We are to remember that the Word has now been uttered and so is already at

[5] In passing we may note here the basis of John Calvin's emphasis in his theology of the sacraments. It is that the sacraments convey the power of God. Calvin rejected the medieval view that the sacraments offered man an infusion of grace.

work within Israel's life; for Israel is just about to be redeemed from the dungeons of Babylon. But the power of the uttered Word—*the oracular utterance of Yahweh* (vs. 8)—cannot cease with that one historical incident. It will continue along its way as the path of Israel's history continues to unfold. The word may indeed remain hidden from mortal eyes for many years on end. That turned out to be the case. Israel unfortunately adopted a less penetrating interpretation of her covenant relationship with Yahweh than DI had revealed. Later generations obscured and even destroyed the vision of what it means for Israel to be the suffering Servant of the Lord. But the potency of the Word uttered is a reality. Thus, from our privileged position of hindsight, we are aware that the Word did finally become flesh in one who was no less than Israel himself. And we believe this because Jesus believed it of himself, as did the early Church (cf. Luke 1:54). Jesus said to John the Baptist: "Suffer it to be so now: for thus it becometh us to fulfill all righteousness," i.e., God's saving purpose (Matt. 3:15). He spoke of giving his life as a ransom for the masses (Mark 10:45). So the Word uttered through the lips of DI finally became effective, as the action of the Servant was meant to be (52:13).

We have still to face the difficult issue that the ideal Servant portrayed in ch. 53 is not a historical figure of the Babylonian period. He is yet only a Word, even though a Word that has, first, been uttered by God and then, second, been enunciated through the lips of DI. DI himself could not have invented the portrait of the ideal Servant, for sinful man cannot imagine or delineate what is perfect. Isa. 53 is therefore nothing less than a Word of revelation. Yet it has been couched in human terms and expressed in human thought forms. Its format in DI's mind may well have been influenced from one or more sources—by the sufferings of his predecessor Jeremiah, or by the willingness of Moses to be an offering for his people, or again, even by his pondering the issues associated with the New Year festival at Babylon. As DI did so, his mind may have given birth to the creative picture that he has given us.

Yet the most potent factor in his whole thinking must have emerged from an element in the genius of his cultural heritage as it was expressed in the Hebrew language that was his mother tongue. Ideally there is no separation between matter and spirit in Hebrew thinking. Yet of course in this world as we know it, a cleavage between these two does exist. It is sin that causes this cleavage. There would be no separation between the realities of word and work if sin were not present to establish the dichotomy.

With God, however, word and work must necessarily be one; with him the verbum is also the opus. He has only to say, "Let light become," and light comes into being. DI would know the words of promise that God had made to Moses, "Certainly I shall become with thee" (Exod. 3:12), words which reveal that the content of God's promise is identical with the essence of his being (Exod. 3:14). DI's forerunner had used this promise as the basis of another divine promise when he named the child who was to be born in the dark days of siege "God-is-with-us" (Isa. 7:14). Now DI takes the step of claiming that this word of promise cannot just remain word, but must become flesh and historical fact. Since the word that has been uttered in the life of Israel is the Word of God, and since what we are confronted with in the Servant is no longer Israel, but God *in* Israel, reconciling the world unto himself, as DI has now declared at five separate points in his argument, then that Word must necessarily become flesh, and become flesh in Israel alone. For the Word cannot return unto God void, any more than the rain can return into the sky. The end product of the rain's coming down is food for the good of man. In the same way, the end product of the Word's coming down into Israel can be nothing less than food for man (cf. vs. 1), beyond all that man can ever hope for or ever hope to understand.

12.

This extraordinary news is world-shattering. Even *the mountains and hills are to burst into shouts of joy . . . , and all the trees of the field will clap their hands*. Later, at chs. 65 and 66, DI's disciple, whom we call Trito-Isaiah for convenience, brings this issue to its logical outcome, for he believes that in the end God will create actually new heavens and a new earth. Then the eschatological significance of this present world will be revealed, and the hopes and fears and joys and aspirations of this world will find their sublime fulfillment.

13.

At the present time, however, the curse of sin rests even upon nonmoral nature. This curse has always clouded the eyes of man, so that the reality of nature red in tooth and claw has been perhaps the one most significant factor militating against belief in a God of good purpose against which men have had to struggle. But before DI's day, Isaiah of Jerusalem had expressed the conviction that with the coming of the messianic Figure, whom he delineated in chs. 9 and 11, there would eventuate the removal of the curse. Nature then would be harmonious and cooperative instead of mutually destructive and cruel (11:6-9). DI here expresses this same faith, but in his own peculiar and poetic manner. We recall that the concept of wilderness is the pictorializing of chaos, *tohu* (45:18). It is there that *thornbushes* and thistles or *briers* grow. These weeds choke the ground and signify the effect of the sin of man upon the soil (Gen. 3:17-18). But now these pests are to be transformed into productive and shade-giving trees; and as they nestle round the peasant homestead, they will witness to the deep-seated joy of the Easterner who wants more than anything else to be one in spirit with the little piece of earth that he loves and tills.

Realize then, says DI (vs. 12), when *you are going forth* from Babylon, you poor, dispirited Israelite exiles, that you will go forth with the *joy* of God in your hearts—for Yahweh dwells in joy, for he knows the end from the beginning (41:4; 44:6; 48:12). Yours will be the inestimable joy of learning that you are sharing in, even acting as the trigger of, the greatest of all divine activities. This movement will now go forward like the inevitable, linked, progressive, onward movement of a chain reaction, or, more properly, like the inevitable, linked, forward movement that proceeds from promise to fulfillment. *You are going forth with joy,* joy at knowing that by grace you have a unique place that no one else can fill in the divine plan of cosmic redemption; *and will be led in peace, shalom,* because by faith you already possess the ultimate expression of that wholeness and fullness of life which it is God's will that all men should know. For being led in the manner that the Good Shepherd leads his sheep (40:11) naturally occasions the sheep a secure sense of *peace.*

Right at the end of his thesis, DI returns to the subject with which he began in ch. 40. There the new exodus was seen to be composed of very ordinary people, trudging along a very ordinary road as they returned from Babylon to Jerusalem. DI does not suggest that this poor struggling group of people could be said per se to constitute revelation. What he is emphasizing is that God has now uttered his Word. This Word has gone forth and therefore cannot return to him fruitless. But since it has been uttered within the form and framework of this particular depressed group of people, this people has therefore become in actuality the very form or body of divine revelation.

DI's last and highly significant words therefore come as a completely fitting climax to his whole message: *Then will be the revelation of Yahweh himself, an eternal sign that shall never be cut down.* That is to say, this Word now spoken must someday and inevitably become flesh, and must inevitably do so within the form of Israel. In fact, what God must necessarily accomplish, now that he has uttered his Word, has several facets to it: (1) The Word must be effective and accomplish what God wills. (2) The Word, now that it has been uttered, must necessarily become flesh, event, or work. (3) The Word must necessarily become flesh only within the form of Israel, for it is within the form of Israel and as an element in her history alone that God has uttered his voice. (4) This Word made flesh will then be no less than the revelation—Hebrew, "name"—of the living God. (5) Once the Word has become flesh, it will then be a fact of history that no one can deny; and so it will be a *sign* (-post) *that shall never be cut down.* (6) This Word will take the form of the Servant who pours out his *nephesh* unto death, as he empties out his life as an *'asham* for the masses. (7) The death of the Servant will not mark the end of God's purpose; rather *he will find satisfaction in* [*his*] *seed; he will prolong* [*his*] *days. . . . He will shed forth* [*light*] *and . . . be satisfied. Therefore I shall divide the many for him as his portion* (53:10-12).

This event will be a *sign* (-post) indeed, a sacramental act, an event in time that reveals the reality of eternity. It will happen through the intervention of God in the life of his unwilling and imperfect Servant Israel (42:19; 49:4), and within the form and body of an Israel who refuses to be the Servant that she is elected to be; in fact who even forces the Holy One of Israel to be the Servant in her stead (43:22-24). Thus, even in the continuity of Word becoming event, there will occur a moment of complete discontinuity. For the Holy One must accomplish his end, not *with* Israel, but *despite* Israel and her constant resistance and disloyalty to his Word. Yet it is just because of this strange paradox that the glory of God is finally revealed (44:23; 49:3). As to the glory of man—why, *sic transit gloria mundi,* even that of the people of the covenant (see at 53:4). But the glory of God is the *revelation* of a love that triumphs in rejection, and in the face of every disloyalty; for it is "the love that will not let me go," the *ḥesedh* that God had long since promised to the David who did not deserve it (55:3); and it is the free grace that can be seen in all its splendor (49:3) only when it is finally and ultimately resisted by the one who is chosen to receive it in full. "Israel is not a sick man who was allowed to recover, but One risen from the dead." [6]

[6] Karl Barth, *Dogmatics in Outline* (London: SCM, 1949), p. 80.

DI began his good news by proclaiming: *Comfort My people, comfort them* (40:1). For he knew that God had a mighty plan in readiness that was to work through his people's present extremity. DI now ends his interpretation of that proclamation with a call that reaches far beyond this handful of miserable Judean exiles. For the Word that he has now uttered in his capacity as the mouthpiece of Israel's God is one that no power on earth can frustrate. It will go forth and bear fruit until that time when the whole creation, groaning and travailing in pain together till now as it is (cf. Rom. 8:22), will finally meet with its Redeemer and Lord. For the creation is to meet this saving Word and work of God in the person of a new David, who will wholly sum up and represent and fulfill in his own person the form and body of the whole people of God, even One whom God had in mind since the foundation of the world.

SUMMARY OF DEUTERO-ISAIAH

DI begins with the contemporary historical situation. The Exile is almost over; God commands the angelic forces to comfort Israel with the assurance that her iniquity that brought about the Exile is pardoned. In grace God has accepted her period of "forced labor" as if it were divine service (40:1-2). Israel will shortly return home across the wilderness, but this march will have cosmic significance. We know this, because God's initial act of redemption at the Exodus was of this nature. This new redemptive act will mean that the invisible God will be revealed (40:5).

The exiles are not all of Israel, but are an *ecclesiola in ecclesia* whom God has made to suffer to educate them for his purposes. In the Exile he has never left them, however, so his presence has been their reward in suffering (40:10).

God has raised up Cyrus the Persian to be his servant (41:1-7). His task is to set Israel free. But Israel is God's servant in a unique sense (41:8), for ever since the days of Abraham, God has been becoming *with* his people. Israel has been bound to God within the covenant; thus even though Israel is a "worm," God has remained his people's Redeemer. His grace has overruled Israel's sin and has subsumed it to his ends of saving love (41:14 *ff.*). In her capacity as "Son of man," Israel will exult when she learns how she is being used by God as his instrument of salvation.

God has chosen Israel not to be saved but to serve. Israel is to bring the true way of life to the masses of humanity who are longing for revelation (42:1-4). Of herself she is nothing; she is but the vehicle of mission. Therefore she is to further her task not by fostering her ego but by "emptying it out." In this way Israel will become God's covenant people for all men (42:6). Only in Israel then will God's glory be found. The manner in which God will work redemptively through his Servant will produce a "new" thing; and as the latter emerges from the death of the old, God himself will feel the pain like a mother in the throes of giving birth. So God suffers. He is the only Savior. Nothing exists but him. Yet he plans to use Israel, although she is a sinner and therefore even non-being herself.

Israel persists in being blind and deaf, in seeing no meaning in her history, in continually rebelling against God's loving plan. She ought to have discovered that she was now the sacrificial beast that God intended to use for the salvation of the world. Instead she makes God into the Servant (43:24). God responds by showing willingness to share Israel's damnation (43:28). For his purpose remains constant, despite the ban he has had to lay on her; it is that through the unique relationship of the covenant he will win all men (44:5; 45:23). The city of Jerusalem is central to the plan (44:26), for God's eschatological purpose is dependent on the particularism of a city and of a human conqueror—Cyrus.

Since Israel is nothing in herself, God has given her his own saving power. This means that God must act, not by means of Israel's faith, but despite her lack of it. He will reveal his glory, not through Israel's co-operation, but through her resistance (46:13), even through her damnation. God foreknew Israel would resist his will (48:4); so as a last resort he tried the refiner's fire. But no silver came out; Israel was wholly rotten (48:10). Yet God persists in acting through this chosen people.

God now addresses Israel in the feminine singular (ch. 49:14 *ff.*). Queen Babylon is the apotheosis of apostasy (ch. 47), but Queen Zion is Yahweh's wife; he loves her even though she is faithless (49:14 *ff.*). The divine Husband would never force her to submit to his will (50:1), instead he chose to leave her alone for a period—in exile—hoping her eyes would open to his love. His hope for her was that she would be wholly submissive, emptying her "self" out of her "body" to make room for the Word to enter. This had been God's plan since the foundation of the world (51:16). But she would not. Instead, like an alcoholic she had drunk herself into delirium. But it was Yahweh who had handed her the cup (51:17). The seed must fall into the ground and die before it can spring forth in new life, and God may have to help it die. Only then can he resuscitate the corpse (51:22). Israel is presently an empty shell. On that day, however, the name of God will dwell within her body (52:6), and God will then be immanent in her. Only then will Israel complete her mission (52:7 *ff.*).

When the Word of Yahweh is thus united as one flesh with the body of the Servant Israel, the Servant will be despised and rejected by humanity (52:13 *ff.*). But the Servant's suffering will be not penal but vicarious (53:4). The new thing is at last revealed. This suffering, which is not merely substitutionary but participative (53:7 *ff.*), is actually *God's* suffering. The Servant is God-in-Israel. Thus God himself is the sin offering *in* the body of Israel (53:10). By grace God identified the perfect Servant with the empirical, sinful Servant, and accounted the latter's suffering in exile as his own remedial suffering for the masses of men.

Almighty God's offering must necessarily be effective, and it cannot be touched by death (53:11-13). Israel, the body with whom the Word has united, will bear God's seed (53:10); and Jerusalem will be filled with his sons (54:1-3). The new life for all men will thus be effected, and God will invite all men to share in it (55:1).

All DI's theology is rooted in historical events. What God has said when his servant Cyrus rescued Israel from the prison house must become cosmic redemption. For God's Word stands forever (40:8) and does not return to him fruitless (55:11). God's purpose of universal redemption has now begun with Cyrus. The Word has been uttered and so must become event. The perfect Servant has now been "spoken," and so must fulfill the plan of God within the context of the covenant which God has chosen to use. The end product of the onward movement of the living Word, the salvation of the world, can be expressed in eschatological language alone; yet its outcome is inevitable (55:12-13).

SELECTED BIBLIOGRAPHY

Albright, William F. *Archaeology and the Religion of Israel.* 4th ed. Baltimore: Johns Hopkins Press, 1956.

———. *From the Stone Age to Christianity.* 2nd ed. Baltimore: Johns Hopkins Press, 1957.

Alt, A. *Staatenbildung der Israeliten in Palästina.* Leipzig: Universität, 1930.

Anderson, Bernhard W. *Understanding the Old Testament.* Englewood Cliffs, N.J.: Prentice-Hall, 1957.

Aytoun, R. A. "The Servant of the Lord in the Targum," *Journal of Theological Studies,* XXIII (1922), 172-80.

Barnes, W. E. "Cyrus, the 'Servant of Jehovah,'" *Journal of Theological Studies,* XXXII (1931), 32-39.

Baron, David. *The Servant of Jehovah, the Sufferings of the Messiah and the Glory That Should Follow.* London: Morgan and Scott, 1922.

Baudissin, Wolf von, "Zur Entwicklung des Gebrauchs von 'ebed im religiosem Sinne." *Beiträge zur Zeitschrift für die Alttestamentliche Wissenschaft,* 1920.

———. *Kyrios.* Vol. III. Giessen: A. Töpelmann, 1929.

Begrich, J. *Studien zu Deuterojesaja.* München: C. Kaiser Verlag, 1938, 1963.

Bentzen, Aage. *King and Messiah.* London: Lutterworth Press, 1955.

———. "On the Ideas of 'the Old' and 'the New' in Deutero-Isaiah," *Studia Theologia,* I (1947), 183-87.

Black, Matthew. "The Servant of the Lord and Son of Man," *Scottish Journal of Theology,* VI (1953), 1-11.

Blank, Sheldon H. "Studies in Deutero-Isaiah," *Hebrew Union College Annual,* 1940, pp. 1-46.

Boer, P. A. H. de, editor. *Second-Isaiah's Message.* (*Oudtestamentische Studiën.* Vol. XI.) Leiden: E. J. Brill, 1950.

Box, G. H. *The Book of Isaiah.* London: Sir Isaac Pitman and Sons, 1908.

Bright, John. *A History of Israel.* Philadelphia: Westminster Press, 1959.

———. *The Kingdom of God.* Nashville: Abingdon Press, 1953.

Brownlee, William H. "The Servant of the Lord in the Qumran Scrolls," *Bulletin of the American Schools of Oriental Research,* 132 (1953); 135 (1954).

Bruno, A. *Jesaja, Eine Rythmische und Textkritische Untersuchung.* Stockholm: Almquist & Wiksell, 1953.

Buber, Martin. *The Prophetic Faith.* New York: The Macmillan Co., 1949.

Budde, Karl. "The Religion of Israel to the Exile," *American Journal of Theology,* III (1899), 499-540.

———. *The So-Called "Ebed-Yahweh Songs."* New York: G. P. Putnam's Sons, 1899.

Cheyne, T. K. *The Prophecies of Isaiah.* 2 vols. 2nd ed. London: Kegan Paul, 1880.

Cornill, C. H. "Die neueste Literatur über Jes 40–66," *Theologische Rundschau,* III (1900), 409-20.

Danell, G. *Studies in the Name Israel in the Old Testament.* Uppsala: Appelberg, 1946.

Delitzsch, Franz. *Biblical Commentary on the Prophecies of Isaiah.* Eng. tr. London: Hodder & Stoughton, 1890.

Dillmann, A. *Der Prophet Jesaia.* (*Kurtzgefasstes exegetisches Handbuch zum Alten Testament.* 5th ed.) Leipzig: S. Hirzel, 1890.

Driver, G. R. "Linguistic and Textual Problems: Isaiah XL-LXVI," *Journal of Theological Studies,* XXXVI (1935), 396-406.

Driver, S. R., and Neubauer, A. *The Fifty-third Chapter of Isaiah According to the Jewish Interpreters.* Oxford: J. Parker & Co., 1876-77.

Duhm, Bernhard. *Das Buch Jesaia.* (*Handkommentar zum Alten Testament.*) Göttingen: Vandenhoek & Ruprecht, 1892.

Eissfeldt, Otto. *Der Gottesknecht bei Deuterojesaja.* Halle: Niemeyer, 1933.

———. "The Ebed-Jahwe in Isaiah xl-lv, in the Light of the Israelite Conceptions of the Community and the Individual, the Ideal and the Real," *Expository Times,* XLIV (1933), 261-68.

———. "The Promise of Grace to David in Isa. 55:1-5," *Israel's Prophetic Heritage,* edited by Bernhard W. Anderson. New York: Harper & Row, 1962, pp. 196 *ff.*

Engnell, Ivan. "The Ebed Yahweh Song and the Suffering Messiah in Deutero-Isaiah," *Bulletin of the John Rylands Library,* XXXI (1948).

———. *Studies in Divine Kingship in the Ancient Near East.* Uppsala: Almquist & Wiksells, 1953.

Fischer, Johannes. "Isaiah's Text and the Septuagint," *Beiheft zur ZAW,* 1930.

Frankfort, Henri. *Kingship and the Gods.* Chicago: University of Chicago Press, 1948.

Frey, Helmut. *Das Buch der Weltpolitik Gottes.* (*Die Botschaft des Alten Testaments.* Vol. 18.) Stuttgart: Calver Verlag, 1937.

Galling, Kurt. *Die Erwählungstraditionen Israels.* Giessen: Töpelmann, 1928.

Gaster, T. H. *Thespis.* Anchor Book; New York: Doubleday & Co., 1950, 1961.

Giesebrecht, F. "Die Idee von Jes. lii.13–liii.12," *Beiträge zur Jesajakritik.* Göttingen: Vandenhoek & Ruprecht, 1890.

Gottwald, Norman. *A Light to the Nations.* New York: Harper & Row, 1959.

Gressmann, H. *Der Ursprung der israelitisch-jüdischen Eschatologie.* Göttingen: Vandenhoek & Ruprecht, 1905.

Grether, Oskar. *Name und Wort Gottes im Alten Testament.* Giessen: Töpelmann, 1934.

Guillaume, Alfred. *Prophecy and Divination.* London: Hodder & Stoughton, 1938.

Gunkel, H. *Schöpfung und Chaos in Urzeit und Endzeit.* Göttingen: Vandenhoek & Ruprecht, 1895.

Hegermann, H. *Jesaja 53 in Hexapla, Targum und Peschitta.* Gütersloh: C. Bertelsmann, 1954.

Hempel, Johannes. "Das Ethos des Alten Testaments," *Beiheft zur ZAW,* 1938.

Hooke, Samuel H., editor. *The Labyrinth.* London: S.P.C.K., 1935.

———. *Myth, Ritual and Kingship.* London: Oxford at the Clarendon Press, 1958.

Hooker, Morna D. *Jesus and the Servant.* London: S.P.C.K., 1959.

Hyatt, J. P. "The Sources of the Suffering Servant Idea," *Journal of Near Eastern Studies,* III (1944), 79-86.

James, Fleming. *Personalities of the Old Testament.* New York: Charles Scribner's Sons, 1939.

Jastrow, Morris. *Aspects of Religious Belief and Practice in Babylonia and Assyria.* New York: G. P. Putnam's Sons, 1911.

————. "The Role of the King in the Jerusalem Cultus," *The Labyrinth.* Edited by Samuel Hooke. London: S.P.C.K., 1935.

Jocz, Jakób. *A Theology of Election.* London: S.P.C.K., 1958.

Johnson, A. R. *The One and the Many in the Israelite Conception of God.* Cardiff: University of Wales Press Board, 1942.

————. *Sacral Kingship in Ancient Israel.* Cardiff: University of Wales Press Board, 1955.

————. *The Vitality of the Individual in the Thought of Ancient Israel.* Cardiff: University of Wales Press Board, 1949.

Kaiser, Otto. *Der Königliche Knecht.* Rev. ed. Göttingen: Vandenhoek & Ruprecht, 1962.

Knight, G. A. F. *A Christian Theology of the Old Testament.* Richmond: John Knox Press; London: S.C.M. Press, 1959. Rev. ed., London: S.C.M. Press, 1964.

Köhler, L. "Deuterojesaja stilkritisch untersucht," *Beiheft zur ZAW,* 1923.

König, Eduard. *Das Buch Jesaja.* Gütersloh: Bertelsmann, 1926.

Kurtz, J. H. *Sacrificial Worship of the Old Testament.* Edinburgh: T. & T. Clark, 1863.

Kuschke, A. "Altbabylonische Texte zum Thema 'Der leidende Gottesknecht,'" *Theologische Literaturzeitung,* 1956, 69 *ff.*

Lambert, Wilfred. *Babylonian Wisdom Literature.* London: Oxford at the Clarendon Press, 1960.

Leeuw, Van der. *De Ebed Jahweh-Profetieen* (with résumé in French). Assen: Van Gorcum, 1956.

Leslie, Elmer A. *Isaiah.* Nashville: Abingdon Press, 1963.

Levy, Reuben. *Deutero-Isaiah.* New York: Oxford University Press, 1925.

Lindblom, Johannes. *The Servant-Songs in Deutero-Isaiah.* Lund: Lund University Press, 1951.

Lindhagen, Curt. *The Servant Motif in the Old Testament.* Uppsala: Lundequistska Bokhandeln, 1950.

Lofthouse, W. F. *Israel After the Exile.* (*Clarendon Bible, Old Testament,* Vol. IV.) London: Oxford University Press, 1928.

————. "Some Reflections on the Servant Songs," *Journal of Theological Studies,* XLVIII (1947), 169-70.

Manson, Thomas W. *The Servant-Messiah.* London: Cambridge University Press, 1953.

————. "The Son of Man in Daniel, Enoch, and the Gospels," *Bulletin of the John Rylands Library,* XXXII (1949-50).

Marti, Karl. *Das Buch Jesaja erklärt.* (*Kurzer Hand-Kommentar Zum Alten Testament.*) Tübingen: Mohr, 1900.

Matthews, Isaac G. *The Religious Pilgrimage of Israel.* New York: Harper & Brothers, 1947.

Mendenhall, George E. *Law and Covenant in Israel and the Ancient Near East.* Pittsburgh: The Biblical Colloquium, 1955.

Morgenstern, Julian. "The Message of Deutero-Isaiah in Its Sequential Unfolding," *Hebrew Union College Annual,* XXX (1939).

Mowinckel, Sigmund. *He That Cometh.* Nashville: Abingdon Press, 1956.

Muilenberg, James. Introduction to "The Book of Isaiah, Chapters 40–66," *The Interpreter's Bible.* Vol. 5. Nashville: Abingdon Press, 1956.

Napier, B. Davie. *Song of the Vineyard.* New York: Harper & Row, 1962.

North, Christopher. "The 'Former Things' and the 'New Things' in Deutero-Isaiah," *Studies in Old Testament Prophecy,* edited by H. H. Rowley. Edinburgh: T. & T. Clark, 1950.

————. *Isaiah 40–55.* (*Torch Bible Commentaries.*) London: S.C.M. Press, 1952.

————. *The Suffering Servant in Deutero-Isaiah.* Rev. ed. New York: Oxford University Press, 1956.

Oesterley, W. O. E. *Studies in Isaiah XL-LXVI.* London: Robert Scott, 1916.
Orlinsky, Harry M. "Studies in the St. Mark's Isaiah Scroll, II," *Journal of Near Eastern Studies,* XI (1952), 153-56.
Ottley, R. R. *Isaiah According to the Septuagint.* 2 Vols. Cambridge: Cambridge University Press, 1904, 1906.
Pákozdy, L. M. von. *Deuterojesajanische Studien I and II* (in Hungarian with summaries in German). Debrecen, Hungary, 1940, 1942.
Palache, J. L. *Semantic Notes on the Hebrew Lexicon.* Leiden: E. J. Brill, 1959.
Peake, Arthur S. *The Problem of Suffering in the Old Testament.* London: Robert Bryant & C. H. Kelly, 1904.
————. *The Servant of Yahweh and Other Lectures.* Manchester: Manchester University Press, 1931.
Pedersen, Johannes. *Israel, Its Life and Culture.* 2 vols. London: Oxford University Press, 1926, 1940.
Pritchard, James B., editor. *Ancient Near Eeastern Texts Relating to the Old Testament.* 2nd ed. Princeton: Princeton University Press, 1955.
Rad, Gerhard von. *Theologie des Alten Testaments.* Vol. II. München: C. Kaiser Verlag, 1960.
Reinwald, G. *Cyrus im zweiten Teil des Buches Isaias, Kap. 40–55.* Bamberg, 1956.
Rendtorff, R. "Die theologische Stellung des Schöpferglaubens bei Deuterojesaja," *Zeitschrift für Theologie und Kirche,* LI (1954).
Rignell, Lars G. *A Study of Isaiah chs. 40–55.* Lund: Gleerup, 1956.
Robinson, Henry W. *The Cross in the Old Testament.* Philadelphia: Westminster Press, 1956.
————. "The Hebrew Conception of Corporate Personality," in "Werden und Wesen des Alten Testaments," *Beiheft zur Zeitschrift für die alttestamentliche Wissenschaft,* LXVI (1936).
————. *Inspiration and Revelation in the Old Testament.* New York: Oxford University Press, 1946.
Rowley, H. H. *The Biblical Doctrine of Election.* London: Lutterworth Press, 1950.
————. *Israel's Mission to the World.* London: S.C.M. Press, 1939.
————. *The Servant of the Lord, and Other Essays on the Old Testament.* London: Lutterworth Press, 1952.
Saydon, P. P. "The Use of Tenses in Deutero-Isaiah," *Biblica* (Rome), XL (1959), 290 *ff.*
Scharbert, J. "The Vicarious Suffering in the Ebed Jahweh Songs," *Biblische Zeitschrift,* 1958.
Seeligmann, Isac L. *The Septuagint Version of Isaiah.* Leiden: E. J. Brill, 1948.
Simon, Ulrich E. *A Theology of Salvation.* London: S.P.C.K., 1953.
Skinner, John, editor. *The Book of the Prophet Isaiah, Chapters XL-LXVI.* Rev. ed. (*Cambridge Bible.*) Cambridge: Cambridge University Press, 1917.
Smart, James D. *The Interpretation of Scripture.* Philadelphia: Westminster Press, 1961.
Smith, Charles R. *The Biblical Doctrine of Salvation.* London: Epworth Press, 1941.
Smith, George A. *The Book of Isaiah, Vol. II.* (*Expositor's Bible.*) London: Hodder & Stoughton, 1890.
Smith, John M. P. *The Prophets and Their Times.* Chicago: University of Chicago Press, 1925.
Smith, Sidney. *Isaiah Chapters XL-LV: Literary Criticism and History.* New York: Oxford University Press, 1940, 1944.
Snaith, Norman H. *The Distinctive Ideas of the Old Testament.* London: Epworth Press, 1944.
————. "The Servant of the Lord in Deutero-Isaiah," *Studies in Old Testament Prophecy.* Edited by H. H. Rowley. Edinburgh: T. & T. Clark, 1950.
Stamm, Johannes. *Das Leiden des Unschuldigen in Babylon und Israel.* Zürich: Zwingli Verlag, 1946.

Stenning, John, editor and translator. *The Targum of Isaiah, with an English Translation.* New York: Oxford Press, 1949.

Stuhlmueller, C. "The Theology of Creation in Second Isaias," *Catholic Biblical Quarterly,* XXI (1959), 429-67.

Swete, Henry B. *An Introduction to the Old Testament in Greek.* London: Cambridge University Press, 1930-34.

Thexton, Stewart C. *Isaiah 40–66.* (*Epworth Preacher's Commentaries.*) London: Epworth Press, 1959.

Thomas, D. Winton, editor. *Documents from Old Testament Times.* London: Thomas Nelson & Sons, 1958.

Torrey, Charles C. *The Second Isaiah, a New Interpretation.* New York: Charles Scribner's Sons, 1928.

Vischer, Wilhelm. *Das Kerygma des Alten Testaments.* Zürich: Zwingli Verlag, 1955.

———. *Les Premiers Prophètes.* Neuchatel and Paris: Delachaux et Niestlé, 1951.

———. *Valeur de l'Ancien Testament: Esaie II.* Geneva: Labor et Fides, n.d.

Vriezen, T. C. *Die Erwählung Israels nach dem Alten Testament.* Zürich: Zwingli Verlag, 1953.

Wade, George W. *The Book of the Prophet Isaiah, with Introduction and Notes.* (*Westminster Commentaries.*) London: Methuen, 1911.

Wardle, W. L. *Isaiah XL-LXVI.* (*Peake's Commentary on the Bible.*) London: T. C. & E. C. Jack, 1931.

Weiser, Artur. *The Psalms, a Commentary.* Eng. tr. Philadelphia: Westminster Press, 1962.

Whitehouse, Owen C. *Isaiah XL-LXVI.* (*Century Bible.*) London: T. C. & E. C. Jack, 1905.

Ziegler, Joseph. *Untersuchungen zur Septuaginta des Buches Isaias.* Göttingen: Vandenhoek and Ruprecht, 1934.

Zimmern, Heinrich. *Das babylonische Neujahrsfest.* Leipzig: J. C. Hinrichs, 1926.

INDEX

MBS Feb/67 KON H. YANG